Windows® 98 For Dummies®

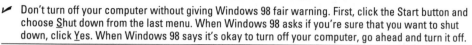

Cheat Sheet

KT-556-615

Helpful hints

✔ Don't turn off your computer without giving Windows 98 fair warning. First, click the Start button and choose Shut down from the last menu. When Windows 98 asks if you're sure that you want to shut down, click Yes. When Windows 98 says it's okay to turn off your computer, go ahead and turn it off.

✔ Don't know what a certain button does in a program? Rest your mouse pointer over the button for a few seconds; a helpful box often pops up to explain the button's purpose.

✔ If you're baffled, try pressing F1, that "function key" in the upper-left corner of your keyboard. A "help" window appears, bringing hints about your current program.

✔ To quickly organize the windows on the desktop, click the taskbar's clock with your *right* mouse button. When a menu appears, click one of the tile options, and all your open windows neatly tile across your screen.

✔ To keep icons organized in neat rows across your desktop or in windows, click the icon's background. When the menu pops up, choose Auto Arrange from the Arrange Icons menu.

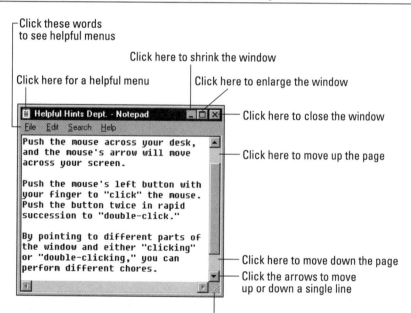

Click these words to see helpful menus

Click here for a helpful menu

Click here to shrink the window

Click here to enlarge the window

Click here to close the window

Click here to move up the page

Click here to move down the page

Click the arrows to move up or down a single line

Point here, hold down the mouse button, and move the mouse to change the window's size

Handling files within a program

To Do This . . .	Do This . . .
Start a new file	Press Alt, F, N.
Open an existing file	Press Alt, F, O.
Save a file	Press Alt, F, S.
Save a file under a new name	Press Alt, F, A.
Print a file	Press Alt, F, P.

...For Dummies®: Bestselling Book Series for Beginners

Windows® 98 For Dummies®

Cheat Sheet

Organizing a pile of windows

To Do This . . .	Do This . . .
See a list of all open windows	Look at the names on the taskbar along the screen's bottom.
Move from one window to another window	Press Alt+Tab+Tab or click the window's name on the taskbar.
Tile the windows across the screen	Click the taskbar's clock with the *right* mouse button and then click Tile Horizontally or Tile Vertically.
Cascade the windows across the screen	Click the taskbar's clock with the *right* mouse button and then click Cascade.
Shrink a window into an icon	Click the window, press Alt+spacebar, and press N.
Make a window fill the screen	Click the window, press Alt+spacebar, and Press X.

Cut and Paste stuff

To Do This . . .	Press These Keys . . .
Copy highlighted stuff to the Clipboard	Ctrl+C or Ctrl+Insert
Cut highlighted stuff to the Clipboard	Ctrl+X or Shift+Delete
Paste stuff from the Clipboard to the current window	Ctrl+V or Shift+Insert
Copy an entire screen to the Clipboard	PrintScreen (Shift+PrintScreen on some keyboards)
Copy the current window to the Clipboard	Alt+PrintScreen

Windows key shortcuts

To Do This . . .	Press This . . .
Display Windows 98 Help	<WindowsKey>+F1
Display the Start menu	<WindowsKey>
Cycle through the taskbar's buttons	<WindowsKey>+Tab
Display Windows Explorer	<WindowsKey>+E
Find files	<WindowsKey>+F
Find other computers on the network	Ctrl+<WindowsKey>+F
Display your computer's properties	<WindowsKey>+Break
Minimize or restore all windows	<WindowsKey>+D
Undo minimize all windows	Shift+<WindowsKey>+M

Windows Explorer and My Computer Programs

To Do This . . .	Do This . . .
Copy a file to another location on the *same* disk drive	Hold down Ctrl and drag it there.
Copy a file to a *different* disk drive	Drag it there.
Move a file to another location on the same disk drive	Drag it there.
Move a file to a different disk drive	Hold down Shift and drag it there.
Make a shortcut while dragging a file	Hold down Ctrl+Shift and drag it there.
Remember how to copy or move files	Hold down the *right* mouse button while dragging and then choose Move Copy Here from the menu.
Select several files	Hold down Ctrl and click the filenames.
Look at a different folder's icon	Double-click that folder.

...For Dummies®: Bestselling Book Series for Beginners

by Andy Rathbone

IDG Books Worldwide, Inc.
An International Data Group Company

Foster City, CA ◆ Chicago, IL ◆ Indianapolis, IN ◆ New York, NY

Windows® 98 For Dummies®

Published by
IDG Books Worldwide, Inc.
An International Data Group Company
919 E. Hillsdale Blvd.
Suite 400
Foster City, CA 94404
www.idgbooks.com (IDG Books Worldwide Web site)
www.dummies.com (Dummies Press Web site)

Library of Congress Catalog Card No.: 99-64197

ISBN: 0-7645-0261-1

Printed in the United States of America

10 9

1B/TQ/QX/ZZ/IN

Distributed in the United States by IDG Books Worldwide, Inc.

Distributed by CDG Books Canada Inc. for Canada; by Transworld Publishers Limited in the United Kingdom; by IDG Norge Books for Norway; by IDG Sweden Books for Sweden; by IDG Books Australia Publishing Corporation Pty. Ltd. for Australia and New Zealand; by TransQuest Publishers Pte Ltd. for Singapore, Malaysia, Thailand, Indonesia, and Hong Kong; by Gotop Information Inc. for Taiwan; by ICG Muse, Inc. for Japan; by Norma Comunicaciones S.A. for Colombia; by Intersoft for South Africa; by Eyrolles for France; by International Thomson Publishing for Germany, Austria and Switzerland; by Distribuidora Cuspide for Argentina; by Livraria Cultura for Brazil; by Ediciones ZETA S.C.R. Ltda. for Peru; by WS Computer Publishing Corporation, Inc., for the Philippines; by Contemporanea de Ediciones for Venezuela; by Express Computer Distributors for the Caribbean and West Indies; by Micronesia Media Distributor, Inc. for Micronesia; by Grupo Editorial Norma S.A. for Guatemala; by Chips Computadoras S.A. de C.V. for Mexico; by Editorial Norma de Panama S.A. for Panama; by American Bookshops for Finland. Authorized Sales Agent: Anthony Rudkin Associates for the Middle East and North Africa.

For general information on IDG Books Worldwide's books in the U.S., please call our Consumer Customer Service department at 800-762-2974. For reseller information, including discounts and premium sales, please call our Reseller Customer Service department at 800-434-3422.

For information on where to purchase IDG Books Worldwide's books outside the U.S., please contact our International Sales department at 317-596-5530 or fax 317-596-5692.

For consumer information on foreign language translations, please contact our Customer Service department at 1-800-434-3422, fax 317-596-5692, or e-mail rights@idgbooks.com.

For information on licensing foreign or domestic rights, please phone +1-650-655-3109.

For sales inquiries and special prices for bulk quantities, please contact our Sales department at 650-655-3200 or write to the address above.

For information on using IDG Books Worldwide's books in the classroom or for ordering examination copies, please contact our Educational Sales department at 800-434-2086 or fax 317-596-5499.

For press review copies, author interviews, or other publicity information, please contact our Public Relations department at 650-655-3000 or fax 650-655-3299.

For authorization to photocopy items for corporate, personal, or educational use, please contact Copyright Clearance Center, 222 Rosewood Drive, Danvers, MA 01923, or fax 978-750-4470.

is a registered trademark or trademark under exclusive license to IDG Books Worldwide, Inc. from International Data Group, Inc. in the United States and/or other countries.

About the Author

Andy Rathbone started geeking around with computers in 1985 when he bought a boxy CP/ M Kaypro 2X with lime-green letters. Like other budding nerds, he soon began playing with null-modem adaptors, dialing up computer bulletin boards, and working part-time at Radio Shack.

In between playing computer games, he served as editor of the *Daily Aztec* newspaper at San Diego State University. After graduating with a comparative literature degree, he went to work for a bizarre underground coffee-table magazine that sort of disappeared.

Andy began combining his two interests, words and computers, by selling articles to a local computer magazine. During the next few years, Andy started ghostwriting computer books for more famous computer authors, as well as writing several hundred articles about computers for technoid publications like *Supercomputing Review, CompuServe Magazine, ID Systems, DataPro,* and *Shareware.*

In 1992, Andy and *DOS For Dummies* author/legend Dan Gookin teamed up to write *PCs For Dummies,* which was runner-up in the Computer Press Association's 1993 awards. Andy subsequently wrote the first edition of *Windows For Dummies,* and a string of other *...For Dummies* books, including *OS/2 For Dummies, Upgrading & Fixing PCs For Dummies, Multimedia & CD-ROMs For Dummies, MORE Windows For Dummies, Dummies 101: Windows 98,* and *Windows NT For Dummies* with Sharon Crawford.

Andy lives with his most excellent wife, Tina, and their cat in San Diego, California. When not writing, he fiddles with his MIDI synthesizer and tries to keep the cat off both keyboards.

ABOUT IDG BOOKS WORLDWIDE

Welcome to the world of IDG Books Worldwide.

IDG Books Worldwide, Inc., is a subsidiary of International Data Group, the world's largest publisher of computer-related information and the leading global provider of information services on information technology. IDG was founded more than 30 years ago by Patrick J. McGovern and now employs more than 9,000 people worldwide. IDG publishes more than 290 computer publications in over 75 countries. More than 90 million people read one or more IDG publications each month.

Launched in 1990, IDG Books Worldwide is today the #1 publisher of best-selling computer books in the United States. We are proud to have received eight awards from the Computer Press Association in recognition of editorial excellence and three from Computer Currents' First Annual Readers' Choice Awards. Our best-selling ...For Dummies® series has more than 50 million copies in print with translations in 31 languages. IDG Books Worldwide, through a joint venture with IDG's Hi-Tech Beijing, became the first U.S. publisher to publish a computer book in the People's Republic of China. In record time, IDG Books Worldwide has become the first choice for millions of readers around the world who want to learn how to better manage their businesses.

Our mission is simple: Every one of our books is designed to bring extra value and skill-building instructions to the reader. Our books are written by experts who understand and care about our readers. The knowledge base of our editorial staff comes from years of experience in publishing, education, and journalism — experience we use to produce books to carry us into the new millennium. In short, we care about books, so we attract the best people. We devote special attention to details such as audience, interior design, use of icons, and illustrations. And because we use an efficient process of authoring, editing, and desktop publishing our books electronically, we can spend more time ensuring superior content and less time on the technicalities of making books.

You can count on our commitment to deliver high-quality books at competitive prices on topics you want to read about. At IDG Books Worldwide, we continue in the IDG tradition of delivering quality for more than 30 years. You'll find no better book on a subject than one from IDG Books Worldwide.

John Kilcullen
Chairman and CEO
IDG Books Worldwide, Inc.

Steven Berkowitz
President and Publisher
IDG Books Worldwide, Inc.

WINNER

Eighth Annual
Computer Press
Awards ➣ 1992

IX WINNER

Ninth Annual
Computer Press
Awards ➣ 1993

X WINNER

Tenth Annual
Computer Press
Awards ➣ 1994

XI WINNER

Eleventh Annual
Computer Press
Awards ➣ 1995

IDG is the world's leading IT media, research and exposition company. Founded in 1964, IDG had 1997 revenues of $2.05 billion and has more than 9,000 employees worldwide. IDG offers the widest range of media options that reach IT buyers in 75 countries representing 95% of worldwide IT spending. IDG's diverse product and services portfolio spans six key areas including print publishing, online publishing, expositions and conferences, market research, education and training, and global marketing services. More than 90 million people read one or more of IDG's 290 magazines and newspapers, including IDG's leading global brands — Computerworld, PC World, Network World, Macworld and the Channel World family of publications. IDG Books Worldwide is one of the fastest-growing computer book publishers in the world, with more than 700 titles in 36 languages. The "...For Dummies®" series alone has more than 50 million copies in print. IDG offers online users the largest network of technology-specific Web sites around the world through IDG.net (http://www.idg.net), which comprises more than 225 targeted Web sites in 55 countries worldwide. International Data Corporation (IDC) is the world's largest provider of information technology data, analysis and consulting, with research centers in over 41 countries and more than 400 research analysts worldwide. IDG World Expo is a leading producer of more than 168 globally branded conferences and expositions in 35 countries including E3 (Electronic Entertainment Expo), Macworld Expo, ComNet, Windows World Expo, ICE (Internet Commerce Expo), Agenda, DEMO, and Spotlight. IDG's training subsidiary, ExecuTrain, is the world's largest computer training company, with more than 230 locations worldwide and 785 training courses. IDG Marketing Services helps industry-leading IT companies build international brand recognition by developing global integrated marketing programs via IDG's print, online and exposition products worldwide. Further information about the company can be found at www.idg.com.   1/24/99

Dedication

To my wife, parents, sister, and cat.

Author's Acknowledgments

Thanks to Dan Gookin and his wife Sandy, Matt Wagner, the Kleskes, the Tragesers, Sandy Blackthorn, Jennifer Ehrlich, Colleen Totz, Allen Wyatt of Discovery Computing, Terrie and David Solomon, and everyone else who's made this book such a success.

Publisher's Acknowledgments

We're proud of this book; please register your comments through our IDG Books Worldwide Online Registration Form located at http://my2cents.dummies.com.

Some of the people who helped bring this book to market include the following:

Acquisitions, Editorial, and Media Development

Project Editor: Colleen Totz
   (Previous Edition: Jennifer Ehrlich)

Acquisitions Editor: Steven H. Hayes

Technical Editor: Discovery Computing

Media Development Manager:
   Heather Heath Dismore

Production

Project Coordinator: Marridee V. Ennis

Layout and Graphics: Angela F. Hunckler, Dave McKelvey, Barry Offringa Brent Savage, Michael A. Sullivan, Brian Torwelle, Mary Jo Weis, Dan Whetstine

Proofreaders: Mary C. Barnack, Christine Berman, Nancy Price, Marianne Santy, Rebecca Senninger

Indexer: Liz Cunningham

Special Help

Suzanne Thomas

General and Administrative

IDG Books Worldwide, Inc.: John Kilcullen, CEO; Steven Berkowitz, President and Publisher

IDG Books Technology Publishing Group: Richard Swadley, Senior Vice President and Publisher; Walter Bruce III, Vice President and Associate Publisher; Steven Sayre, Associate Publisher; Joseph Wikert, Associate Publisher; Mary Bednarek, Branded Product Development Director; Mary Corder, Editorial Director

IDG Books Consumer Publishing Group: Roland Elgey, Senior Vice President and Publisher; Kathleen A. Welton, Vice President and Publisher; Kevin Thornton, Acquisitions Manager; Kristin A. Cocks, Editorial Director

IDG Books Internet Publishing Group: Brenda McLaughlin, Senior Vice President and Publisher; Diane Graves Steele, Vice President and Associate Publisher; Sofia Marchant, Online Marketing Manager

IDG Books Production for Dummies Press: Michael R. Britton, Vice President of Production; Debbie Stailey, Associate Director of Production; Cindy L. Phipps, Manager of Project Coordination, Production Proofreading, and Indexing; Shelley Lea, Supervisor of Graphics and Design; Debbie J. Gates, Production Systems Specialist; Robert Springer, Supervisor of Proofreading; Laura Carpenter, Production Control Manager; Tony Augsburger, Supervisor of Reprints and Bluelines

◆

The publisher would like to give special thanks to Patrick J. McGovern, without whom this book would not have been possible.

◆

Contents at a Glance

Cartoons at a Glance

By Rich Tennant

"HEY DAD, IS IT ALL RIGHT IF I WINDOW YOUR COMPUTER?"

page 7

"THE PHONE COMPANY BLAMES THE MANUFACTURER, WHO SAYS IT'S THE SOFTWARE COMPANY'S FAULT, WHO BLAMES IT ON OUR MOON BEING IN VENUS WITH SCORPIO RISING."

page 65

"IT'S A MEMO FROM SOFTWARE DOCUMENTATION. IT'S EITHER AN EXPLANATION OF HOW THE NEW SATELLITE COMMUNICATIONS NETWORK FUNCTIONS, OR DIRECTIONS FOR REPLACING BATTERIES IN THE SMOKE DETECTORS."

page 285

"GENTLEMEN, I SAY RATHER THAN FIX THE 'BUGS,' WE CHANGE THE DOCUMENTATION AND CALL THEM 'FEATURES.'"

page 315

"It still bothers me that I'm paying a lot of REAL dollars to a REAL university so you can get a degree in ARTIFICIAL intelligence."

page 179

Fax: 978-546-7747 • E-mail: the5wave@tiac.net

Table of Contents

Introduction

● ●

*W*elcome to *Windows 98 For Dummies!*

This book boils down to this simple fact: Some people want to be Windows wizards. They love interacting with dialog boxes. While sitting in front of their computers, they randomly press keys on their keyboards, hoping to stumble onto a hidden, undocumented feature. They memorize long strings of computer commands while rinsing dishes to go in the dishwasher.

And you? Well, you're no dummy, that's for sure. In fact, you're much more developed than most computer nerds. You can make casual conversation with a neighbor without mumbling about ordering pizzas over the Internet, for example. But when it comes to Windows and computers, the fascination just isn't there. You just want to get your work done, go home, fill the pet's water dish, and relax for a while. You have no intention of changing, and there's nothing wrong with that.

That's where this book comes in handy. It won't try to turn you into a Windows wizard, but you'll pick up a few chunks of useful computing information while reading it. Instead of becoming a Windows 98 expert, you'll know just enough to get by quickly, cleanly, and with a minimum of pain so that you can move on to the more pleasant things in life.

About This Book

Don't try to read this book in one sitting; there's no need to. Instead, treat this book like a dictionary or an encyclopedia. Turn to the page with the information you need and say, "Ah, so that's what they're talking about." Then put down the book and move on.

Don't bother trying to remember all the Windows 98 buzzwords, such as "Select the menu item from the drop-down list box." Leave that stuff for the computer gurus. In fact, if anything technical comes up in a chapter, a road sign warns you well in advance. That way you can either slow down to read it or speed on around it.

You won't find any fancy computer jargon in this book. Instead, you'll find subjects like these, discussed in plain old English:

- Preparing your computer to run Windows 98
- Finding the file you saved yesterday
- Moving those little windows around on the screen with the mouse
- Running your favorite old programs under Windows 98
- Performing chores in Windows 98 that you used to do in older versions of Windows
- Figuring out which of the many Windows versions you're using

There's nothing to memorize and nothing to learn. Just turn to the right page, read the brief explanation, and get back to work. Unlike other books, this one enables you to bypass any technical hoopla and still get your work done.

How to Use This Book

Something in Windows 98 will eventually leave you scratching your head. No other program brings so many buttons, bars, and babble to the screen. When something in Windows 98 has you stumped, use this book as a reference. Look for the troublesome topic in this book's table of contents or index. The table of contents lists chapter and section titles and page numbers. The index lists topics and page numbers. Page through the table of contents or index to the spot that deals with that particular bit of computer obscurity, read only what you have to, close the book, and apply what you've read.

If you're feeling spunky and want to learn something, read a little further. You can find a few completely voluntary extra details or some cross-references to check out. There's no pressure, though. You won't be forced to learn anything that you don't want to or that you simply don't have time for.

If you have to type something into the computer, you'll see easy-to-follow text like this:

```
http://www.vw.com
```

In the preceding example, you type the cryptic string of letters **http://www.vw.com** and then press the keyboard's Enter key. Typing words into a computer can be confusing, so a description of what you're supposed to type usually follows. That way, you can type the words exactly as they're supposed to be typed.

Whenever I describe a message or information that you see on-screen, I present it in the same way, as follows:

```
This is a message on-screen.
```

This book doesn't wimp out by saying, "For further information, consult your manual." No need to pull on your wading boots. This book covers all the basic information you need to begin using Windows 98. (And if you're still having trouble with your old DOS programs, the best crowbar is this book's grandfather, *DOS For Dummies,* 3rd Edition, by Dan Gookin, published by IDG Books Worldwide, Inc.)

You also won't find information about running specific Windows software packages. Windows 98 is complicated enough on its own! Luckily, other *...For Dummies* books mercifully explain most popular software packages.

Don't feel abandoned, though. The book covers some of the more popular Windows programs in enough detail for you to get the job done.

Finally, keep in mind that this book is a *reference*. It's not designed to teach you how to use Windows 98. Instead, this book dishes out enough bite-sized chunks of information so that you don't *have* to learn Windows. If you prefer a complete tutorial that gently takes you by the hand and teaches you how to use Windows 98, please pick up one of my other books, *Dummies 101: Windows 98* (published by IDG Books Worldwide, Inc.).

Please Don't Read This!

Computers thrive on technical stuff. Luckily, you're warned in advance when you're heading for something even vaguely obtuse. Chances are it's just more minute detail concerning something you've already read about. Feel free to skip any section labeled Technical Stuff. Those niblets of information aren't what this book is about. But, if you're feeling particularly ornery, keep reading and you may learn something. (Just don't let anybody see you do it.)

And What about You?

Well, chances are that you have a computer. You have Windows 98, or are thinking about picking up a copy. You know what *you* want to do with your computer. The problem lies in making the *computer* do what you want it to do. You've gotten by one way or another, hopefully with the help of a computer guru — either a friend at the office or somebody down the street. Unfortunately, though, that computer guru isn't always around. This book can be a substitute during your times of need. Keep a Jack-in-the-Box Jumbo Jack gift certificate nearby, however, just in case you need a quick bribe.

How This Book Is Organized

The information in this book has been well sifted. This book contains six parts, and each part is divided into chapters related to the part's theme. Each chapter is divided into short sections to help you navigate the stormy seas of Windows 98. Sometimes, you may find what you're looking for in a small, boxed tip. Other times, you may need to cruise through an entire section or chapter. It's up to you and the particular task at hand.

Here are the categories (the envelope, please):

Part I: Bare-Bones Windows 98 Stuff (Start Here)

This book starts out with the basics. You find out how to turn on your computer and how to examine your computer's parts and what Windows 98 does to them. It explains all the Windows 98 stuff that everybody thinks you already know. It explains the new features in Windows 98, separating the wheat from the chaff while leaving out any thick, technical oatmeal. You discover whether your computer has enough oomph to run Windows 98. And you end this part (with great relief) by turning off your computer.

Part II: Making Windows 98 Do Something

The program sits on the screen, playing jazzy tunes and flashing exciting pictures. But how do you make the darn thing do something *useful?* Here, you find ways to overcome the frustratingly playful tendencies of Windows 98 and force it to shovel the walkway or blow leaves off the driveway.

Part III: Using Windows 98 Applications (And Surfing the Web, Should the Mood Strike)

Windows 98 comes with a whole bunch of free programs. In this part, you find practical information about your new word processor and WebTV for Windows, as well as ways to start playing with that World Wide Web thing everyone is mumbling about suspiciously. You discover what the funky, new

Windows 98 Active Desktop is all about, and why your computer screen now looks like a billboard for Microsoft products. In fact, if you punch the right buttons, you can also turn your wallpaper into a Web page, with separate channels for Disney, _The Wall Street Journal,_ and Warner Brothers. Zounds!

Part IV: Help!

Are your windows stuck? Broken? Do you need new screens? Although glass doesn't shatter when Windows 98 crashes, it can still hurt. In this part, you find some soothing salves for the most painful and irritating maladies. Plus, you find ways to unleash the Troubleshooting Wizards and automatic Update programs in Windows 98. Imagine: A computer that can finally grab a wrench and fix itself!

Part V: The Part of Tens

Everybody loves lists (except during tax time). This part contains lists of Windows-related trivia — ten aggravating things about Windows 98 (and how to fix them), ten ways to fix confusing Internet problems, ten weird Windows 98 icons and what they mean, ten expensive things that make Windows 98 easier, and other shoulder-rubbing solutions for tense problems.

Appendixes

Windows 98 didn't come preinstalled on your computer? Flip to the back of the book for tips on transferring the software from the box onto your computer. The official Windows 98 glossary lurks back here, too, ready to explain funky computer terms like "32-bit."

Icons Used in This Book

Already seen Windows? Then you've probably noticed its _icons,_ which are little pictures for starting various programs. The icons in this book fit right in. They're even a little easier to figure out:

Watch out! This signpost warns you that pointless technical information is coming around the bend. Swerve away from this icon, and you'll be safe from the awful technical drivel.

This icon alerts you about juicy information that makes computing easier. Handy little stuff, like how to cheat in FreeCell, or banish that annoying Password screen that appears whenever you turn on your computer.

Don't forget to remember these important points. (Or at least dog-ear the pages so that you can look them up again a few days later.)

The computer won't explode while you're performing the delicate operations associated with this icon. Still, wearing gloves and proceeding with caution is a good idea when this icon is near.

Already familiar with Windows 95, the predecessor to Windows 98? This icon marks information that can ease the transition from the two systems.

Where to Go from Here

Now you're ready for action. Give the pages a quick flip and maybe scan through a few sections that you know you'll need later. Oh, and this is *your* book — your weapon against the computer criminals who've inflicted this whole complicated computer concept on you. So pretend that you're Xena, the Warrior Princess, and personalize your sword: Circle the paragraphs you find useful, highlight key concepts, cover up the technical drivel with sticky notes, and draw gothic gargoyles in the margins next to the complicated stuff. The more you mark up the book, the easier it will be for you to find all the good stuff again.

Part I
Bare-Bones Windows 98 Stuff (Start Here)

The 5th Wave   By Rich Tennant

"HEY DAD, IS IT ALL RIGHT IF I WINDOW YOUR COMPUTER?"

In this part . . .

Windows 98 is an exciting, new way to use the computer. That means it's as confusing as a new car's dashboard. Even the most wizened old computer buffs stumble in this strange new land of boxes, bars, and bizarre oddities like push technology.

Never used a computer before but bought Windows 98 because it's "easy to use?" Well, Windows 98 can be intuitive, but that doesn't mean it's as easy to figure out as a steak knife.

In fact, most people are dragged into Windows 98 without a choice. Your new computer probably came with a version of Windows 98 already installed. Or maybe you had installed Windows 98 at the office, where everyone has to learn it except for Jerry, who moved over to the Art Department and got his own Macintosh. Or perhaps the latest version of your favorite program, like Microsoft Word, requires Windows 98, so you've had to learn to live with the darn thing.

No matter how you were introduced, you can adjust to Windows 98, just like you eventually learned to live comfortably with that funky college roommate who kept leaving hair clogs in the shower.

Whatever your situation, this part keeps things safe and sane, with the water flowing smoothly. If you're new to computers, the first chapter answers the question you've been afraid to ask around the lunch room: "Just what is this Windows 98 thing, anyway?"

Chapter 1

What Is Windows 98?

In This Chapter

▶ Understanding what Windows 98 is and what it does

▶ Finding out how Windows 98 affects your current programs

▶ Deciding whether you should upgrade to Windows 98

One way or another, you've probably already heard about Microsoft Windows. Windows posters line the walls of computer stores. While you're stuck in traffic, the Microsoft roadside billboards cheerfully ask, "Where do you want to go today?" Everybody who's anybody talks breezily about Windows, the Internet, and the World Wide Web. Weird code words, like www.vw.com, stare out cryptically from magazine, newspaper, and television advertisements.

To help you play catch-up in the world of Windows, this chapter fills you in on the basics of the latest version of Windows, called *Windows 98*. The chapter explains what Windows 98 is and what it can do. You can also examine how Windows 98 works with your older Windows programs.

What Are Windows and Windows 98?

Windows is just another piece of software, like the zillions of others lining the store shelves. But it's not a program in the normal sense — something that lets you write letters or lets your coworkers play Bozark the Destroyer over the office network after everybody else goes home. Rather, Windows controls the way you work with your computer.

For years, computers have clung to a "typewriter" style of work. Just as on a typewriter, people type letters and numbers into the computer. The computer listens and then places letters and numbers onto the screen. This time-tested system works well. But it takes a long time to learn, and it's as boring as reading the ingredients on a jar of reduced-fat mayonnaise.

The method is boring because computer engineers designed computers for other computer engineers many moons ago. They thought that computers would be forever isolated in narrow hallways where somber youngsters with crewcuts, clipboards, and white lab coats jotted down notes while the big reels whirled. Nobody expected normal people to use computers — especially not in their offices, their dens, or, heaven help us, their kitchens.

- ✔ Windows software dumps the typewriter analogy and updates the *look* of computers. Windows replaces the words and numbers with pictures and fun buttons. It's smooth and shiny, like an expensive, new coffeemaker.

- ✔ Because Windows software looks and acts differently from traditional computer programs, understanding it can take a few days. After all, you probably couldn't make perfect coffee the first day, either.

- ✔ Windows 98 is the most powerful version of Windows software — software that's been updated many times since starting to breathe in January 1985.

- ✔ Programmer types say Windows software is big enough and powerful enough to be called an *operating system*. That's because Windows "operates" your computer. Most computer users, however, call Windows lots of other names, including some that my editor won't let me publish here.

- ✔ Okay, I lied. *Windows 2000* is Microsoft's biggest, most powerful version of Windows. Stronger and more full-featured, Windows 2000 is favored mostly by large office networks so all the computers can talk to each other. In fact, Microsoft eventually plans to discontinue its Windows 98 line in favor of its Windows 2000 series. (That means it also gets its own book, *Windows 2000 For Dummies*, written by me and Sharon Crawford, and published by IDG Books Worldwide, Inc.)

What Does Windows Do?

Like the mother with the whistle in the lunch court, Windows controls all the parts of your computer. You turn on your computer, start Windows, and start running programs. Each program runs in its own little *window* on-screen, as shown in Figure 1-1. Yet Windows keeps things safe, even if the programs start throwing food at each other.

Windows gets its name from all the cute little windows on-screen. Each window shows some information: a picture, perhaps, or a program that you're running. You can put several windows on-screen at the same time and jump from window to window, visiting different programs.

Some people say that colorful windows and pictures make Windows easier to use; others say that Windows is a little too arty. To write a letter in Windows 98, for example, do you select the picture of the notepad, the quill, or the clipboard? And what potential problems can emerge with the icons of the spinning globe and the bomb?

✔ A computer environment that uses little pictures and symbols is called a *graphical user interface,* or *GUI.* (It's pronounced *gooey,* believe it or not.) Pictures require more computing horsepower than letters and numbers, so Windows 98 requires a relatively powerful computer. (You can find a list of its requirements in Chapter 2.)

✔ When the word *Windows* starts with a capital letter, it refers to the Windows program. When the word *windows* starts with a lowercase letter, it refers to windows you see on-screen. When the word *Windows* ends with the number *98,* it refers to the latest version of the Windows software, Windows 98.

Because Windows uses graphics, it's much easier to use than to describe. To tell someone how to move through a Windows document you say, "Click in the vertical scroll bar beneath the scroll box." Those directions sound awfully weird, but after you've done it, you'll say, "Oh, is that all? Golly!" (Plus, you can still press the PgDn key in Windows. You don't have to "click in the vertical scroll bar beneath the scroll box" if you don't want to.)

With Windows 98, your desktop doesn't have to look like a typewritten page *or* a desktop. Now, it can look like an Internet Web page, as shown in Figure 1-2. (You can find more about Web pages and the Internet in Chapter 13.) In fact, the chameleon-like Windows 98 can run like a Web page, use the "Classic Windows 95" settings, or let you customize it with any combination. That introduces many more ways for things to go wrong.

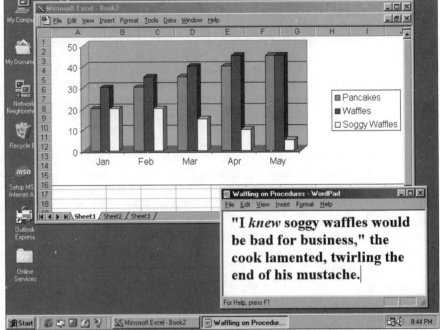

Figure 1-1:
The Windows 98 desktop runs programs in little on-screen windows.

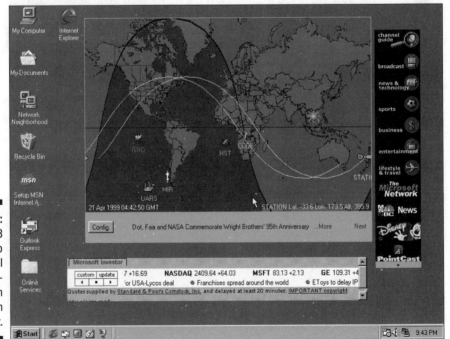

Figure 1-2:
Windows 98 lets "Web surfers" fill their desktop with pages from the Internet.

How Does Windows 98 Affect My Older Programs?

Windows 98 can still run most of your older Windows programs, too, thank goodness. So after upgrading to Windows 98, you won't have to immediately buy expensive new software. It runs almost all Windows 95 programs and many Windows 3.1 programs.

Finally upgrading from an old computer that uses DOS? Windows 98 can probably still run your old DOS programs. (Your dusty old computer probably won't have enough oomph to run Windows 98, but you probably wanted a new one, anyway.)

✔ When people say *Windows 3.1,* they're often referring to several older versions of Windows: *Windows 3.11, Windows for Workgroups 3.1,* and *Windows for Workgroups 3.11.* Each version is just a slightly improved reworking of its predecessor, however: *Windows 3.1* is easiest to say, so that's the phrase most people use. (Some programmers use the term *Windows 3.x,* however, just to add a scientific touch.)

✔ Most programs from the Windows 3.0 generation or earlier simply can't keep up with Windows 98: Retire them.

✔ You can't take Windows 98, install it onto your five-year-old computer and expect it to run well. No; Windows 98 is a big operating system for a big computer. You'll probably have to buy a new one or add bigger shoulders to your older one. (In computer language, big shoulders translate to a faster CPU chip, more memory, a larger hard drive, and a CD-ROM drive.) Unfortunately, adding bigger shoulders often costs more than buying a new PC.

When people say Windows 98 is *backward compatible,* that just means it can run software that was written for older versions of Windows. You can still run most Windows 95 and Windows 3.1 software on Windows 98, for example, as well as most DOS software. (Don't even think about running Macintosh software, though.)

Should I Bother Using Windows 98?

Windows 95 users are elbowing each other nervously by the water cooler and whispering the Big Question: Why bother buying Windows 98, going through the hassle of installing it, and learning all its new programs?

Here's why: Windows 98 comes preinstalled on most new computers, so many people are simply stuck with it. Also, Windows 98 offers quite a few improvements over earlier versions, as you'll find out in the next two sections.

Basically, the upgrade question boils down to this answer: If your computer crashes a lot when using Windows 95, it might be time to upgrade. But if you're happy with your current computer setup, don't bother. After all, why buy new tires if your old ones still have some life left?

Upgrading from Windows 95

Upgrading from Windows 95? Then you'll find Windows 98 easier to install. Plus, it handles files faster and more efficiently on today's powerhouse PCs.

It can automatically run background maintenance tasks to keep itself "tuned up" and ready to run. If you have access to the Internet, Windows 98 can diagnose itself to see if it's up to date, and then automatically grab the latest files it needs to keep running smoothly.

Technolusters who like the latest and greatest gadgets will like the new "TV Tuner" programs for watching TV on their monitors (provided you shell out a hundred bucks or so for a TV card). Or, if your desk is big enough, splurge on another monitor. Windows 98 lets you arrange your desktop across both monitors, doubling your workspace. Whoopee!

If you're an Internet devotee, you'll like the way Windows 98 wraps itself around Microsoft's Web browser, Internet Explorer. Not only can you make your computer look like a Web page, but you can also have parts of Web pages embedded in your desktop and running in the background — where the boss can't notice 'em as much.

Finally, Windows makes the Internet act more like a television, with easily switchable — and customizable — Channels. You'll find Channels for Disney, America Online, Warner Brothers, and other large corporate conglomerations.

Upgrading from Windows 3.1

Windows 3.1 users who skipped Windows 95 will be pleasantly surprised: They won't have to point and click as much to find files and start programs. For example, Windows 98 remembers the names of files or programs you've recently used and stores their names in a special spot. Do you want to load the file again? Just click on the file's name from the pop-up list — no wading through menus or opening programs: White-gloved Windows 98 opens the car door and lets you start moving immediately.

Should I upgrade from Windows 95 to Windows 98?

Here's the ugly truth about Windows 98 that you might not hear anyplace else. Windows 98 is really just a slightly polished version of Windows 95. Although Microsoft tossed in a few extra doodads, Windows 98 looks and acts almost identically to its three-year-old cousin.

The big difference? Microsoft massaged its Internet Web browser program, Internet Explorer, into the skin of Windows 98. The result? Your desktop can look and act like an Internet Web page.

Some people will be excited by this new-tech change. Others will search for a way to turn it off. (Chapter 21 reveals that secret.) And others will wonder if it's even worth the upgrade in the first place. Only you can decide.

You see lots more little buttons with pictures on them — *icons* — used in Windows 98 programs. You don't know what the icon with the little policeman picture is supposed to do? Then just rest your mouse pointer over the icon; after a few seconds, a message often pops up on-screen, explaining the policeman button's role on the streets of Windows. The most helpful messages appear when you rest the pointer over the unlabeled buttons that hang out along the tops of programs, like word processors and spreadsheets — in their toolbar areas.

Windows 98 allows longer filenames, just like Windows 95. After 15 years of frustration, PC users can call their files something more descriptive than RPT45.TXT. In fact, Windows offers you 255 characters to describe your creations.

✔ Ready to upgrade your computer? Windows 98 can give you a hand with its upgraded "Plug and Play" concept. A new Windows 98 "Wizard" keeps better track of the parts inside your computer and can alert you when internal brawls start. Better yet, it prevents many brawls from even starting by making sure that two computer parts aren't assigned the same areas of your computer's memory.

✔ Windows 98 automates many computing chores. To install a program, for example, just push the floppy disk (or compact disc) into the drive and click the Control Panel's Add/Remove Programs button (which I cover in Chapter 9, by the way). Windows searches all your drives for the installation program and runs it automatically. Windows 98 can automatically search for any new hardware you've installed as well, recognizing quite a few of the most popular upgrades.

✔ Are you tired of twiddling your thumbs while Windows formats a floppy? Windows 98 can handle floppy chores in the background so that you can continue playing your card game. (The card game, FreeCell, is an incredibly delicious time-waster.)

Bracing Yourself (And Your Computer) for Windows 98

With Windows, everything happens at the same time. Its many different parts run around like hamsters with an open cage door. Programs cover each other up on-screen. They overlap corners, hiding each other's important parts. Occasionally, they simply disappear.

Be prepared for a bit of frustration when things don't behave properly. You may be tempted to stand up, bellow, and toss a nearby stapler across the room. After that, calmly pick up this book, find the trouble spot listed in the index, and turn to the page with the answer.

✔ Windows software may be accommodating, but that can cause problems, too. For example, Windows 98 often offers more than three different ways for you to perform the same computing task. Don't bother memorizing each command. Just choose one method that works for you and stick with it. For example, Andrew and Deirdre Kleske use scissors to cut their freshly delivered pizza into slices. It stupefies most of their house guests, but it gets the job done.

✔ Windows 98 runs best on a powerful new computer with the key words *Pentium, Pentium Pro, Pentium II, Pentium III* or *testosterone* somewhere in the description. Look for as much *RAM* (Random-Access Memory) and as many *gigabytes* as you can afford. You can find the detailed rundown of the Windows 98 finicky computer requirements in Chapter 2.

Chapter 2

Ignore This Chapter on Computer Parts

*T*his chapter introduces computer gizmos and gadgets. Go ahead and ignore it. Who cares about what all your PC gadgetry is called? Unless your PC's beeping at you like a car alarm (or not beeping when it's supposed to beep), don't bother messing with it. Just dog-ear the top of this page, say, "So, that's where all that stuff is explained," and keep going.

In Windows 98, you just press the buttons. Windows 98 does the dirty work, scooting over to the right part of your computer and kick-starting the action. In case Windows 98 stubs a toe, this chapter explains where you might need to put the bandages. And, as always, the foulest-smelling technical chunks are clearly marked; just hold your nose while stepping over them gingerly.

The Computer

The computer is that box with all the cables. Officially, it probably answers to one of two names: IBM (called *True Blue* when people try to dump their old ones in the classifieds) or an *IBM compatible* or *clone*.

However, most people just call their computers *PCs* because that's what IBM called its first *personal computer* back in 1981. In fact, the first IBM PC started this whole personal computing craze, although some people lay the blame on video games.

The concept of a small computer that could be pecked on in an office or den caught on well with the average Joe, and IBM made gobs of money. So much money, in fact, that other companies immediately ripped off the IBM design. They *cloned,* or copied, IBM's handiwork to make a computer that worked just like it. Made by companies like Dell and Gateway, they're *compatible* with IBM's own PC; they can all use the same software as an IBM PC without spitting up.

IBM-compatible computers generally have an obscure brand name and a lower price on their invoice, but they often work just as well (or better) than IBM's own line of computers. In fact, more people own compatibles than IBM's own line of personal computers. (Just look at the recent IBM quarterly earnings statements for proof.)

✔ Windows 98 runs equally well on IBM-compatible computers and on IBM's own computers; the key word is *IBM.* Computers from other planets, like the Macintosh, don't run Windows 98, but their owners don't care. They just smile pleasantly when you try to figure out how to create a Windows 98 "file association."

✔ Okay, so a Macintosh can *run* some third-party versions of Windows software, but you need a special (and expensive) breed of Windows-emulating software. These days, you're probably better off sticking with either a Mac or a PC — don't try to interbreed their brands of software.

✔ Most newer computers are designed to work sideways. These upright PCs are called *tower PCs.* The tilt doesn't affect their performance, but it makes them look cool. In fact, some muscular people heft their old desktop PCs onto one side and put them in a special stand so they look cool, too.

✔ As other companies built *compatible* computers, they strayed from the original IBM design. They added sound, color, and other bits of whig-maleerie. Windows 98 can now identify what computer parts it's dealing with automatically, so it knows what tone of voice to use when speaking with them. Most problems pop up when first installing Windows 98 — a topic covered step by step in this book's Appendix A.

✔ Laptop and notebook computers can run Windows 98 with no problems. Palmtops and other handheld computers can't; they can only run an itty-bitty version of Windows called Windows CE — now in its second edition.

When laptopping on an airplane, drop a few smoked almonds on your neighboring passenger's thigh. If he doesn't wake up, you can use his kneecap as a makeshift mousepad for a few double-clicks.

The Microprocessor (CPU)

The computer's brain is a small chip of silicon buried deep inside the computer's case. Resembling a Girl Scout's Thin Mint with square corners, this flat little wafer is the *microprocessor,* but nerds tend to call it a *central processing unit,* or *CPU.* (You may have seen flashy microprocessor TV commercials that say, "Intel Inside." Intel is a leading CPU developer.)

The computer's microprocessor determines how fast and powerful the computer can toss information around. Refer to Table 2-1 for a look at the power of your particular computer.

Table 2-1	Microprocessor Power Ratings
Computer	*Comments*
XT, AT, 386SX, 386DX	Nearly obsolete, these chips can't handle Windows 98. These computers make great gifts to friends and charities.
486SX, 486DX	A few of these chips can run Windows 98, but much too slowly. Get rid of 'em.
Pentium (sometimes called 586 or AMD-K6)	A Pentium runs Windows 98 much faster than a 486, meaning less thumb-twiddling while opening programs and files. (Computer games play much smoother, too.)
Pentium Pro	The Pentium Pro was designed specifically to run the more powerful versions of Windows, like Windows 98 and Windows NT. So it runs Windows 98 faster than a plain old Pentium.
Pentium II	These are basically fast Pentium Pros with special "MMX" technology tossed in for faster graphics and videos. (*MMX* once stood for *Multi Media eXtensions*, but Intel registered the acronym as a brand name so nobody could rip it off.)
Pentium III	Intel's latest chip is basically a polished and sped-up Pentium II with a bit more graphics technology sprinkled on top.
"Celeron", "Xeon", and Mobile	Pentium chips labeled "Celeron" are the budget models without as much oomph as the more luxurious and powerful Xeon chips. The Mobile models, designed for laptops, are small, cool, and power-conscious.

(continued)

Table 2-1 *(continued)*

Computer	Comments
AMD and Cyrix chips	Intel isn't the only chipmaker, just the most expensive. AMD (Advanced Micro Devices) and Cyrix grab the budget market with chips below Intel's cutting edge offerings but delivering high-performance at a low price. Windows 98 prefers a AMD K-6 CPU or higher, or a Cyrix M-II or MediaGX processor.

✔ A microprocessor is the current evolution of the gadget that powered those little 1970s pocket calculators. It performs all the computer's background calculations, from juggling spreadsheets to swapping dirty jokes through office e-mail.

✔ Microprocessors are described by several numbers. Generally, the bigger the numbers, the faster and more powerful the chip.

✔ Intel assigns three numbers to its Pentium chips. The chip's model number — Pentium, Pentium II, Pentium III — comes in Roman numerals. The chip's processing speed is measured in *megahertz,* or *MHz.* The *cache* size (pronounced "cash") is measured in kilobites, like 512K. When comparing Pentiums, just remember that the bigger the number, the faster Windows performs.

Disks and Disk Drives

The computer's *disk drive,* that thin slot in its front side, is like the drawer at the bank's drive-up teller window. That disk drive enables you to send and retrieve information from the computer. Instead of making you drop information into a cashier's drawer, the computer makes you send and receive your information from disks. The main types — the floppy disk, the compact disc, the hard disk, the DVD, and the Zip drive — appear in the next four sections.

Not sure what kilobyte (K), megabyte (MB) and gigabyte (GB) mean? Head for that section a few pages later on in this chapter.

Floppy disks

You can shove anything that's flat into a floppy drive, but the computer recognizes only one thing: *floppy disks.* Things get a little weird here, so hang on tight. See, by some bizarre bit of mechanical wizardry, computers store information on disks as a stream of magnetic impulses.

A disk drive spits those little magnetic impulses onto the floppy disk for safe storage. The drive can slurp the information back up, too. You just push the disk into the disk drive and tell Windows whether to spit or slurp information. That's known as *copy to* or *copy from* in computer parlance.

Floppy disks are sturdy 3 ½-inch squares that are slowly losing popularity in favor of the compact disc, or CD, described next.

- ✔ A disk drive automatically grabs the 3 ½-inch disk when you push it in far enough. You hear it *clunk,* and the disk sinks down into the drive. If it doesn't, you're putting it in the wrong way. (The disk's silver edge goes in first, with the little round silver thing in the middle facing down.) To retrieve the disk, push the button protruding from around the drive's slot and then grab the disk when the drive kicks it out.

- ✔ Computer stores sell blank floppy disks so that you can copy your work onto them. Unless your new box of blank disks has the word *preformatted,* you can't use them straight out of the box. They must be *formatted* first. This merry little chore is covered in Chapter 11.

- ✔ Computers love to *copy* things. When you're copying a file from one disk to another, you aren't *moving* the file. You're just placing a copy of that file onto that other disk. (Of course, you can *move* the files over there, if you want, as described in Chapter 11.)

Compact discs (CD-ROM drive stuff)

Computer technicians snapped up compact disc technology pretty quickly when they realized that the shiny discs could store numbers as well as music. Today, most companies sell their programs and information on compact discs. A single compact disc holds more information than hundreds of floppy disks.

To use a disc, however, your computer needs its own compact disc drive. The CD player with your stereo won't cut it. Luckily, most compact disc drives let you access programs *and* play music through your PC. Now you can sell the CD player attached to your stereo. (It's getting old anyway.)

CDs enter your computer in a more dignified way than a floppy disk. Push a button on your compact disc drive, and the drive spits out a little platter. Place the CD on the platter, label side down, and push the little button again. The computer grabs the CD, ready for action. (If the button's too hard to reach, just nudge the platter and it'll retreat.)

✔ For years, you couldn't copy files onto a compact disc — you could only read information from them. Only the people at the CD factory could copy files to CDs, and that's because they had a whoppingly expensive machine. Now, many cheap compact disc drives let you read *and* copy files and music to your own discs. In fact, copyright attorneys are holding international conferences to make sure that nobody can create copies of their favorite Pearl Jam albums and sell them to their friends.

✔ A CD that only stores information until it's full is known as a CD-R; a CD that can read, write, and erase information is called CD-RW. Naturally, the CD-RW discs cost about five times as much.

✔ Compact disc is spelled with a *c* to confuse people accustomed to seeing disk ending with a *k*.

✔ Multimedia computers need a sound card as well as a compact drive; the drive alone isn't enough. This requirement is the computer industry's special way of making people spend more money. And, of course, most of today's computers come with a built-in CD-ROM drive and sound card.

✔ In fact, some multimedia computers come with a compact disc drive that plays DVD discs — the CDs with movies on them — as well as compact discs. They get their own section coming up next.

✔ Windows 98 offers technology called *Autoplay.* Just pop the CD into the CD-ROM drive, and Windows 98 automatically revs it up, whether the disc contains music, programs, or trendy videos of glassblowers in Italy. Autoplay is one more step toward eliminating installation hassles. If Windows 98 doesn't Autoplay your CD, see Chapter 18 for the fix.

DVD discs

Although it's hard to tell the difference between a DVD disc and a compact disc by looking, the computer certainly knows. A DVD disc holds a *lot* more information — enough information to hold an entire movie in several languages and extra perks like a director's voiceover explaining why a certain actress giggled during certain shots.

A DVD player costs a bit more, but it can play back DVD discs — the kind you rent or buy in video stores — as well as music CDs.

The biggest problem? Why would the family gather around a 15-inch computer monitor to watch a movie when they can buy a cheap DVD player, attach it to the living room's TV, and watch everything on a bigger screen?

Although nearly every sound card works with a DVD player, only special DVD-compatible sound cards can play the extra "surround sound" stored on a DVD.

Iomega drives

The robotic-sounding Zip, Jaz and the laptop-ready Clik drives from Iomega are thick plastic disks that hold 100MB or more of information, making them convenient for backing up garage-sized boxes of data.

They're as convenient as shoeboxes — not only for people who always run out of data space, but for people who've been burned a few times and always like to keep plenty of backups.

- ✔ Iomega's Zip drives are the small, portable gadgets that look sort of like a Sony Walkman. The Jaz drives hold up to 2 gigabytes; they fit into the computer like a regular floppy drive, but with a bigger slot. The portable Clik drives fit into a shirt pocket, ready to store 40 megabytes of information from a laptop or digital camera.

- ✔ Zip, Jaz and Clik drives are an easy way to move large amounts of data from the office to home and back — if you're forced to even consider such a thing.

Hard disks

Not everybody has a compact disc drive, Iomega drive, or even a floppy drive, but just about everybody has a hard disk: thick little Frisbees inside the computer that can hold thousands of times more information than floppy disks. Hard disks are also much quicker at reading and writing information. (They're a great deal quieter, too, thank goodness.) Windows 98 insists on a hard disk because it's such a huge program.

The programs that run under Windows 98 can be pretty huge, too. The Microsoft Monster Truck Madness game grabs 200MB of hard disk space if you install all the coolest options. Microsoft recommends a 2 gigabyte hard drive for video cards that let you watch TV.

- ✔ The point? Buy the largest hard disk you can afford. If you're shopping for a computer, make sure that it has room to add a second hard disk. You'll eventually need the room.

- ✔ If a program has a lot of *multimedia* — sounds, graphics, or movies — you need a huge hard disk. That type of information eats up the most space on a hard disk.

Windows 98 comes with "DriveSpace" and "Drive Converter" that claim to tweak your computer's hard disk so that you can fit many more files on it. Don't bother — installing them can do more harm than good. Save disk tweaking for people who *like* to play with their computer's ailing innards. Hard disks are relatively cheap these days, so just buy a big one.

What disk drives does Windows 98 like?

Windows 98 can easily eat up 300MB of space, depending on how much of it you choose to install. Your Windows 98 programs can eat up even more space. Nobody will laugh if you buy a 8 gigabyte or larger hard drive for Windows 98 and your Windows 98 programs. (A single gigabyte equals roughly 1,000 megabytes.)

You also want a CD-ROM drive. You may not actually need one, but it's better to copy from (or copy to) a single CD-ROM than to stand in front of the computer, feeding it floppy disks for more than an hour. In fact, buy one that can both read and write to the CD-R compact discs explained a few sections ago. Those discs only cost a few dollars, and they're a quick and easy way to back up your computer.

What does write-protected mean?

Write protection is supposed to be a helpful safety feature, but most people discover it through an abrupt bit of computer rudeness: Windows 98 stops them short with the threatening message shown in Figure 2-1 while they are trying to copy a file to a floppy disk.

A *write-protected disk* has simply been tweaked so that nobody can copy to it or delete the files it contains. Write protection is a simple procedure, surprisingly enough, requiring no government registration. You can write-protect and unwrite-protect disks in the privacy of your own home.

 ✔ To write-protect a 3 ½-inch floppy disk, look for a tiny black sliding tab in a square hole in its corner. Slide the tab with a pencil or your thumbnail so that the hole is uncovered. The disk is now write-protected.

 ✔ To remove the write protection on a 3 ½-inch disk, slide the little black plastic thingy so that the hole is covered up.

 ✔ If you encounter the write-protect error shown in Figure 2-1, wait until the drive stops making noise. Remove the disk, unwrite-protect the disk, and put it back in the drive. Then repeat what you were doing before you were so rudely interrupted.

Disk do's and doughnuts

✔ Do label your disks so that you know what's on them. (You can write on the top side of compact discs with a permanent felt pen.)

✔ Do at least make a valiant effort to peel off a disk's old label before sticking on a new one. (After a while, those stacks of old labels make the disk too fat to fit into the drive.)

✔ Do feel free to write on the label after it has been placed on the disk.

✔ Do not write on the disk's sleeve instead of the label. Disks always end up in each other's sleeves, leading to mistaken identities and faux pas.

✔ Do copy important files from your hard disk to floppy disks or compact discs on a regular basis. (This routine is called *backing up* in computer lingo. Windows comes with special backup software to make this chore a little easier — not much, but a little.)

✔ Do not leave disks lying in the sun.

✔ Do not place 3 ½ disks next to magnets. Don't place them next to magnets disguised as paper clip holders, either, or next to other common magnetized desktop items, such as older telephones.

✔ Do handle compact discs by their edges, not their surfaces. Keep the backside of the disc as clean as possible.

Figure 2-1:
Windows 98 sends an error message if the disk is write-protected

The Mouse and That Double-Click Stuff

The *mouse* is that rounded plastic thing that looks like a bar of electronic soap. Marketing people thought that the word *mouse* sounded like fun, so the name stuck. Actually, think of your mouse as your electronic finger, because you use it in Windows 98 to point at stuff on-screen.

A mouse has a little roller, or mouse ball, embedded in its belly. (Where were the animal-rights people?) When you move the mouse across your desk, the ball rubs against electronic sensor gizmos. The gizmos record the mouse's movements and send the information down the mouse's tail, which connects to the back of the computer.

As you move the mouse, you see an *arrow,* or *pointer,* move simultaneously across the computer screen. Here's where your electronic finger comes in: When the arrow points at a picture of a button on-screen, you press and release, or *click,* the left button on the mouse. The Windows 98 button is selected, just as if you'd pressed it with your finger. It's a cool bit of 3-D computer graphics that makes you want to click buttons again and again.

- You control just about everything in Windows 98 by pointing at it with the mouse and clicking the mouse button. (The mouse pitches in with a helpful clicking noise when you press its button.)

- The plural of mouse is *mice,* just like the ones cats chew on. It's not *mouses.*

- Some laptops come with a *touch-pad* — a little square thing for you to slide your finger over. As you move the tip of your finger across the pad, you move the mouse pointer across the screen. Other laptops, like IBM's suave black Thinkpads, have a *Trackpoint,* a little pencil eraser that sticks up out of the keyboard, wedged above the b key and below the g and h. Just push the eraser in the direction you want the mouse to move, and the mouse pointer scurries.

- If your mouse doesn't work with Windows 98 (it gets the shivers, it scurries around at random, or the arrow doesn't move), visit Chapter 14 for help.

- Microsoft's fairly new IntelliMouse has what looks like a tiny water-wheel protruding from the mouse's neck. By slowly rolling the water-wheel back and forth with your index finger, you can scroll up or down in your current work, line by line. Fun! Plus, pushing down once on the water-wheel is equivalent to an automatic double-click. (You can customize the buttons' actions, too.)

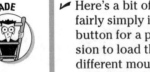

- Here's a bit of Windows 98 upgrade ugliness: For years, a mouse worked fairly simply in Windows. You pointed at something on the screen — a button for a program, for instance — and clicked twice in rapid succession to load that particular program. Now, Windows 98 comes with three different mouse "modes." Sometimes a single click loads a program, other times it takes two clicks. Still other times, the click factor depends on the program's lineage — whether it hails from the Internet. See Chapter 5 for the rundown on these new complications.

The mouse arrow changes shape, depending on what it's pointing at in Windows 98. When it changes shape, you know that it's ready to perform a new task. Table 2-2 is a handy reference for the different uniforms the mouse pointer wears for different jobs.

Table 2-2	The Various Shapes of the Mouse Pointer	
Shape	*What It Points At*	*What to Do When You See It*
▨	Just about anything	Use this pointer for moving from place to place on-screen. Then click to bring that place to Windows' attention.
✛	A single window	Uh-oh. You've somehow selected the annoying size or move option from the Control menu. Moving the mouse or pressing the cursor-control keys now makes the current window bigger or smaller. Press Enter when you're done, or press Esc if you want to get away from this uncomfortable bit of weirdness.
↕	The top or bottom edge of a window	Hold down the mouse button and move the mouse back and forth to make the window grow taller or shorter. Let go when you like the window's new size.
↔	The left or right side of a window	Hold down the mouse button and move the mouse back and forth to make the window fatter or skinnier. Let go when you like the window's new size.
↖	The corner of a window	Hold down the mouse button and move the mouse anywhere to make the window fat, skinny, tall, or short. Let go when you're through playing.
I	A program or box that accepts text (this pointer is called an I-beam)	Put the pointer where you want words to appear, click the button, and start typing the letters or numbers.
🖑	A word with a hidden meaning in the Windows' help system	Click the mouse, and Windows 98 trots out some more helpful information about that particular subject
⧗	Nothing (Windows is busy ignoring you)	Move the mouse in wild circles and watch the hourglass spin around until Windows catches up with you. This shape usually appears when you are loading files or copying stuff to a floppy disk.

(continued)

Table 2-2 (continued)

Shape	What It Points At	What to Do When You See It
⏳	Anything	Keep working. This pointer means that Windows 98 is doing something in the background, so it may work a little more slowly.
?⃝	Anything	By clicking the little question mark found in the top-right corner of some boxes, you create this pointer. Click confusing on-screen areas for helpful informational handouts.
⊘	Something forbidden	Press the Esc key, let go of the mouse button, and start over. (You're trying to drag something to a place where it doesn't belong.)

Don't worry about memorizing all the various shapes that the pointer takes on. The pointer changes shape automatically at the appropriate times. The shapes are described here so that you won't think that your pointer's goofing off when it changes shape.

The Microsoft Intellimouse — the one with the little wheel — comes with bunches of cutesy pointers. Double-click the mouse icon next to your on-screen clock, choose the Pointers tab, and choose S̲cheme to see them all. When all the cutesy stuff becomes overwhelming, choose None to return to the more reassuring arrow pointer.

Video Cards and Monitors

The *monitor* is the thing you stare at all day until you go home to watch TV. The front of the monitor, called its *screen* or *display,* is where all the Windows 98 action takes place. The screen is where you can watch the windows as they bump around, cover each other up, and generally behave like nine people eyeing a recently delivered eight-slice pizza.

Monitors have *two* cords so they won't be mistaken for a mouse. One cord plugs into the electrical outlet; the other heads for the *video card,* a special piece of electronics poking out from the computer's back. The computer tells the video card what it's doing; the card translates the events into graphics information and shoots it up the cable into the monitor, where it appears on-screen.

Ignore these awful graphics terms

Some people describe their monitors as "boxy" or "covered with cat hair"; others use the following strange scientific terms:

Pixel: A pixel is a fancy name for an individual dot on-screen. Everything on-screen is made up of bunches of dots, or pixels. Each pixel can be a different shade or color, which creates the image. (Squint up close and you may be able to make out an individual pixel.)

Resolution: The resolution is the number of pixels on a screen — specifically, the number of pixels across (horizontal) and down (vertical). More pixels mean greater resolution: smaller letters and more information packed onto the same-sized screen. People with small monitors usually use 640 x 480 resolution. People with larger monitors often switch to 800 x 600 or 1024 x 768 resolution so that they can fit more windows on-screen.

Color: This term describes the number of colors the card and monitor display on-screen. The number of colors can change, however, depending on the current resolution. When the card runs at a low resolution, for example, it can crank out more colors. At super-duper-high 1280 x 1024 resolution, you may see only 256 colors on-screen. With a lower resolution of 640 x 480, you can probably see up to 16.7 million colors. Windows 98 runs fastest with 256 colors, but looks better on the screen with more colors — the traditional sacrifice of speed versus beauty: your call. Hint: Color settings are adjustable, as you see in Chapter 9. Set it for "High Color" or "16 bit"; you're usually safe there.

Mode: A predetermined combination of pixels, resolution, and colors is described as a graphics *mode*. Right out of the box, Windows 98 uses a mode that works for just about everybody. You don't need to know any of this stuff, though. If you're feeling particularly modular, however, you can change the Windows 98 graphics modes after reading Chapter 9.

✔ Like herbivores and cellulose-digesting gut microorganisms, monitors and video cards come in symbiotic pairs. Neither can function without the other, and you buy them in matched sets so that they'll get along.

✔ Unlike other parts of the computer, the video card and monitor don't require any special care and feeding. Just wipe the dust off the screen every once in a while. (And at least *try* to keep the cat off the monitor.)

✔ Spray plain old glass cleaner on a rag and then wipe off the dust with the newly dampened rag. If you spray glass cleaner directly on the screen, it drips down into the monitor's casing, annoying the trolls who sleep under the bridge.

✔ Some glass cleaners contain alcohol, which can cloud the antiglare screens found on some fancy new monitors. When in doubt, check your monitor's manual to see if glass cleaner is allowed. My Nanao monitor came with its own special rag for cleaning the glass.

✔ When you first install Windows 98, it interrogates the video card and monitor until they reveal their brand name and orientation. Windows 98 almost always gets the correct answer from them and sets itself up automatically so that everything works fine the first time.

✔ Windows 98 may be dominating, but it's accommodating, too. It can handle a wide variety of monitors and cards. In fact, most monitors and cards can switch to different *modes,* putting more or fewer colors on-screen and shrinking the text so that you can cram more information onto the screen. Windows 98 enables you to play around with all sorts of different video settings, if you're in that sort of mood. (If you are, check out Chapter 9.)

Hallelujah! If you have lots of money, a big desk, and a case of Windows Lust, Windows 98 lets you do two new things: First, you can plug a special TV card inside your computer that lets you watch TV on the monitor. Second, you can plug a second video card inside your computer, heft a second monitor onto your desk, and watch Windows on two monitors — *at the same time!* Scurry to Chapter 17 for the lowdown on both new features.

Keyboards

Computer keyboards look pretty much like typewriter keyboards with a few dark growths around the perimeter. In the center lie the familiar white typewriter keys. The grayish keys with obtuse code words live along the outside edges. They're described next.

Groups of keys

Obtuse code-word sorters divvy those outside-edge keys into key groups:

Function keys: These keys either sit along the top of the keyboard in one long row or clump together in two short rows along the keyboard's left side. Function keys boss around programs. For example, you can press F1 to demand help whenever you're stumped in Windows 98.

Numeric keypad: Zippy-fingered bankers like this thingy: a square, calculator-like pad of numbers along the right edge of most keyboards. (You have to press a key called Num Lock above those numbers, though, before they'll work. Otherwise, they're *cursor-control keys,* described next.)

Cursor-control keys: If you *haven't* pressed the magical Num Lock key, the keys on that square, calculator-like pad of numbers are the cursor-control keys. These keys have little arrows that show which direction the cursor moves on-screen. (The arrowless 5 key doesn't do anything except try to

Can I load Windows 98 with the Num Lock key turned off?

If you're not a zippy-fingered banker, you might want to use the number pad as cursor-control keys. Luckily, your Num Lock key's setting can be toggled through your computer's BIOS in its Setup area, which can usually be accessed by pressing Delete, Esc, or another key combination as your computer is first turned on.

When you find the Setup screen's Keyboard area, look for a Num Lock key setting, and set it either on or off. If that doesn't work, here's another thing to try: Your computer keeps some settings in another special place, a file called CONFIG.SYS. To edit that file, type SYSEDIT into your Start button's Run box. When the Sysedit program loads, click in the CONFIG.SYS window, and add the line NUMLOCK = OFF or NUMLOCK = ON (depending on your preference). Although you need to use a separate line, that line can appear anywhere in the file.

When your computer boots up, it should set your Num Lock key to the position you prefer.

overcome its low self-esteem.) Some keyboards have a second set of cursor-control keys next to the numeric keypad. Both sets do the same thing. Additional cursor-control keys are Home, End, PgUp, and PgDn (or Page Up and Page Down). To move down a page in a word-processing program, for example, you press the PgDn key.

Pressing the cursor keys doesn't move the little mouse-pointer arrow around on the screen. Instead, cursor keys control your position inside a program, letting you type information at the right place.

The Windows Key: Eager to make money from selling keyboards *and* software, Microsoft came out with a bold new design: a keyboard with a special key marked "Windows." (The key's little "Windows" icon looks like the icon on your Start button.) What does the key do? It opens the Start menu, which can be done at the click of a mouse, anyway. Ho hum. Table 2-3 shows more things the Windows key can do — if you can remember them.

Table 2-3	Windows Key Shortcuts
To Do This	*Press This*
Display Windows 98 Help	<WindowsKey>+F1
Display the Start menu	<WindowsKey>
Cycle through the taskbar's buttons	<WindowsKey>+Tab

(continued)

Table 2-3 (continued)

To Do This	Press This
Display Windows Explorer	\<WindowsKey\>+E
Find files	\<WindowsKey\>+F
Find other computers on the network	Ctrl+\<WindowsKey\>+F
Display your computer's properties	\<WindowsKey\>+Break
Minimize or restore all windows	\<WindowsKey\>+D
Undo minimize all windows	Shift+\<WindowsKey\>+M

More key principles

These keyboard keys may sound confusing, but Windows still makes you use them a lot:

Shift: Just as on a typewriter, this key creates uppercase letters or the symbols %#@$, which make great G-rated swear words.

Alt: Watch out for this one! When you press Alt (which stands for *Alternate*), Windows moves the cursor to the little menus at the top of the current window. If you're trapped up there and can't get out, you probably pressed Alt by mistake. Press Alt again or Esc to free yourself.

Ctrl: This key (which stands for *Control*) works like the Shift key, but it's for weird computer combinations. For example, holding down the Ctrl key while pressing Esc (described next) brings up the Windows 98 Start menu. (Check out "The Way-Cool Taskbar" section in Chapter 6.)

Esc: This key (which stands for *Escape*) was a pipe dream of the computer's creators. They added Esc as an escape hatch from malfunctioning computers. By pressing Esc, the user was supposed to be able to escape from whatever inner turmoil the computer was currently going through. Esc doesn't always work that way, but give it a try. It sometimes enables you to escape when you're trapped in a menu or a dastardly dialog box. (Those traps are described in Chapter 5.)

Scroll Lock: This one's too weird to bother with. Ignore it. (It's no relation to a *scroll bar,* either.) If a little keyboard light glows next to your Scroll Lock key, press the Scroll Lock key to turn it off. (The key's often labeled Scrl Lk or something equally obnoxious.)

Delete: Press the Delete key (sometimes labeled Del), and the unlucky character sitting to the *right* of the cursor disappears. Any highlighted information disappears as well. Poof.

Backspace: Press the Backspace key, and the unlucky character to the *left* of the cursor disappears. The Backspace key is on the top row, near the right side of the keyboard; it has a left-pointing arrow on it. Oh, and the Backspace key deletes any highlighted information, too.

If you've goofed, hold down Alt and press the Backspace key. This action undoes your last mistake in most Windows 98 programs.

Insert: Pressing Insert (sometimes labeled Ins) puts you in Insert mode. As you type, any existing words are scooted to the right, letting you add stuff. The opposite of Insert mode is Overwrite mode, where everything you type replaces any text in its way. Press Insert to toggle between these two modes.

Ugly disclaimer: Some Windows 98 programs — Notepad, for example — are always in Insert mode. There's simply no way to move to Overwrite mode, no matter how hard you pound the Insert key.

Enter: This key works pretty much like a typewriter's Return key, but with a big exception: Don't press Enter at the end of each line when typing documents. A word processor can sense when you're about to type off the edge of the screen. It herds your words down to the next line automatically. So just press Enter at the end of each paragraph.

You'll also want to press Enter when Windows 98 asks you to type something — the name of a file, for example, or the number of pages you want to print — into a special box. (Clicking a nearby OK button often performs the same task.)

Caps Lock: If you've mastered the Shift Lock key on a typewriter, you'll be pleased to find no surprises here. (Okay, there's one surprise: Caps Lock affects only your letters. It has no effect on punctuation symbols or the numbers along the top row.)

Tab: There are no surprises here, either, except that Tab is equal to five spaces in some word processors and eight spaces in others. Still, other word processors enable you to set Tab to whatever number you want. Plus, a startling Tab Tip follows.

Press Tab to move from one box to the next when filling out a form in Windows 98. (Sometimes these forms are called *dialog boxes.*)

✔ A mouse works best for most Windows 98 tasks, like starting programs or choosing among various options. Sometimes the keyboard comes in handy, however. Windows 98 comes with *shortcut keys* to replace just about anything you can do with a mouse. Sometimes pressing a few keys can be quicker than wading through heaps of menus with a mouse. (The shortcut keys are described in Chapter 4 in the section on when to use the keyboard.)

✔ If you don't own a mouse or a trackball, you can control Windows 98 exclusively with a keyboard. But it's awkward, like when Freddy from *Nightmare on Elm Street* tries to floss his back molars.

✔ Finally, some keyboards come with special keys installed by the manufacturer. My Gateway's keyboard lets me adjust the sound, log onto the Internet, control my CD or DVD, or make the computer go to sleep. Information about these keys lives in my computer's Control Panel under an icon named "Multi-function Keyboard."

Print Screen: The one, fun, weird code key

Windows fixed something dreadfully confusing about an IBM computer's keyboard: the Print Screen key (sometimes called PrtScr, Print Scrn, or something similar). In the old days of computing, pressing the Print Screen key sent a snapshot of the screen directly to the printer. Imagine the convenience!

Unfortunately, nobody bothered to update the Print Screen key to handle graphics. If a screen showed anything other than straight text, pressing the Print Screen key sent a wild jumble of garbled symbols to the printer. And, if the printer wasn't connected, turned on, and waiting, the computer would stop cold.

Windows fixes those Print Screen woes. Pressing the Print Screen key now copies a picture of the screen to a special place in Windows 98 that is known as the *Clipboard.* When the image is on the Clipboard, you can *paste* it into your programs or save it to disk. You can even print the screen's picture if you paste the image from the Clipboard into Paint, the Windows 98 drawing program.

✔ Want to just capture a particular window, not the entire screen? Then click in your desired window and hold down Alt while pressing the PrintScreen key. That window immediately heads for the Clipboard for later action.

✔ With some older computers, you have to hold down Shift while you press Print Screen, or you get just an asterisk on-screen — not nearly as much fun.

✔ The Clipboard is described in Chapter 8. You'll find all that cut, copy, and paste stuff explained there, too.

✔ Want to peek onto your Clipboard and see what you've copied there? Use the Clipbook Viewer, a program also covered in Chapter 8. (Windows 98 doesn't automatically install Clipbook Viewer onto every computer, though.) If you can't find Clipbook Viewer listed on your Start menu's Accessories page, head for Chapter 9. That chapter shows how to use Control Panel's Add/Remove Programs feature to install the Clipbook Viewer onto your own computer.

Modems and the Internet

I admit it. I used my modem the other night to order Cuban food from the place down the street. How? My wife and I dialed up "Gourmet on the Road" through the Internet, chose our items from the on-screen menu, and punched in our phone number. A few minutes later, the plantains were steaming on the dining room table.

Modems are little mechanical gadgets that translate a computer's information into squealing sounds that can be sent and received over plain, ordinary phone lines. We clicked on the check mark next to Baked Plantain on our computer, a modem at the credit card company tabulated the whole process, and the electric registers started ringing.

Most new computers come with modems, as well as ways to join trendy online services like America Online, CompuServe, or, if you're really hungry, the Internet or World Wide Web. In fact, if you bought a new computer, you probably already have everything you need to jump on the Internet band-wagon. Not wanting to be left out, Microsoft made sure Windows 98 comes with software called Internet Explorer. You can choose to let it blanket your desktop, as shown in Figure 2-2, giving it an ultra-modern look of a Web page. Elaborate Web site art will fill your desktop like posters along the walls of Parisian streets.

✔ Chapter 13 covers the Internet and the Web. It doesn't say what baked plantains taste like, though.

✔ The computers on both ends of the phone lines need modems in order to talk to each other. Luckily, most online services have hundreds, or even thousands, of modems for your computer's modem to talk to over the phone lines.

✔ Modems need special *communications software* to make them work. Windows 98 comes with Internet Explorer to access the Internet; it also comes with software for America Online (AOL), CompuServe, Prodigy Internet, The Microsoft Network, and AT&T WorldNet.

✔ Yes, all this software is free with Windows 98. But you have to pay monthly fees in order to use any of these services.

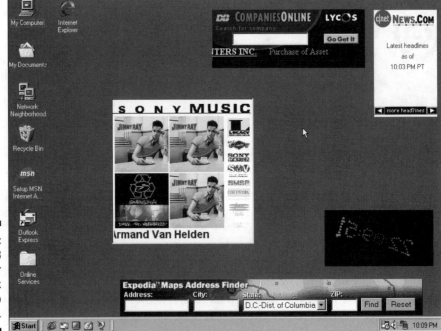

Figure 2-2:
Windows 98
lets your
desktop look
like a Web
page.

✔ Windows 98 also includes a simple communications program called HyperTerminal. It's a mere wooden tub in a world of tile Jacuzzis, and most people have abandoned it for more glamorous Web browsers and the World Wide Web. But it gets a brief mention in Chapter 12.

✔ Your computer doesn't have a modem? You'll find installation instructions in one of my other books, *Upgrading and Fixing PCs For Dummies,* 4th Edition (IDG Books Worldwide, Inc.). (My wife, Tina, actually wrote that chapter, although I forgot to give her credit for it. And, if you're *really* curious about modems, check out her epic tome *Modems For Dummies,* 3rd Edition.)

Printers

Realizing that the paperless office still lies several years down the road, Microsoft made sure that Windows 98 can shake hands and send friendly smoke signals to more than 300 different types of printers. When you install Windows 98, you need to click the name and manufacturer of your printer. Windows checks its dossiers, finds your printer, and immediately begins speaking to it in its native language.

That's all there is to it. Unless, of course, your printer happens to be one of the several hundred printers *left off* the Windows 98 master list. In that case, cross your fingers that your printer's manufacturer is still in business. You have to get a *driver* from the manufacturer before your prose can hit the printed page. (For information on printers, see Chapter 9.)

✔ Printers must be turned on before Windows 98 can print to them. (You'd be surprised how easily you can forget this little fact.)

✔ Windows 98 prints in a *WYSIWYG* (what you see is what you get) format, which means that what you see on-screen is reasonably close to what you'll see on the printed page.

Networks

Networks connect PCs so that people can share information. They can all send stuff to a single printer, for example, or send messages to each other asking whether Marilyn has passed out the paychecks yet.

Some networks are relatively small — less than ten computers in an office or school, for example. Other networks span the world; the Internet runs on a huge computer network that sprawls through nearly every country.

✔ You're probably on a network if you can answer "yes" to any of these questions: Can you and your friends or coworkers share a printer, data, or messages without standing up or yelling across the room? When your computer stops working, does everybody else's computer stop working, too?

✔ When networks are running correctly, you usually don't notice them. But for tips on what to do when you *do* notice them, see the section on networks in Chapter 3.

Sound Cards (Making Barfing Noises)

For years, PC owners looked enviously at Macintosh owners — especially when their Macs ejected a disk. The Macintosh would simultaneously eject a floppy disk from its drive and make a cute barfing sound. Macs come with sound built in; they can barf, giggle, and make *really* disgusting noises that won't be mentioned here.

But the tight shirts at IBM decided there was no place for sound on a Serious Business Machine. Microsoft fixed that mistake, and Windows 98 can make the accounting department's computers barf as loudly as the ones in the art department down the hall.

- ✔ Before your computer can barf, it needs a *sound card.* A sound card looks just like a video card. In fact, all cards look alike: long, green, or brown flat things that nestle into long flat slots inside the computer. Speakers plug into a sound card like a monitor plugs into a video card.

- ✔ Just as computers mimic IBM's original computer design, sound cards mimic the designs of the two most popular sound cards: AdLib and Sound Blaster. The AdLib card sets a standard for playing music; the Sound Blaster design is the current standard for playing music *and* for making noises.

- ✔ Windows works with a wide variety of sound cards, but you'll do best with cards that are compatible with Sound Blaster. Although most new computers come with sound cards already installed, most companies constantly release new software for making them work better. (Chapter 14's section on installing a driver can help knock a miscreant sound card back into action.)

- ✔ Windows 98 comes with a wide variety of noises, but it doesn't have any barf noises. Most computer gurus can either find a copy for you or personally record one. In fact, most new sound cards come with a microphone, and the Windows 98 Sound Recorder program is ready to capture your own efforts. (This book's sequel, *MORE Windows 98 For Dummies,* from IDG Books Worldwide, Inc., covers sound and video recording in much more detail.)

- ✔ The latest, fanciest computers come with DVD drives, special sound cards, software, and extra speakers so that you can hear "surround sound" when watching DVD movies. Better clear off your desk for the big woofer and extra speakers that go with it.

- ✔ Just like the Macintosh, Windows enables you to assign cool sounds to various Windows 98 functions. For example, you can make your computer scream louder than you do when it crashes. For more information, refer to the section in Chapter 9 on making cool sounds with multimedia.

Ports

The back of your computer contains lots of connections for pushing out and pulling in information. The deeper you fall into the Windows lifestyle, the more likely you'll hear the following words bantered about. Plus, when something falls off the back of your computer, Table 2-4 shows you where it should plug back in.

Table 2-4	What Part Plugs into What Port?	
This Port...	*...Looks Like This...*	*...And Accepts This*
Keyboard	New Style Old Style (Pre-1994)	Your keyboard — old style or new. (Some laptops let a mouse plug into the new style keyboard ports, too.)
Mouse	New Style	Your mouse. (Some laptops let a keyboard plug into it, too.)
Video		Your monitor's smallest cable. (The monitor's biggest cable plugs into the power outlet.)
Serial (COM)	Old Style (Pre-1952) New Style	External modems.
Parallel (LPT)		Your printer.
USB		Universal Serial Bus gadgets. (Still rather rare.)
Sound		A sound card has three of these ports: one for headphones, one for the microphone, and the other for an external sound source like a radio, tape recorder, camcorder, TV card, and so on.
Cable TV		TV cards accept your TV cable here.
Telephone		Run a telephone line from the wall to here on a modem. (The modem's second jack lets you plug in the telephone. Look closely for a label.)

Parts Required by Windows 98

Table 2-5 compares what Windows 98 asks for on the side of the box with what you *really* need before it works well.

Table 2-5	What Windows 98 Requires	
Requirements Politely Touted by Microsoft	*What You Really Need*	*Why?*
A 486 66MHz microprocessor	A Pentium II	While at the store, compare Windows 98 running on different computers. The faster the computer, the less time you spend waiting for Windows 98 to do something exciting.
16MB of memory (RAM)	At least 32MB of memory	Windows 98 crawls across the screen with only 16MB and moves much more comfortably with 32MB. RAM is cheap; if you plan to run several large programs or use WebTV, quickly bump that to 64MB. Power users may want to consider 128MB or more.
195MB of hard disk space	At least 4GB	A full installation of Windows 98 requires 300MB; Windows programs quickly rope off their sections of the hard drive, too. Plus, all that sound and video you're going to be grabbing off the Internet and your digital camera will take a whole *lotta* space. (You'll need at least a gigabyte to watch WebTV.) Don't be afraid to buy a hard disk that's 8GB (eight gigabytes) or larger.
A 3 ½-inch high-density disk drive	Same	A few Windows programs still come packaged on high-density, 3½-inch floppy disks. Plus, floppy disks are a handy way to move your files to other computers.
Color VGA card	Super VGA PCI bus card with16- or 24-bitcolor	Because Windows 98 tosses so many colorful little boxes on-screen, get an accelerated high-resolution 3-D Super VGA card at least 4MB of RAM.

Requirements Politely Touted by Microsoft	What You Really Need	Why?
Windows 95, Windows 3.1,Windows for Workgroups (Windows 3.11 or later)	Same	Microsoft is selling Windows 98 as an upgrade to its older products. Not upgrading an older version of Windows? Then you'll have to buy the more expensive "complete" version of Windows 98.
Miscellaneous	A 15-inch monitor or larger	The bigger your monitor, the bigger your desktop: Your windows won't overlap so much. Unfortunately, super-large monitors are super-expensive.
Miscellaneous	CD-ROM or DVD drive	You might be able to find Windows 98 on disks, but it's a lot easier to install off a compact disc than handfuls of floppy disks. (A DVD drive can read normal CDs, so it'll work fine.)
Miscellaneous	Modem	You don't need a modem, but if your computer isn't on a network, you need a modem to dial up the online services that come packaged with Windows 98, and you can't play with Internet Explorer.

Chapter 3

Windows 98 Stuff Everybody Thinks You Already Know

In This Chapter

▶ Explanations of the strange terms used in Windows 98

▶ Information on where to look for more details on these strange terms

*W*hen Windows first hit the market in 1985, it failed miserably. The overpriced, under-powered computers of the day busted a bearing over Windows' attempts at fancy graphics. Back then, Windows was not only slow, but it looked dorky and awkward with ugly colors.

Today's best-selling computers come with custom-rigged V8 engines: They can easily whip Windows 98 into shape. With faster computers, perseverance, and a dozen fashionably healthy new color schemes, such as Eggplant, Plum, and Wheat, Windows 98 has turned into a trendy best-seller.

But because Windows has been around for so long, a lot of computer geeks have had a head start. To help you catch up, this chapter is a tourist's guidebook to those Windows words the nerds have been batting around for more than ten years.

Backing Up a Disk

Computers store *bunches* of files on their hard drives. And that multitude of files can be a problem. When the computer's hard drive eventually dies (nothing lives forever), it takes all your files down with it. Pffffft. Nothing left.

Computer users who don't like anguished *pffffft* sounds *back up* their hard drives religiously. They do so in three main ways.

Some people copy all their files from the hard disk to a bunch of floppy disks. Although backup programs make this task easier, it's still a time-consuming chore. Who wants to spend half an hour backing up computer files *after* finishing work?

Other people buy a *tape backup* unit. This special computerized tape recorder either lives inside your computer like a floppy disk or plugs into the computer's rear. Either way, the gizmo tape-records all the information on your hard disk. Then, when your hard disk dies, you still have all your files. The faithful tape backup unit plays back all your information onto the new hard drive. No scrounging for floppy disks.

Finally, some people buy special *cartridge* storage units. These mechanisms work like hard drives you can slide in and out of your computer. Iomega's Jaz drives, for example, can store up to 2 gigabytes of information on a single cartridge. That can take up a *lot* less space than hundreds of floppies. (More information about Iomega's drives lurks in Chapter 2.)

 ✔ Windows 98 comes with Microsoft Backup, a program that automatically copies your hard drive's information to someplace else, be it a floppy, a tape backup system, or a fancier Iomega drive. The program hides in the System Tools section of your Accessories folder, which lurks in your Programs folder, which pops up when you click your Start button.

 ✔ Don't use backup programs that weren't designed specifically for Windows 95 or Windows 98. Many old backup programs won't know how to back up files that have names longer than eight characters. If you try to use an old backup program with Windows 98, the backup won't be reliable.

 ✔ Can't find Microsoft Backup listed on your Start button? That's because Windows 98 doesn't always install it automatically. The Control Panel's Add/Remove Programs icon lets you tell Windows 98 to install the Backup program, however. (You can find more instructions in Chapter 9.)

 ✔ The average cost of a backup unit runs from $150–$400, depending on the size of your computer's hard drive. Some people back up their work every day, using a new tape or backup disk for each day of the week. If they discover on Thursday that last Monday's report had all the best stuff, they can pop Monday's backup into the unit and grab the report.

Clicking

Computers make plenty of clicking sounds, but one click counts the most: the one that occurs when you press a button on a mouse. You'll find yourself clicking the mouse hundreds of times in Windows 98. For example, to push the on-screen button marked Push Me, you move the mouse across your desk until the little on-screen arrow rests over the Push Me button and then click the mouse button.

- When you hear people say, "Press the button on the mouse," they leave out an important detail: *Release* the button after you press it. Press the button with your index finger and release it, just as you press a button on an elevator.

- Most mice have 2 buttons; some have 3, and some esoteric models for traffic engineers have more than 32. Windows 98 listens mostly to clicks coming from the button on the *left* side of your mouse. It's the one under your index finger if you're right-handed (or if you're left-handed and lucky enough to find a left-handed mouse). Refer to Chapter 9 for more mouse button tricks.

- Windows 98 listens to clicks coming from both the left *and* the right buttons on your mouse. The older Windows 3.1 listens only to clicks coming from the button on the *left* side of your mouse.

- Don't confuse a *click* with a *double-click*. For more rodent details, see the sections, "The Mouse," "Double-Clicking," and "Pointers/Arrows," later in this chapter. The insatiably curious can find even more mouse stuff in Chapter 2, including the new Microsoft IntelliMouse with the little spinning wheel doohickey.

The Cursor

Typewriters have a little mechanical arm that strikes the page, creating the desired letter. Computers don't have little mechanical arms (except in science fiction movies), so they have *cursors*: little blinking lines that show where that next letter will appear in the text.

- Cursors appear only when Windows 98 is ready for you to type text, numbers, or symbols — usually when you write letters or reports.

- The cursor and the mouse pointer are different things that perform different tasks. When you start typing, text appears at the cursor's location, not at the pointer's location.

- You can move the cursor to a new place in the document by using the keyboard's *cursor-control keys* (the keys with little arrows). Or you can point to a spot with the mouse pointer and click the button. The cursor leaps to that new spot.

Filling out a form? Here's a trick for the lazy: Press Tab after filling out each blank. At each press, the Tab key kicks the cursor to the next line on the form. That saves a lot of pointing and clicking to get the cursor to the right place.

You can distinguish between the cursor and the mouse pointer with one look: Cursors always blink steadily; mouse pointers never blink.

For more information, check out the section, "Pointers/Arrows" in this chapter or Table 2-2 in Chapter 2.

Defaults (And the Any Key)

Finally, a computer term that can be safely ignored. Clap your hands and square dance with a neighbor! Here's the lowdown on the, er, hoedown: Some programs present a terse list of inexplicable choices and casually suggest that you select the only option that's not listed: the *default option.*

Don't chew your tongue in despair. Just press Enter.

Those wily programmers have predetermined what option works best for 99 percent of the people using the program. So, if people just press Enter, the program automatically makes the right choice and moves on to the next complicated question.

- ✔ The default option is similar to the oft-mentioned *Any key* because neither of them appears on your keyboard (or on anybody else's, either — no matter how much money they paid).

- ✔ *Default* can also be taken to mean *standard option* or *what to select when you're completely stumped.* For example, strangers riding together in elevators stare at their shoes by default.

- ✔ When a program says to press any key, simply press the spacebar. (The Shift keys don't do the trick, by the way.)

Desktop (And Wallpapering It)

To keep from reverting to revolting computer terms, Windows 98 uses familiar office lingo. For example, all the action in Windows 98 takes place on the Windows 98 desktop. The *desktop* is the background area of the screen where all the windows pile up.

Windows 98 comes with a drab green desktop. To jazz things up, you can cover the desktop with simple pictures, or *wallpaper*. Windows 98 comes with several arty pictures you can use for wallpaper (and Chapter 9 can help you hang it up).

You can customize the wallpaper to fit your own personality: pictures of little kittens, for example, or centipedes. You can draw your own wallpaper with the built-in Windows 98 Paint program, which saves your work in one of the special wallpaper formats.

Internet Explorer and other Internet browsers let you automatically grab any picture you find on a Web site and turn it into your desktop's wallpaper. Click the cool picture with your right mouse button and choose the Set as Wallpaper option.

The Windows 98 Active Desktop option lets you use your favorite Web page as your desktop: Your stock market quotes or pictures of French poodles can be just a click away!

Disk Compression (DriveSpace, FAT32)

It sounds too good to be true: Right-click on a hard drive icon from within My Computer, choose Properties, and the tab called Compression promises to salvage oodles of extra hard drive space from your hard drive.

Another promises to save space by converting drives to the FAT32 system.

Don't bother. Hard drives are cheap right now, and it's easier to simply add a second, larger hard drive to your system. Drive compression tools are for people who love tweaking their computer innards. Chances are, you'd rather spend less time with your computer than more.

(And if you have any doubts, just read the seven paragraphs of warnings that come with the FAT32 system.)

The DOS Prompt

Some people haven't switched to the newer, Windows breed of programs. They're still using the programs they bought nearly a decade ago, when it was trendy to use a DOS program. Luckily, Windows 98 can not only run DOS programs, but it can also provide an age-old DOS prompt for the needy. Click the Start button, click the word Programs, and click MS-DOS Prompt from the menu.

The DOS prompt rhymes with *the boss chomped,* and it's a symbol that looks somewhat like this:

```
C:\>
```

Type the name of your program at the DOS prompt, press Enter, and the program begins.

If you've been rudely dumped at the DOS prompt, you can scoot quickly to Windows 98 by typing the following no-nonsense word:

```
C:\> EXIT
```

That is, you type **EXIT** (lowercase works, too) and follow it with a press of the Enter key.

To appease the DOS hounds, Windows 98 waits in the background while you run a DOS session.

Double-Clicking

Windows 98 places a great significance on something pretty simple: pressing a button on the mouse and releasing it. Pressing and releasing the button once is known as a *click.* Pressing and releasing the button twice in rapid succession is a *double-click.*

Windows 98 watches carefully to see whether you've clicked or double-clicked on its more sensitive parts. The two actions are completely different.

- A click and a double-click often mean two different things to Windows programs. They're not the same.

- A double-click can take some practice to master, even if you have fingers. If you click too slowly, Windows 98 thinks that you're simply clicking twice — not double-clicking. Try clicking a little faster next time, and Windows 98 will probably catch on.

- Can't click fast enough for Windows 98 to tell the difference between a mere click and a rapid-fire double-click? Grab the office computer guru and say that you need to have your Control Panel called up and your clicks fixed. If the guru is at the computer store, tiptoe to the section on tinkering with the Control Panel in Chapter 9.

Windows 98 now emulates the Web, if you prefer, so it can banish the double-click. Simply pointing at an icon selects it; then, when you click it, the program leaps into action. (To fiddle with these settings — the ever-confusing Windows lets you configure it in more than three different ways — march to Chapter 9.)

Dragging and Dropping

Although the term *drag and drop* sounds as if it's straight out of a hitman's handbook, it's really a nonviolent mouse trick in Windows 98. Dragging and dropping is a way of moving something — say, a picture of an egg — from one part of your screen to another.

To *drag,* put the mouse pointer over the egg and *hold down* the mouse button. As you move the mouse across your desk, the pointer drags the egg across the screen. Put the pointer/egg where you want it and release the mouse button. The egg *drops,* uncracked.

✔ Big Tip Dept.: If you hold down the *right* mouse button while dragging, Windows 98 tosses a little menu in your face, asking if you're sure that you want to move that egg across the screen.

✔ For more mouse fun, see the sections, "Clicking," "Double-Clicking," "The Mouse," and "Pointers/Arrows" in this chapter and, if you're not yet weak at the knees, the information on the parts of your computer in Chapter 2.

✔ Started dragging something and realized in midstream that you're dragging the wrong thing? Breathe deeply like a yoga instructor and press Esc. Then let go of your mouse button. Whew!

Drivers

Although Windows 98 performs plenty of work, it hires help when necessary. When Windows 98 needs to talk to unfamiliar parts of your computer, it lets special *drivers* do the translation. A driver is a piece of software that enables Windows 98 to communicate with parts of your computer.

Hundreds of computer companies sell computer attachables, from printers to sound cards to sprinkler systems. Microsoft requires these companies to write drivers for their products so that Windows 98 knows the polite way to address them.

✔ Sometimes computer nerds say that your *mouse driver* is all messed up. They're not talking about your swerving hand movements. They're talking about the piece of software that helps Windows 98 talk and listen to the mouse.

✔ Computer products often require new, improved drivers. The best way to get these new drivers is from the Web, usually on the Web site of the company that made the gadget. Sometimes the Microsoft Web page itself will have the proper driver, too.

✔ If you send a begging letter to the company that made your mouse, the company may mail you a new, updated driver on a floppy disk. Occasionally, you can get these new drivers from the wild-haired teenager who sold you your computer. Find a computer guru to install the driver, however, or check out the section on installing drivers in Chapter 14.

✔ Windows 98 comes with an aptly named new program called "Update Product." Described in Chapter 12, it dials a special spot on the Internet, where a stethoscope examines your computer's internal parts and inserts updated software where needed.

Files

A *file* is a collection of information in a form that the computer can play with. A *program file* contains instructions telling the computer to do something useful, like adding up the number of quarters the kids spent on Sweet Tarts last month. A *data file* contains information you've created, like a picture of an obelisk you drew in the Windows 98 Paint program.

✔ Files can't be touched or handled; they're invisible, unearthly things. Somebody figured out how to store files as little magnetic impulses on a round piece of specially coated plastic, or *disk*. (Yep, these are the disks I cover in Chapter 2.)

✔ A file is referred to by its *filename*. Older computers made people call files by a single word containing no more than eight characters. For example, FILENAME could be the name of a file, as could REPORT, SPONGE, or X. Yes, it was difficult to think up descriptive filenames.

✔ It's so difficult that Windows breaks the barrier: It lets you call files by bunches of words, as long as they don't total more than 255 characters.

✔ Filenames have optional *extensions* of up to three letters that usually refer to the program that created them. For example, the Windows 98 Paint program automatically saves files with the extension BMP. Microsoft realized that most people don't care about file extensions, so Windows 98 no longer lists a file's extension when it's displaying filenames. (You can make it display them, however, if you're curious enough to struggle through the file-and-folder display details in Chapters 9 and 11.)

✔ Be careful if you'll be transferring files between a Windows 98 computer and a Windows 3.1 computer. Your Windows 98 file that's named Kayaking in the Rockies will be automatically renamed KAYAKI˜1 on the Windows 3.1 computer. The filename's ending is simply truncated, never to be seen again.

✔ Filenames still have more rules and regulations than the Jacuzzi at the condo's clubhouse.

✔ For more information than you'll ever want to know about filenames, flip to Chapter 11.

Folders (Directories)

In your everyday paper world, files are stored in folders in a cabinet. In the computer world, files are stored in a *directory* on a disk. Dusty old file cabinets are boring, but directories are even more dreadfully boring: They *never* hold any forgotten savings bonds.

So Windows 98 swapped metaphors. Instead of storing files in directories, Windows 98 holds files in *folders*. You can see the little pictures of the folders on your monitor.

The folders in Windows 98 are *really* just directories, if you've already grown used to working with directories.

Maintaining files and working with folders can be painful experiences, so they're explained in Chapter 11. In the meantime, just think of folders as separate work areas to keep files organized. Different folders hold different projects; you move from folder to folder as you work on different things with your computer.

✔ A file cabinet's Vegetables folder could have an Asparagus folder nested inside for organizing material further. In fact, most folders contain several other folders in order to organize information even more. You need to be pretty fastidious around computers; that's the easiest way of finding your work again.

✔ Technically, a folder in a folder is a nested *subdirectory* that keeps related files from getting lost. For example, you can have folders for Steamed Asparagus and Raw Asparagus in the Asparagus folder, which lives in the Vegetables folder.

Graphical User Interfaces

The way people communicate with computers is called an *interface*. For example, the *Enterprise*'s computer used a *verbal interface*. Captain Kirk just told it what to do.

Windows 98 uses a *graphical user interface*. People talk to the computer through *graphical symbols,* or pictures. A graphical user interface works kind of like travel kiosks at airports — you select some little button symbols right on the screen to find out which hotels offer free airport shuttles.

- ✔ A graphical user interface is called a *GUI,* pronounced *gooey,* as in *Huey, Dewey, Louie,* and *GUI.*

- ✔ Despite what you read in the Microsoft full-page ads, Windows 98 isn't the only GUI for a personal computer. IBM's OS/2 Warp works like Windows 98. Although still on the shelves, OS/2 Warp's scary name frightened customers, killing sales of my *OS/2 Warp For Dummies* book and leaving everybody stuck with Windows 98.

- ✔ You'll eventually hear people raving about a new operating system called Linux (pronounced LINE-uhx, after Linus, the operating system's creator). Programmers and computer tweakers love Linux, but this new operating system can't run nearly as many programs as Windows. Don't buy a new PC with Linux installed unless you're a professional programmer or married to one.

- ✔ The little graphical symbols or buttons in a graphical user interface are called *icons.*

- ✔ Some computers with sound cards can talk to us. A few of the best software packages can actually speak a few words, but even they stumble when asked to comment on the sacrifice of Isaac in Kierkegaard's *Fear and Trembling.*

Hardware and Software

Alert! Alert! Fasten your seat belt so that you don't slump forward when reading about these two particularly boring terms: hardware and software.

Your CD player is *hardware;* so are the stereo amplifier, speakers, and batteries in the boom box. By itself, the CD player doesn't do anything but hum. It needs music to disturb the neighbors. The music is the *software,* or the information processed by the CD player.

✔ Now you can unfasten your seat belt and relax for a bit. Computer *hardware* refers to anything you can touch, including hard things like a printer, a monitor, disks, and disk drives.

✔ *Software* is the ethereal stuff that makes the hardware do something fun. A piece of software is called a *program*. Programs come on disks (or CDs, too, if you've anted up for the latest computer gear).

✔ Software has very little to do with lingerie.

✔ When somber technical nerds (STNs) say, "It must be a hardware problem," they mean that something must be wrong with your computer itself: its disk drive, keyboard, or central processing unit (CPU). When they say, "It must be a software problem," they mean that something is wrong with the program you're trying to run from the disk.

Here's how to earn points with your computer gurus: When they ask you the riddle, "How many programmers does it take to change a light bulb?," pretend that you don't know this answer: "None; that's a hardware problem."

Icons

An *icon* is a little picture. Windows 98 fills the screen with little pictures, or icons. You choose among them to make Windows 98 do different things. For example, you'd choose the Printer icon, the little picture of the printer, to make your computer print something. Icons are just fancy names for cute buttons.

✔ Windows 98 relies on icons for nearly everything, from opening files to releasing the winged monkeys.

✔ Some icons have explanatory titles, like Open File or Terrorize Dorothy. Others make you guess; for example, the Little Juggling Man icon opens the network mail system.

✔ For more icon stuff, see the section, "Graphical User Interfaces" earlier in this chapter.

The Internet

In the late 1960s, the U.S. government worried that enemies could drop bombs on its main cluster of Department of Defense computers, quickly turning circuits into slosh. So, the scientists moved the computers away from each other, connecting them globally with high-speed phone lines and a unique system of information forwarding.

If a computer in Hawaii blew up, for example, the data chain from surrounding computers wouldn't simply stop there. The other computers would automatically reroute their information to other computers in the network, and everybody would still have e-mail waiting the next morning (except for the folks in Hawaii, of course).

With this sprawling chain of new networks running automatically in the background, enemies no longer have a single target to destroy. The system has proven quite durable, and thousands of other networks have hopped on for a ride. Many academic institutions climbed aboard as well, helping the system grow to gigantic proportions. Now known as the *Internet,* the information chain's built-in independence keeps it difficult to use, completely uncensored, and rampantly random in quality.

Anybody can use the Internet and its trendy World Wide Web to sample the information strewn about the globe. Windows 98 includes most of the tools you need to jump aboard.

  ✔ In fact, Windows 98 includes tools to create your own spot — a Web page — on the Internet for everybody to visit. It includes software for cruising the Web, creating Web pages, watching video clips, and listening to radio stations from around the world.

  ✔ There's one problem. In order to use Windows 98's tools and visit the Web, you need to sign up with a Internet service provider (ISP). These businesses usually charge a monthly fee, just any other utility company.

  ✔ For more Internet fun, see Chapter 13. To turn off any Windows 98's Internet components like the Active Desktop, flip forward to Chapter 21.

Kilobytes, Megabytes, and So On

Figuring out the size of a real file folder is easy: Just look at the thickness of the papers stuffed in and around it. But computer files are invisible, so their size is measured in bytes (which is pronounced like what Dracula does).

A *byte* is pretty much like a character or letter in a word. For example, the word *sodium-free* contains 11 bytes. (The hyphen counts as a byte.) Computer nerds picked up the metric system much more quickly than the rest of us, so bytes are measured in kilos (1,000), megas (1,000,000), and gigas (way huge).

A page of double-spaced text in Notepad is about 1,000 bytes, known as 1 kilobyte, which is often abbreviated as 1K. One thousand of those kilobytes is a megabyte, or 1MB. One thousand megabytes is a gigabyte, which brings us to your computer's sales slip: Most hard drives today are 2 gigabytes or larger.

✔ Just about all floppy disks these days can hold 1.44MB. Today's programs are huge, so they usually come on compact discs, which hold more than 600MB.

✔ All files are measured in bytes, regardless of whether they contain text. For example, that leafy forest background art some people put on their Windows 98 desktop takes up 66,146 bytes. (For information on changing to the forest desktop, see Chapter 9.)

✔ A page of double-spaced text in Notepad takes up about 1K, but that same page in Microsoft Word consumes much more space. That's because Word sticks in lots more information: font size, the author's name, bookmarks, spell-check results, and just about anything else you can think of.

✔ The Windows 98 Explorer or My Computer programs can tell you how many bytes each of your files consumes. To find out more, check out the information on Explorer in Chapter 11. (***Hint for anxious users:*** Click the file's name with your right mouse button and choose Properties from the menu that pops up; you find more information about a file than you want to know.)

One kilobyte doesn't *really* equal 1,000 bytes. That would be too easy. Instead, this byte stuff is based on the number two. One kilobyte is really 1,024 bytes, which is 2 raised to the 10th power, or 210. (Computers love mathematical details, especially when a 2 is involved.) For more byte-size information, see Table 3-1.

Table 3-1	Ultra-Precise Details from the Slide-Rule Crowd		
Term	*Abbreviation*	*Rough Size*	*Ultra-Precise Size*
Byte	byte	1 byte	1 byte
Kilobyte	K or KB	1,000 bytes	1,024 bytes
Megabyte	M or MB	1,000 kilobytes	1,048,576 bytes
Gigabyte	G or GB	1,000 megabytes	1,073,741,824 bytes

Loading, Running, Executing, and Launching

Files are yanked from a file cabinet and placed onto a desk for easy reference. On a computer, files are *loaded* from a disk and placed into the computer's memory so that you can do important stuff with them. You can't work with a file or program until it has been loaded into the computer's memory.

When you *run, execute,* or *launch* a program, you're merely starting it up so that you can use it. *Load* means pretty much the same thing, but some people fine-tune its meaning to describe when a program file brings in a data file.

- ✔ The Windows 98 Start button enables picture lovers to start programs by using icons. The Windows 98 Explorer program enables text-and-word lovers to start programs by clicking the mouse on their names in a list (although Explorer lets you click icons, too, if you prefer).

- ✔ If you're feeling particularly bold, you can load programs by using the command line hidden in the Start button as well. For the full dirt, check out the information on the Start button in Chapter 10 and the information on Explorer in Chapter 11.

Memory

Whoa! How did this complicated memory stuff creep in here? Luckily, it all boils down to one key sentence:

The more memory a computer has available, the more pleasantly Windows 98 behaves.

- ✔ Memory is measured in bytes, just like a file. The computer at the garage sale probably came with 640 kilobytes, or 640K, of memory. Last year's computer models usually came with at least 8MB of memory. Today's computers often come with at least 32MB of memory installed.

- ✔ Windows 98 requires computers to have at least 16 megabytes, or 16MB, of memory, or it won't even bother to come out of the box.

Memory and hard disk space are both measured in bytes, but they're two different things: *Memory* is what the computer uses for quick, on-the-fly calculations when programs are up and running on-screen. *Hard disk space* is what the computer uses to store unused files and programs.

Everybody's computer contains much more hard disk space than memory because hard disks — also known as *hard drives* — are so much cheaper. Also, a hard disk remembers things even when the computer is turned off. A computer's memory, on the other hand, is washed completely clean whenever someone turns it off or pokes its reset button.

Not sure about all that kilobyte and MB stuff? Skip a few pages back to the "Kilobytes, Megabytes, and So On" section.

The Mouse

A *mouse* is a smooth little plastic thing that looks like Soap on a Rope. It rests on a little roller, or *ball,* and its tail plugs into the back of the PC. When you push the mouse across your desk, the mouse sends its current location through its tail to the PC. By moving the mouse around on the desk, you move a corresponding arrow across the screen.

You can wiggle the mouse in circles and watch the arrow make spirals. Or, to be practical, you can maneuver the on-screen arrow over an on-screen button and click the mouse button to boss Windows 98 around. (Refer to the sections, "Clicking," "Double-Clicking," and "Pointers/Arrows," and, if you haven't run out of steam, turn to Chapter 2 for information on the parts of your computer.)

Multitasking and Task Switching

Windows 98 can run two or more programs at the same time, but computer nerds take overly tedious steps to describe the process. So skip this section because you'll never need to know it.

Even though the words *task switching* and *multitasking* often have an exclamation point in computer ads, there's nothing really exciting about them.

When you run two programs, yet switch back and forth between them, you're *task switching.* For example, if Jeff calls while you're reading a book, you put down the book and talk to Jeff. You are task switching: stopping one task and starting another. The process is similar to running your word processor and then stopping to look up a phone number in your handy business card database program.

But when you run two programs simultaneously, you're *multitasking.* For example, if you continue reading your book while listening to Jeff talk about the Natural History Museum's new Grecian urns, you're multitasking: performing two tasks at the same time. In Windows 98, multitasking can be playing its solitaire game or adding a huge spreadsheet while you print something in the background.

These two concepts differ only subtly, and yet computer nerds make a big deal out of the difference. Everybody else shrugs and says, "So what?"

Networks

Networks connect PCs with cables so that people can share equipment and information. Every computer can send stuff to one printer, for example, or people can send messages back and forth talking about Jane's new hairstyle.

You, as a Windows 98 beginner, are safely absolved from knowing anything about networks. Leave network stuff to that poor person in charge.

✔ This book provides more information about networks in case you need to know about the subject. Chapter 4, for example, explains logging on and off. Chapter 11 shows how to push and pull files off of other computers that may be networked with your own computer.

✔ Unless you're working on a computer in an office, however, you probably won't have to worry about networks.

✔ For information about dial-up networks, like connecting to the Internet through the Windows 98 Internet Explorer, head for Chapter 13.

Pointers/Arrows

This idea sounds easy at first. When you roll the mouse around on your desk, you see a little arrow move around on-screen. That arrow is your *pointer,* and it is also called an *arrow.* (Almost everything in Windows 98 has at least two names.)

The pointer serves as your *electronic index finger.* Instead of pushing an on-screen button with your finger, you move the pointer over that button and click the left button on the mouse.

So what's the hard part? Well, that pointer doesn't always stay an arrow. Depending on where the pointer is located on the Windows 98 screen, it can turn into a straight line, a two-headed arrow, a four-sided arrow, an hourglass, a little pillar, or a zillion other things. Each of the symbols makes the mouse do something slightly different. Luckily, you can find these and other arrowheads covered in Chapter 2.

Plug and Play

Historically, installing new hardware devices has required substantial technical expertise to configure and load hardware and software. Basically, that means that only geeks could figure out how to fix their computers and add new gadgets to them.

So a bunch of computer vendors hunched together around a table and came up with *Plug and Play* — a way for Windows 98 to set up new gadgets for your computer automatically, with little or no human intervention. You plug in your latest gadget and Windows 98 "interviews" it, checking to see what special settings it needs. Then Windows 98 automatically flips the right switches.

Because Windows 98 keeps track of which switches are flipped, none of the parts argue over who got the best settings. Better yet, users don't have to do anything but plug the darn thing into their computers and flip the On switch.

✔ Of course, the process couldn't be *that* simple. Only gadgets that say "Plug and Play" on the box allow for this automatic switch flipping. With the others, you probably need to flip the switches yourself. (But at least they still work when the right switches are flipped.)

✔ Plug-and-Play laptops and palmtops often work well with "docking stations." For example, when you plug the laptop into the docking station, Windows 98 automatically detects the new monitor, keyboard, mouse, sound card, and whatever other goodies the owner could afford. Then Windows 98 automatically sets itself up to use those new goodies — without the owner having to fiddle with the settings.

✔ Some people call Plug and Play "PnP."

✔ Other, more skeptical, people refer to Plug and Play as "Plug and Pray." (It can't recognize everything, particularly older computer parts.)

Quitting or Exiting

When you're ready to throw in the computing towel and head for greener pastures, you need to stop, or quit, any programs you've been using. The terms *quit* and *exit* mean pretty much the same thing: making the current program on-screen stop running so that you can go away and do something a little more rewarding.

Luckily, exiting Windows 98 programs is fairly easy because all of them are supposed to use the same special exit command. You simply click the little X in the upper-right corner of the program's window. Or, if you prefer using the keyboard, you hold down the Alt key (either one of them, if you have two) and press the key labeled F4. (The F4 key is a *function key;* function keys are either in one row along the top of your keyboard or in two rows along its leftmost edge.)

Never quit a program by just flicking off your computer's power switch. Doing so can foul up your computer's innards. Instead, you must leave the program responsibly so that it has time to perform its housekeeping chores before it shuts down.

- ✔ When you press Alt+F4 or click the little X in the upper-right corner, the program asks whether you want to save any changes you've made to the file. Normally, you click the button that says something like "Yes, by all means, save the work I've spent the last three hours trying to create." (If you've muffed things up horribly, click the No button. Windows 98 disregards any work you've done and lets you start over from scratch.)

- ✔ If, by some broad stretch of your fingers, you press Alt+F4 by accident, click the button that says Cancel, and the program pretends that you never tried to leave it. You can continue as if nothing happened.

- ✔ Windows 3.1 programs have a square button in their uppermost left corner that looks like an aerial view of a single-slot toaster. Double-clicking that toaster exits the program. Windows 98 still lets you close most Windows programs by double-clicking in their uppermost left corner (although the programs don't have that toaster anymore). However, it's usually easier to single-click the X in the program's uppermost *right* corner. But either action tells the program that you want to close it down.

- ✔ Save your work before exiting a program or turning off your computer. Computers aren't always smart enough to save it automatically.

Save Command

Save means to send the work you've just created on your computer to a disk for safekeeping. Unless you specifically save your work, your computer thinks that you've just been fiddling around for the past four hours. You need to specifically tell the computer to save your work before it will safely store the work on a disk.

Thanks to Microsoft's snapping leather whips, all Windows 98 programs use the same Save command, no matter what company wrote them. Press and release the Alt, F, and S keys in any Windows 98 program, and the computer saves your work.

If you're saving something for the first time, Windows 98 asks you to think up a filename for the work and pick a folder to stuff the new file into. Luckily, this stuff's covered in Chapter 4 in the section, "Saving Your Work."

✔ You can save files to a hard disk or a floppy disk; some people save files on Zip drives, or writable compact discs. (Check out Chapter 2 for more drive specifics.) Or, if you're working in a networked office, you can often save files onto other computers.

✔ If you prefer using the mouse to save files, click the word *File* from the row of words along the top of the program. After a menu drops down, click the word Save. Some programs even have a little picture of a floppy disk along their top edge; clicking the picture saves the file.

✔ Choose descriptive filenames for your work. Windows 98 gives you 255 characters to work with, so a file named "June Report on Squeegee Sales" is easier to relocate than one named "Stuff."

✔ Some programs, like Microsoft Word for Windows, have an *autosave* feature that automatically saves your work every five minutes or so.

Save As Command

Huh? Save as *what?* A chemical compound? Naw, the Save As command just gives you a chance to save your work with a different name and in a different location.

Suppose that you open the Random Musings file in your Miscellaneous Stuff directory and change a few sentences around. You want to save the changes, but you don't want to lose the original stuff. So you select Save As and type the new name, **Additional Random Musings**.

✔ The Save As command is identical to the Save command when you're first trying to save something new: You can choose a fresh name and location for your work.

✔ The world's biggest clams can weigh up to 500 pounds.

ScanDisk

You've probably seen this program, usually abruptly, and at the worst times. When your computer crashes — or when it's turned off without using the Start button's Shut Down command — the ScanDisk program hops onto the big blue screen.

Greet it with relief. ScanDisk is a disk detective that examines your hard drive for errors, and then repairs them before allowing Windows 98 to reappear on the screen.

In fact, if your computer is behaving oddly, run ScanDisk yourself. Open My Computer, right-click on a disk drive, and choose Properties. Click the Check Now button to bring ScanDisk to life. Highlight all your disk drives, click the Standard and Automatically fix errors boxes, and click the box's Start button.

ScanDisk will examine your hard drives for anything askew and automatically repair it. It's not a cure-all; it merely restores the way information is stored on your disk. But if your computer often freezes, it's worth a try.

Shortcuts

The shortcut concept is familiar to most people: Why bother walking around the block to get to school when a shortcut through Mr. McGurdy's backyard can get you there twice as fast?

It's the same with Windows 98. Instead of wading through a bunch of menus to get somewhere, you can create a shortcut and assign it to an icon. Then, when you double-click the Shortcut icon, Windows 98 immediately takes you to that location.

You can create a shortcut to your word processor, for example, and leave the shortcut icon sitting on your desktop within easy reach. Double-click the word processor's shortcut icon, and Windows 98 automatically wades through your computer's folders and files, grabs the word processor, and throws it onto the screen.

A *shortcut* is simply a push button that loads a file or program. You can even make shortcuts for accessing your printer or a favorite folder.

To create a desktop shortcut to your favorite program, open My Computer or Explorer and right-click on your coveted program's icon. Drag it to your desktop and let go of the button. Then choose Create Shortcut(s) Here from the pop-up menu. Fun!

Here's the important thing to remember about Windows 98: Deleting a shortcut doesn't delete the file or program that the shortcut points to. It merely deletes one of the push buttons that quickly brings up that file or program. You can still get to the program by moving through the menus on the Start button or using Windows Explorer.

✔ Internet-crazy Windows 98 even lets you create shortcuts to your favorite spots on the Internet and sprinkle them around your desktop for easy access.

- ✔ The ever-helpful Start button automatically makes a shortcut to the last 15 documents you've opened. Click the Start button, click the word Documents, and you see shortcuts waiting for you to discover them.

- ✔ Unfortunately, the Start button only keeps track of the last 15 documents you've opened. If you're looking for the *16th* one, you won't find a shortcut waiting. Also, not all programs tell the Start button about recently opened documents; the shortcuts then don't appear on the list. (It's not your fault, if that makes you feel better.)

- ✔ A shortcut in Windows 98 is the same thing that an icon used to be in Windows 3.1 Program Manager: a push button that starts a program. If you delete a shortcut, you haven't deleted the program; you've just removed a button that started that program.

Temp Files

Like children who don't put away the peanut butter jar, Windows 98 also leaves things lying around. They're called *temp files* — secret files Windows 98 creates to store stuff in while it's running. Windows 98 normally deletes them automatically when you leave the program. It occasionally forgets, however, and leaves them cluttering up your hard drive. Stern lectures leave very little impression.

- ✔ Temp files usually (but not always) end with the letters TMP. Common temp filenames include ~DOC0D37.TMP, ~WRI3F0E.TMP, the occasional stray ~$DIBLCA.ASD, and similar-looking files that usually start with the wavy ~ thing. (Typographically correct people call it a *tilde*.)

- ✔ If you exit Windows 98 the naughty way — by just flicking the computer's off switch — Windows 98 won't have a chance to clean up its temp file mess. If you keep doing it, you'll eventually see hundreds of TMP files lying around your hard drive. Be sure to exit Windows 98 the Good Bear way: by clicking the Start button and choosing Shut Down from the menu that pops up.

- ✔ To free up wasted disk space, feel free to delete any TMP files in your Windows Temp folder — but make sure they're at least one week old.

The Windows

Windows 98 enables you to run several programs at the same time by placing them in *windows*. A window is just a little on-screen box.

You can move the boxes around. You can make them bigger or smaller. You can make them fill your entire screen. You can make them turn into little icons at the bottom of your screen. You can spend hours playing with windows. In fact, most frustrated new Windows 98 users do.

- You can put as many windows on-screen as you want, peeping at all of them at the same time or just looking into each one individually. This activity appeals to the voyeur in all of us.

- For instructions on how to move windows or resize them, head to Chapter 6. To retrieve lost windows from the pile, head immediately to Chapter 7.

The World Wide Web

The World Wide Web, known simply as the Web, is merely a way for sending and receiving pictures, sound, and other information on the Internet network. (See the section, "The Internet," earlier in this chapter, or Chapter 13, if you're *really* interested.)

Part II
Making Windows 98 Do Something

The 5th Wave   By Rich Tennant

"THE PHONE COMPANY BLAMES THE MANUFACTURER, WHO SAYS IT'S THE SOFTWARE COMPANY'S FAULT, WHO BLAMES IT ON OUR MOON BEING IN VENUS WITH SCORPIO RISING."

In this part . . .

Windows 98 is more fun than cheap tattoos from the bottom of a Cracker Jack box. It's especially fun to show friends the built-in screen savers, like the one that cruises past the stars at warp speed. You can even adjust the ship's pace by using the Control Panel.

Unfortunately, some spoil-sport friend will eventually mutter the words that bring everything back to Earth: "Let's see Windows 98 do something useful, like balance a checkbook or teach the kids to rinse off their plates and put them in the dishwasher."

Toss this eminently practical part at them to quiet 'em down.

Chapter 4

Starting Windows 98

● ●

In This Chapter

▶ Revvin' up Windows 98

▶ Starting a program

▶ Finding the secret pull-down menus

▶ Loading a file

▶ Putting two programs on the screen

▶ Using the keyboard

▶ Printing your work

▶ Saving your work

▶ Quitting Windows 98

● ●

*H*old on to your hat! Then try to type at the same time. No, let the hat fly by the wayside because this is a hands-on Windows 98 chapter that demonstrates some dazzling special effects. First, you make Windows 98 leap to your screen, ready to load a program!

Then, at the click of the mouse, you launch a second program, running at the same time as the first! Plus, you discover secret magic tricks to bypass the mouse and use the keyboard instead!

Finally, you find out how to print your work so that you'll have some hard copy to show those doubting friends of yours.

Oh, and you also find out how to save your work so that you can find it again the next day. So warm up those fingers, shake out your sleeves, and get ready for action.

Beware, however, that you can set up Windows 98 in a zillion different ways. Because most of them are described here, you'll have to ignore the ones that don't apply to your own computer. (Luckily, most people are happiest when ignoring their computers.)

Revvin' Up Windows 98

If your PC came with Windows 98 already installed (most of them do these days), Windows 98 probably leaps to your screen automatically when you first turn on the computer. If not, perhaps some evil soul left you at a "DOS prompt." Try opening the cage door manually by typing the following command at the C:\> prompt:

```
C:\> EXIT
```

That is, you type **EXIT** (lowercase works, too) and follow it with a deft press of the Enter key.

If Windows 98 has been installed on your computer, a chore described in this book's Appendix B, it pops up on the screen, and its Start button is ready for action. Windows 98 is like an elevator that moves around your computer, and the Start button is like a panel of elevator buttons. By pushing the Start button, you tell Windows 98 where to go and what to do.

✔ When you start Windows 98, you may hear pleasant synthesizer sounds singing from the computer's sound card. If you don't have a sound card, you don't hear anything but a strong inner urge driving you toward the computer store's sound-card aisles. (Sound cards range in price from $75–$250.)

✔ Can't hear cheery synthesized greetings when Windows 98 loads itself? If the desktop speakers are turned up, Windows 98 may have its sound options turned off. To activate the sounds yourself, choose the Sounds icon from the Control Panel and select a new sound Scheme, a not-too-laborious process described in Chapter 9.

It wants me to enter a password!

Your computer may be part of a *network* — a bunch of computers linked with cables or through the phone lines. A network lets you sit at your own computer in your own cubicle, but swap files with Grace's computer in her cubicle — and neither of you has to get up.

But how do you make sure nobody uses your computer to steal Grace's files? How can you set up your computer so that nobody else can mess with your own files? Or, if several people share the same computer, how can they make sure that their Windows 98 desktop is customized to their own special needs?

Typing a password solves some of those problems. After Windows 98 wakes up and figures out that it's part of a network, it cautiously sends out the box shown in Figure 4-1.

Running Windows 98 for the first time

Just installed Windows 98 or turned on your new computer for the first time? Then you're treated with a few extra Windows 98 spectacles.

First, a hip little box appears on the screen, demonstrating that Windows 98 can indeed create cool colors and noises.

Then Windows 98 leaves you at a box with the following four buttons:

Register Now: Click here to "register" Windows 98. This wakes up the Registration Wizard, which can get a little complicated. Basically, it tells Microsoft that you're a new owner of Windows 98, so they'll bother to talk to you. It also installs the goods necessary for your computer to call a special Microsoft Web spot on the Internet called Windows Update. By calling the Windows Update area, your computer can automatically keep itself up to date on new software fixes.

Connect to the Internet: The Windows Update area requires an Internet connection, unfortunately. And despite the Registration Wizard's hand-holding, Internet configurations often lead to some rough questions. (Although Chapter 13 explains how to navigate the Internet, the *MORE Windows 98 For Dummies* book from IDG Books Worldwide, Inc., tackles the more odious chores of configuring an Internet account.)

Discover Windows 98: By all means, click here. Windows 98 merrily unveils its new features, offers quick lessons for beginners, and teaches basic computing to first-time users. (For later access, this "Welcome to Windows" feature lives under System Tools, which lives under Accessories in the Start button's Programs area. If it doesn't work, try inserting your Windows 98 CD, or reading the section in Chapter 9 about adding missing Windows 98 programs.)

Maintain Your Computer: Want the built-in mechanic to run automatic service and maintenance calls? Click here to tell Windows when to run tune-ups on your computer (mine works every night at 3 a.m.); the "fix-it" software will show up at the scheduled time, ready to squirt the digital oil. You'll find more information in "The Techie Programs" section of Chapter 12.

Figure 4-1:
Type your name in the box, press Tab, type any assigned password into the bottom box, and click OK to log on to your computer.

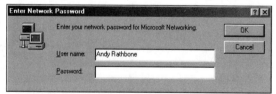

By typing your name in the Uder name box and making up a password to type into the Password box, you enable your computer to immediately recognize you: You're logged on.

- Depending on your network's level of security, a password can let you do many things. Sometimes entering the password merely lets you use your own computer. Other times, it lets you share files on a network.

- Because networks can be notoriously difficult to set up, most networked offices have a full-time network administrator who tries to make the darn thing work. (That's the person to bug if something goes wrong.)

- If you are not working on a network where security is an issue, don't type anything in the Password box, shown in Figure 4-1. If you leave the box blank and click the OK button, Windows 98 just lets you type in your name to log on to the computer — nothing to remember, and nothing to forget.

- Have you forgotten your password already? Just click on the Cancel button, shown in Figure 4-1. Unless you're on a strict network, Windows 98 still lets you in. Because it doesn't recognize you, however, you might not be able to see your favorite wallpaper, desktop, and other Windows 98 accoutrements.

- Keep your password short and sweet: the name of your favorite vegetable, for example, or the brand of your dental floss. (See your network administrator if Windows 98 doesn't accept your password.)

- Passwords are case-sensitive. That means that a password of caviar is different from Caviar. The computer notices the capital C and considers them to be two different words.

Make Windows stop asking me for a password!

Windows asks for your name and password only when it needs to know who's tapping on its keys. And it needs that information for only two reasons:

- Your computer is part of a network, and your identity determines what goodies you can access.

- You share your computer with other people, and each person customizes how Windows 98 looks and behaves.

If you're not working on a network, disable the network password request by double-clicking the Control Panel's Network icon and choosing Windows Logon in the Primary Network Logon box. Click the OK button and follow any instructions.

If you don't share your machine with other users — or everybody uses the same desktop — head for the Control Panel's Passwords icon. Under the User Profiles tab, choose the button marked All users of this computer use same preferences and desktop settings.

By choosing these two settings, Windows 98 should never ask for a password again.

It wants me to choose whether to click or double-click!

We are entering a historical moment in the computing world as programmers ponder the big question: Should we click or double-click the mouse to get things done on-screen?

For years, Windows owners have "double-clicked" to make things happen; Macintosh owners have single-clicked. Internet aficionados do both. To please everybody, Microsoft makes Windows 98 users fill out a form to determine how their mouse button should behave.

For example, when you choose the new Web style folder option to make Windows 98 look like a Web page (a procedure covered in the Active Desktops section of Chapter 21), Windows 98 slings out a clicking etiquette question, as shown in Figure 4-2.

Basically, it asks whether you prefer single-clicking or double-clicking your desktop's icons to bring them to life.

Figure 4-2:
Windows 98
lets you
choose
between
single-click-
ing or
double-
clicking.

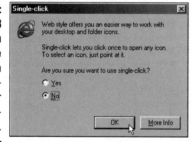

 That's because Windows 98 can mimic Web software on the Internet. And with the Web, a simple click on a button makes things happen — just like controlling an elevator. So, if you enjoy using the Internet's Web — and you want your desktop to look and act like the Web — then choose the single-click option.

But if you're not a big Web user — or you don't even know what the Web is — then choose No to remain with the Windows traditional double-click option, called, sentimentally enough, Classic style.

Keep this in mind, too: The single-click/double-click choice only applies to the folders and icons on the Windows 98 desktop. Even if you choose to single-click folders and icons in Windows 98, you still end up double-clicking occasionally when inside most Windows programs.

✔ Because Windows 98 now lets people customize the desktop to such an extreme, Windows 98 can act very differently on different people's computers. Chapter 5 shows how to fiddle with all the folder settings until you come up with something comfortable.

✔ To *really* start fiddling with your desktop's Web page options, however, troop to Chapter 21 and read about something called The Active Desktop.

Starting your favorite program with the Start button

When Windows 98 first takes over your computer, it turns your screen into a desktop. However, the desktop is merely a fancy name for a plate of buttons with labels underneath them. Click a button, and programs hop to the screen in their own little windows. Click the Start button in the bottom-left corner of the screen, and you'll have even more buttons to choose from, as shown in Figure 4-3.

Figure 4-3:
The Start button in Windows 98 hides dozens of menus for starting programs.

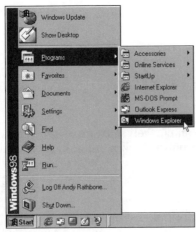

Because the buttons have little pictures on them, they're called *icons.* Icons offer clues to the program they represent. For example, the icon of the stamped envelope stands for Microsoft Outlook Express, a program that lets people send and receive electronic mail on their computers.

See the dark bar shading the Windows Explorer icon's title in Figure 4-3? The bar means that the Windows Explorer program is *highlighted:* It's queued up and ready to go. If you press the Enter key while Windows Explorer is high-lighted, Explorer hops to the forefront. (Don't press Enter, though, because Explorer is too boring to play with right now.)

Look at the little arrow sitting by itself in the corner of your screen. Roll your mouse around until that arrow hovers over the button that says Start.

Click your mouse button, and the Start menu pops up on the screen, shown in Figure 4-4. Next, click the Programs button, and another menu full of but-tons shoots out, as shown in Figure 4-5. Click Accessories to see yet another menu, shown in Figure 4-6. Click Games to see the last menu on the chain (see Figure 4-7). And, if you're not too exhausted, click FreeCell to check out the great Windows 98 Solitaire game.

Figure 4-4:
To start a
program in
Windows
98, click the
Start
button...

✔ The Start button is just a big panel of buttons. When you press one of the buttons by pointing at it and clicking with the mouse, the program assigned to that button heads for the top of the screen and appears in a little window.

✔ You don't have to click your way through all those buttons hiding beneath the Start button. Click the Start button and then just hover your mouse pointer over the other menu areas you want to open. Windows 98 opens them without even waiting for your clicks.

✔ Icons can stand for files as well as for programs. Clicking the Documents button usually brings up shortcut buttons that take you to 15 of your most recently used documents.

✔ Microsoft has already set up the Start button to include icons for the most popular programs and files Windows 98 found as it installed itself on your computer — stuff like Microsoft Word or Excel. If you want to add some other programs and files, however, check out the section in Chapter 10 on customizing your Start button.

✔ If you're kind of sketchy about all this *double-click* stuff, head to the end of Chapter 5; you're not alone.

Figure 4-5:
... and then click *Programs* and follow the menu as it grows.

Figure 4-6:
Click the type of program you'd like to load...

TIP

✔ Do you despise mice? You don't need a mouse for the Start button. Hold down Ctrl and press Esc to make the Start menu appear. Then push your arrow keys to navigate the various menus. Highlighted the program you want? Press Enter, and the program begins to run.

✔ If the icon you're after in the Start menu has a little black bar around its name, it's *highlighted*. If you just press Enter, the highlighted program loads itself into a little window. Or you can still double-click it to load it. Windows 98 lets you do things in a bunch of different ways.

✔ This chapter gives you just a quick tour of Windows 98. You can find glowing descriptions of the Start button in Chapter 10.

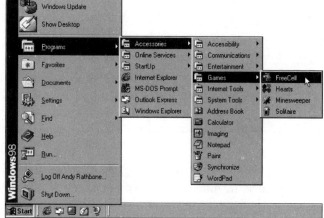

Figure 4-7:
... and then click your program's name to load it.

Pull-down menus

Windows 98, bless its heart, makes an honest effort toward making computing easier. For example, the Start button puts a bunch of options on the screen in front of you. You just choose the one you want, and Windows 98 takes it from there.

But if Windows 98 put all its options on the screen at the same time, it would look more crowded than a 14-page menu at the Siam Thai restaurant. To avoid resorting to fine print, Windows 98 hides some menus in special locations on the screen. When you click the mouse in the right place, more options leap toward you.

For example, begin loading Windows' simple word-processing program, WordPad, by clicking the Start button. When the Start menu pops up, choose Programs, click Accessories, and click WordPad to bring it to the screen.

See the row of words beginning with File that rests along the top edge of WordPad? You find a row of words across the top of just about every Windows 98 program. Move your mouse pointer over the word File and click.

A menu opens from beneath File. This menu is called a *pull-down menu,* if you're interested, and it looks somewhat like what you see in Figure 4-8.

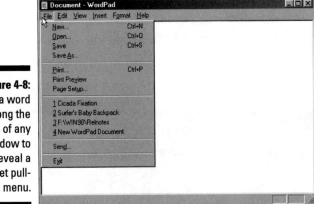

Figure 4-8: Click a word along the top of any window to reveal a secret pull-down menu.

- ✔ Pull-down menus open from any of those key words along the top of a window. Just click the mouse on the word, and the menu tumbles down like shoeboxes falling off a closet shelf.

- ✔ To close the menu, go back up and click the mouse again, but click it someplace away from the menu.

- ✔ Different Windows 98 programs have different words across the menu bar, but almost all of the bars begin with the word File. The File pull-down menu contains file-related options, like Open, Save, Print, and Push Back Cuticles.

- ✔ You find pull-down menus sprinkled liberally throughout Windows 98.

Loading a file

First, here's the bad news: Loading a file into a Windows 98 program can be a mite complicated sometimes. Second, *loading* a file means the same thing as *opening* a file.

Now that those trifles have been dispensed with, here's the good news: All Windows 98 programs load files in the exact same way. So, after you know the proper etiquette for one program, you're prepared for all the others!

Here's the scoop: To open a file in any Windows 98 program, look for the program's *menu bar,* that row of important-looking words along its top. Because you're after a *file,* click File.

A most-welcome pull-down menu descends from the word File. The menu has a list of important-looking words. Because you're trying to *open* a file, move the mouse to the word Open and click once again.

Yet another box hops onto the screen, shown in Figure 4-9, and you see this box named *Open* appear over and over again in Windows 98.

See the list of filenames inside the box? Point at one of them with the mouse, click the button, and that file's name shows up in the box called File name. Click the Open button, and WordPad opens the file and displays it on the screen. If you don't have a mouse, press the Tab key until a little square appears around one of the file's names. Then press the arrow keys until the file you want is highlighted, and press Enter.

Figure 4-9:
Almost
every
Windows 98
program
tosses this
box at you
when you
load or save
a file.

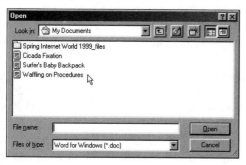

You've done it! You've loaded a file into a program! Those are the same stone steps you walk across in any Windows 98 program, whether it was written by Microsoft or by the teenager down the street. They all work in the same way.

✔ Sometimes you won't immediately spot the file you're after. It's just not listed in that little box. That means that you'll have to do a little spelunking. Just like most people store their underwear and T-shirts in different dresser drawers, most computers store their files in different places called folders. If you're having trouble finding a file for your program to open, head for the section on folders in Chapter 11.

✔ You can speed things up by simply double-clicking a file's name right from a menu; that action tells Windows 98 to load the file as well. Or you can click the name once to highlight it (it turns black) and then press the Enter key. Windows 98 is full of multiple options like that (different strokes for different folks and all).

If you set up Windows 98 to work with the "single-click" option (making your desktop work like the Internet Explorer), then just single-clicking a file will load the file and the program that created it.

✔ Whenever you load a file into a program and change it, even by an accidental press of the spacebar, Windows 98 assumes that you've consciously changed the file for the better. If you try to load another file into the program, Windows 98 cautiously asks whether you want to save the changes you've made to the current file. Click the No button unless you do, indeed, want to save that version you've haphazardly changed.

✔ The Open box has a bunch of options in it. You can open files that are stored in different folders or on other disk drives. You can also call up files that were created by certain programs, filtering out the ones you won't be needing. Chapter 5 explains all this Open box stuff. *Tip:* Don't know what those little icons along the top are supposed to do? Let the mouse pointer rest over them, and a box will appear, announcing their occupation.

✔ Now, here's some more bad news: Only Windows 98 and Windows 95 programs can handle long filenames. If you're using Windows 3.1 programs in Windows 98, you are still stuck with the old versions of the Open and Save boxes, and the long filenames won't work right in these programs.

✔ Some newly revamped Windows 98 programs, like Media Player, dare to be different. Instead of immediately showing you a list of files to open, they make you click a button called Browse. Then you get to choose the files.

✔ If you're still a little murky on the concepts of *files, folders, directories,* and *drives,* flip to Chapter 11 for an explanation of Windows Explorer.

Putting two programs on-screen simultaneously

After spending all your money for Windows 98 and a computer powerful enough to cart it around, you're not going to be content with only one program on your screen. You want to *fill* the screen with programs, all running in their own little windows.

How do you put a second program on the screen? Well, if you've opened WordPad by clicking its icon in the Start button's Accessories area (that area's listed under the Programs area), you're probably already itching to load FreeCell, the Solitaire game. Simply click the Start button and start moving through the menus, as described in the "Starting your favorite program with the Start button" section earlier in this chapter.

- ✔ This section is intentionally short. When working in Windows 98, you almost always have two or more programs on the screen at the same time. There's nothing really special about it, so there's no need to belabor the point here.

- ✔ The special part comes when you move information between the two programs, which is explained in Chapter 8. (Moving information between windows is known as "cutting and pasting" in Windows parlance.)

- ✔ If you want to move multiple windows around on the screen, move yourself to Chapter 6.

- ✔ If you've started up FreeCell, you're probably wondering where the WordPad window disappeared to. It's now hidden behind the FreeCell window. To get it back, check out the information on retrieving lost windows in Chapter 7. (Or, if you see a button called WordPad along the bottom of your screen, click it.)

- ✔ To switch between windows, just click them. When you click a window, it immediately becomes the *active* window — the window where all the activity takes place. For more information on switching between windows, switch to Chapter 6.

- ✔ Can't find FreeCell *anywhere*? Unfortunately, Windows 98 doesn't automatically install FreeCell on everybody's computers. To correct this oversight, use the Control Panel's Add/Remove Programs icon, as described in Chapter 9.

Using the Keyboard

It's a good thing Microsoft doesn't design automobiles. Each car would have a steering wheel, a joystick, a remote control, and handles on the back for people who prefer to push. Windows 98 offers almost a dozen different ways for you to perform the most simple tasks.

For example, check out the top of any window where that important-looking row of words hides above secret pull-down menus. Some of the words have certain letters underlined. What gives? Well, it's a secret way for you to open their menus without using the mouse. This sleight of hand depends on the Alt key, that dark key resting next to your keyboard's spacebar.

Press (and release) Alt and keep an eye on the row of words in the WordPad *menu bar*. The first word, File, darkens immediately after you release Alt. You haven't damaged it; you've selected it, just as if you'd pointed to it with the mouse. The different color means that it's highlighted.

Now, see how the letter F in File is underlined? Press the letter F, and the pull-down menu hidden below File falls recklessly down, like a mushroom off a pizza.

That's the secret underlined-letter trick! And pressing Alt and F is often faster than plowing through a truckload of mouse menus — especially if you think that the whole mouse concept is rather frivolous, anyway.

- ✔ You can access almost every command in Windows 98 by using Alt rather than a mouse. Press Alt, and then press the key for the underlined letter. That option, or command, then begins to work.

- ✔ If you accidentally press Alt and find yourself trapped in Menu Land, press Alt again to return to normal. If that doesn't work, try pressing Esc.

- ✔ As pull-down menus continue to appear, you can keep plowing through them by selecting underlined letters until you accomplish your ultimate goal. For example, pressing Alt and then F brings down the File pull-down menu. Pressing O subsequently activates the Open files option from the File menu and immediately brings the Open file box to the front of the screen.

When you see a word with an underlined letter in a menu, press and release Alt. Then press that underlined letter to choose that menu item.

Printing Your Work

Eventually, you'll want to transfer a copy of your finely honed work to the printed page so that you can pass it around. Printing something from any Windows 98 program (or application, or applet, whatever you want to call it) takes only three keystrokes. Press and release Alt, and then press the letters F and P. What you see on your screen will be whisked to your printer.

Pressing Alt activates the words along the top, known as the *menu bar*. The letter F wakes up the File menu, and the letter P tells the program to send its stuff to the printer — pronto. (Some fancier programs bring up a special Print box that makes you click the OK button first.)

- ✔ Alternatively, you can use the mouse to click the word File and then click the word Print from the pull-down menu. Depending on the RPM of your mouse ball and the elasticity of your wrist, both the mouse and the keyboard method can be equally quick.

- ✔ If nothing comes out of the printer after a few minutes, try putting paper in your printer and making sure that it's turned on. If it still doesn't work, cautiously tiptoe to Chapter 14.

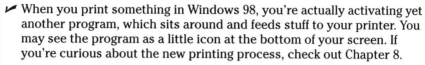

✔ When you print something in Windows 98, you're actually activating yet another program, which sits around and feeds stuff to your printer. You may see the program as a little icon at the bottom of your screen. If you're curious about the new printing process, check out Chapter 8.

✔ Some programs, such as WordPad, have a little picture of a printer along their top. Clicking on that printer icon is a quick way of telling the program to shuffle your work to the printer.

Saving Your Work

Anytime you create something in a Windows 98 program, be it a picture of a spoon or a letter to *The New York Times* begging for a decent comics page, you'll want to save it to disk.

Saving your work means placing a copy of it onto a disk, either the mysterious hard disk inside your computer or a floppy disk, one of those things you're always tempted to use as beverage coasters. (Don't try it, though.)

Luckily, Windows 98 makes it easy for you to save your work. You need only press three keys, just as if you were printing your work or opening a file. To save your work, press and release Alt, press F, and then press S.

If you prefer to push the mouse around, click File from the Windows 98 menu bar. When the secret pull-down menu appears, click Save. Your mouse pointer turns into an hourglass, asking you to hold your horses while Windows 98 shuffles your work from the program to your hard disk or a floppy disk for safekeeping.

That's it!

✔ If you're saving your work for the first time, you see a familiar-looking box: It's the same box you see when opening a file. See how the letters in the File name box are highlighted? The computer is always paying attention to the highlighted areas, so anything you type appears in that box. Type in a name for the file and press Enter.

✔ If Windows 98 throws a box in your face saying something like "A filename cannot contain any of the following characters," you haven't adhered to the ridiculously strict filename guidelines spelled out in Chapter 11.

✔ Just as files can be loaded from different directories and disk drives, they can be saved to them as well. You can choose between different directories and drives by clicking various parts of the Save box. All this stuff is explained in Chapter 5.

Quitting Windows 98

Ah! The most pleasant thing you'll do with Windows 98 all day could very well be to stop using it. And you do that the same way you started: by using the Start button, that friendly little helper that popped up the first time you started Windows 98.

Other Windows 98 programs come and go, but the Start button is always on your screen somewhere. (Sometimes you have to press Ctrl+Esc to bring it out of hiding.)

First, make the Start menu pop to the forefront by clicking the Start button or holding down Ctrl and pressing Esc at the same time. Next, click the Shut Down command from the Start button's menu. Windows 98, tearful that you're leaving, sends out one last plea, shown in Figure 4-10.

Figure 4-10: Be sure to shut down Windows 98 before turning off your computer.

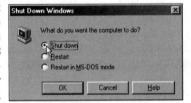

If you mean business, click the OK button or press Enter. Windows 98 starts to put all of its parts away, preparing to leave the screen of your computer. If, by some odd mistake, you've clicked the Shut Down command in error, click the Cancel button, and Windows 98 ignores your faux pas. (Keyboard users must press Tab to highlight the Cancel button and then press Enter.)

- ✔ Be sure to shut down Windows 98 through its official Shut Down program before turning off your computer. Otherwise, Windows 98 can't properly prepare your computer for the event, leading to future troubles.

- ✔ When you tell Windows 98 that you want to quit, it searches through all your open windows to see whether you've saved all your work. If it finds any work you've forgotten to save, it tosses a box your way, letting you click the OK button to save it. Whew!

- ✔ Holding down Alt and pressing F4 tells Windows 98 that you want to stop working in your current program and close it down. If you press Alt+F4 while no programs are running, Windows 98 figures that you've had enough for one day, and it acts as though you clicked its Shut Down command.

✔ If you happen to have any DOS programs running, Windows 98 stops and tells you to quit your DOS programs first. See, Windows 98 knows how to shut down Windows 98 programs because they all use the same command. But all DOS programs are different. You have to shut the program down manually, using whatever exit sequence you normally use in that program.

✔ If you want to run a cranky DOS program that doesn't like to run with Windows 98, select the last option, Restart the computer in MS-DOS mode. (To return to Windows 98 from DOS, type **EXIT** at the C:\> prompt thing.)

✔ You don't *have* to shut down Windows 98. In fact, some people leave their computers on all the time. Just be sure to turn off your monitor; those things like to cool down when they're not being used.

Chapter 5

Field Guide to Buttons, Bars, Boxes, Folders, and Files

. . . .

In This Chapter

▶ Looking at a typical window

▶ Getting into bars

▶ Changing borders

▶ Getting to know the button family

▶ Disregarding the dopey Control-menu button

▶ Exploring dialog box stuff: text boxes, drop-down list boxes, list boxes, and other gibberish

▶ Finding out how to open a file

▶ Changing your folder viewing options

▶ Knowing when to click and when to double-click

▶ Knowing when to use the left mouse button and when to use the right mouse button

. . . .

*A*s children, just about all of us played with elevator buttons until our parents told us to knock it off. An elevator gave such an awesome feeling of power: Push a little button, watch the mammoth doors slide shut, and feel the responsive push as the spaceship floor begins to surge upward. . . . What fun!

Part of an elevator's attraction still comes from its simplicity. To stop at the third floor, you merely press the button marked 3. No problems there.

Windows 98 takes the elevator button concept to an extreme, unfortunately, and it loses something in the process. First, some of the Windows 98 buttons don't even *look* like buttons. Most of the Windows 98 buttons have ambiguous little pictures rather than clearly marked labels. And the worst part is the Windows 98 terminology: The phrase *push the button* becomes *click the scroll bar above or below the scroll box on the vertical scroll bars.* Yuck!

When braving your way through Windows 98, don't bother learning all these dorky terms. Instead, treat this chapter as a field guide, something you can grab when you stumble across a confusing new button or box that you've never encountered before. Just page through until you find its picture. Read the description to find out whether that particular creature is deadly or just mildly poisonous. Then read to find out where you're supposed to poke it with the mouse pointer.

You'll get used to the critter after you've clicked it a few times. Just don't bother remembering the scientific name *vertical scroll bar,* and you'll be fine.

A Typical Window

Nobody wants a field guide without pictures, so Figure 5-1 shows a typical window with its parts labeled.

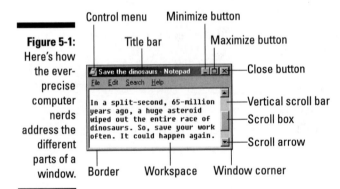

Figure 5-1: Here's how the ever-precise computer nerds address the different parts of a window.

Control menu   Minimize button

Title bar   Maximize button

Close button

Vertical scroll bar

Scroll box

Scroll arrow

Border   Workspace   Window corner

Just as boxers grimace differently depending on where they've been punched, windows behave differently depending on where they've been clicked. The following sections describe the correct places to click and, if that doesn't work, the best places to punch.

✔ Windows 98 is full of little weird-shaped buttons, borders, and boxes. You don't have to remember their Latin or Greek etymologies. The important part is just finding out what part you're supposed to click. Then you can start worrying about whether you're supposed to single-click or double-click. (And that little dilemma is explained near the end of this chapter.)

✔ Not sure whether Windows 98 is set up for single-clicking or double-clicking? Click cautiously once. If that doesn't do the trick — the click doesn't prod your program into action, for instance — then double-click by clicking twice in rapid succession.

 ✔ After you click a few windows a few times, you realize how easy it really is to boss them around. The hard part is finding out everything for the first time, just like when you stalled the car while learning how to use the stick shift.

Bars

Windows 98 is filled with bars; perhaps that's why some of its programs seem a bit groggy and hung over. Bars are thick stripes along the edges of a window. You find several different types of bars in Windows 98.

The title bar

The title bar is that topmost strip in any window (see Figure 5-2). It lists the name of the program, as well as the name of any open file. For example, the title bar in Figure 5-2 comes from the Windows 98 Notepad. It contains an untitled file because you haven't had a chance to save the file yet. (For example, the file may be full of notes you've jotted down from an energetic phone conversation with Ed McMahon.)

Figure 5-2:
A title bar
lists the
program's
name along
the top of a
window.

Windows 98 often chooses the name New Text Document for untitled Notepad files; you choose a more descriptive name for that file when you save it for the first time. That new filename then replaces the admittedly vague New Text Document in the title bar.

✔ The title bar merely shows the name of the current program and file. If you've just started to create a file, the title bar refers to that file's name as New Text Document, or something similar, depending on the program.

✔ The title bar can serve as a *handle* for moving a window around on-screen. Point at the title bar, hold down the mouse button, and move the mouse around. An outline of the window moves as you move the mouse. When you've placed the outline in a new spot, let go of the mouse button. The window leaps to that new spot and sets up camp.

✔ When you're working on a window, its title bar is *highlighted,* meaning that it's a different color from the title bar of any other open window. By glancing at all the title bars on-screen, you can quickly tell which window is currently being used.

TIP

To enlarge a window so that it completely fills the screen, double-click its title bar. It expands to full size, making it easier to read and covering up every-thing else. No mouse? Then press Alt, the spacebar, and then X. Maximized windows can't be moved, however; double-click their titlebars to return them to window size. Then they can be moved once again.

The menu bar

Windows 98 has menus *everywhere.* But if menus appeared all at once, every-body would think about deep-fried appetizers rather than computer commands. So Windows 98 hides its menus in something called a *menu bar* (see Figure 5-3).

Figure 5-3:
A menu bar
provides a
handy
place for
Windows 98
to hide its
cluttersome
menus.

Lying beneath the title bar, the menu bar keeps those little menus hidden behind little words. To reveal secret options associated with those words, click one of those words.

TIP

If you think that mice are for milksops, use the brawny Alt key instead. A quick tap of the Alt key activates the menu words across the top of the window. Press the arrow keys to the right or left until you've selected the word you're after and then press the down arrow key to expose the hidden menu. (You can also press a word's underlined letter to bring it to life, but that tip is explained in Chapter 4 and later in more detail.)

For example, to see the entrees under Edit, click your mouse button on Edit (or press Alt and then E). A secret menu tumbles down from a trap door, shown in Figure 5-4, presenting all sorts of *edit-related* options.

Figure 5-4:
Select any
word in the
menu bar
to reveal
its secret
hidden
menu.

Keep the following points in mind when using menus:

✔ When you select a key word in a menu bar, a menu comes tumbling down. The menu contains options related to that particular key word.

✔ Just as restaurants sometimes run out of specials, a window sometimes isn't capable of offering all its menu items. Any unavailable options are *grayed out,* as the Undo, Cut, Copy, Paste, and Delete options are in Figure 5-4.

✔ If you accidentally select the wrong word, causing the wrong menu to jump down, just sigh complacently. (S-i-i-i-i-igh.) Then select the word you *really* wanted. The first menu disappears, and the new one appears below the new word.

✔ If you want out of a program's Menu Land completely, click the mouse pointer back down on your work in the window's *workspace* — usually the area where you've been typing stuff. (Or press your Alt key; whichever method comes to mind sooner.)

✔ Some menu items have *shortcut keys* listed next to them, such as the Ctrl+Z key combination next to the Undo option in Figure 5-4. Just hold down the Ctrl key and press the letter Z to undo your last effort. The Undo option takes place immediately, and you don't have to wait for the menu to tumble down.

If you find yourself performing the same task on a menu over and over, check to see whether a shortcut key is next to it. By pressing the shortcut key, you can bypass the menu altogether, performing that task instantly.

The scroll bar

The scroll bar, which looks like an elevator shaft, is along the edge of a window (see Figure 5-5). Inside the shaft, a little freight elevator (the *scroll box*) travels up and down as you page through your work. In fact, by glancing at the little elevator, you can tell whether you're near the top of a document, the middle, or the bottom.

Figure 5-5:
Scroll bars
enable you
to page
through
everything
that's in the
window.

For example, if you're looking at stuff near the *top* of a document, the elevator box is near the top of its little shaft. If you're working on the bottom portion of your work, the elevator box dangles near the bottom. You can watch the little box travel up or down as you press the PgUp or PgDn key. (Yes, it's easy to get distracted in Windows 98.)

Here's where the little box in the scroll bar comes into play: By clicking in various places on that scroll bar, you can quickly move around in a document without pressing the PgUp or PgDn key.

- ✔ Instead of pressing the PgUp key, click in the elevator shaft *above* the little elevator (the *scroll box*). The box jumps up the shaft a little bit, and the document moves up one page, too. Click *below* the scroll box, and your view moves down, just as with the PgDn key.

- ✔ To move your view up line by line, click the boxed-in arrow (*scroll arrow*) at the top of the scroll bar. If you hold down the mouse button while the mouse pointer is over that arrow, more and more of your document appears, line by line, as it moves you closer to its top. (Holding down the mouse button while the pointer is on the bottom arrow moves you closer to the bottom, line by line.)

✔ Scroll bars that run along the *bottom* of a window can move your view from side to side rather than up and down. They're handy for viewing spreadsheets that extend off the right side of your screen.

✔ If the scroll bars don't have a little scroll box inside them, you have to use the little arrows to move around. There's no little elevator to play with. Sniff. Sniff.

✔ Want to move around in a hurry? Then put the mouse pointer on the little elevator box, hold down the mouse button, and *drag* the little elevator box up or down inside the shaft. For example, if you drag the box up toward the top of its shaft and release it, you can view the top of the document. Dragging it and releasing it down low takes you near the end.

✔ Windows 98 adds another dimension to some scroll bars: the little elevator's *size*. If the elevator is swollen up so big that it's practically filling the scroll bar, the window is currently displaying practically all the information the file has to offer. But if the elevator is a tiny box in a huge scroll bar, you're only viewing a tiny amount of the information contained in the file. Don't be surprised to see the scroll box change size when you add or remove information from a file.

✔ Clicking or double-clicking the little elevator box itself doesn't do anything, but that doesn't stop most people from trying it anyway.

REMEMBER

Undoing what you've just done

Windows 98 offers a zillion different ways for you to do the same thing. Here are three ways to access the Undo option, which unspills the milk you've just spilled:

✔ Hold down the Ctrl key and press the Z key. (This little quickie is known as the *shortcut key method*.) The last mistake you made is reversed, sparing you from further shame.

✔ Hold down the Alt key and press the Backspace key. (This other quickie often works when the Ctrl+Z trick fails.)

✔ Click Edit and then click Undo from the menu that falls down. (This approach is known as *wading through the menus*.) The last command you made is undone, saving you from any damage.

✔ Press and release the Alt key, and then press the letter E (from Edit), and then press the letter U (from Undo). (This *Alt key method* is handy when you don't have a mouse.) Your last bungle is unbungled, reversing any grievous penalties.

Don't feel like you have to learn all three methods. For example, if you can remember the Ctrl+Z key combination, you can forget about the menu method or the Alt key method.

Or, if you don't want to remember *anything*, stick with the menu method. Just pluck the Undo command as it appears on the menu.

Finally, if you don't have a mouse, you'll have to remember the Alt key or Ctrl key business until you remember to buy a mouse.

✔ If you don't have a mouse, you can't play on the elevator. To view the top of your document, hold down Ctrl and press Home. To see the bottom, hold down Ctrl and press End. Or press the PgUp or PgDn key to move one page at a time.

The taskbar

Windows 98 converts your computer monitor's screen into a desktop. But because your newly computerized desktop is probably only 15 inches wide, all your programs and windows cover each other up like memos tossed onto a spike.

To keep track of the action, Windows 98 introduces the taskbar. It usually clings to the bottom of your screen and simply lists what windows are currently open. If you've found the Start button, you've found the taskbar — the Start button lives on the taskbar's left or top end.

✔ Whenever you open a window, Windows 98 tosses that window's name onto a button on the taskbar. If you open a lot of windows, the taskbar automatically shrinks all its buttons so they'll fit.

✔ To switch from one window to another, just click the desired window's name from its button on the taskbar. Wham! That window shoots to the top of the pile.

✔ Are all those open windows looking too crowded? Click a blank part of the taskbar with your right mouse button and choose the Minimize All Windows option. All your currently open windows turn into buttons on the taskbar.

✔ In Windows 3.1, double-clicking the desktop in the background brings up the Task List, a taskbarlike program that lists open windows so you can choose between them, and tile them across your screen for easy access. In Windows 98, clicking the taskbar with the right mouse button brings up the Task List's equivalent — a menu for organizing your open windows.

✔ You can't find your taskbar? Try pointing off the edge of your screen, slowly, trying each of the four sides. If you hit the correct side, some specially configured taskbars will stop goofing around and come back to the screen. But be wary: Windows 98 computers can use more than one monitor, and the taskbar can live on *any* of those monitor's edges — and that can lead to a lot of searching. (Ignore the mouse, hold down Control, and press Escape to bring the darn thing out into the open.)

✔ You can find more information about the taskbar in Chapter 10.

Borders

A *border* is that thin edge enclosing a window. Compared with a bar, it's really tiny.

✔ You use borders to change a window's size. I discuss how to do that in Chapter 6.

✔ You can't use a mouse to change a window's size if the window doesn't have a border. A few unruly borders keep the window locked at its current size, no matter how much you fiddle.

✔ If you like to trifle in details, you can make a border thicker or thinner through the Windows 98 Control Panel, which is discussed in Chapter 9. In fact, laptop owners often thicken their windows' borders to make them a little easier to grab with those awkward trackballs.

✔ Other than that, you won't be using borders much.

The Button Family

Three basic species of buttons flourish throughout the Windows 98 environment: command buttons, option buttons, and minimize/maximize buttons. All three species are closely related, and yet they look and act quite differently.

Command buttons

Command buttons may be the simplest to figure out — Microsoft labeled them! Command buttons are most commonly found in *dialog boxes,* which are little pop-up forms that Windows 98 makes you fill out before it will work for you.

For example, when you ask Windows 98 to open a file, it sends out a form in a dialog box. You have to fill out the form, telling Windows 98 what file you're after, where it's located, and equally cumbersome details.

Table 5-1 identifies some of the more common command buttons that you encounter in Windows 98.

Table 5-1	Common Windows 98 Command Buttons	
Command Button	**Habitat**	**Description**
OK	Found in nearly every pop-up dialog box	A click on this button says, "I'm done filling out the form, and I'm ready to move on." Windows 98 then reads what you've typed into the form and processes your request. (Pressing the Enter key does the same thing as clicking the OK button.)
Cancel	Found in nearly every pop-up dialog box	If you've somehow loused things up when filling out a form, click the Cancel button. The pop-up box disappears, and everything returns to normal. Whew! (The Esc key does the same thing.)
(help icon)	Found in nearly every pop-up dialog box	Stumped? Click this button. Yet another box pops up, this time offering help with your current situation. (The F1 function key does the same thing.)
< Back / Next > / Finish	Found when you must answer a string of questions as you fill out a form	Boy, would this have come in handy in elementary school! By clicking the Back button, Windows returns you to the previous window so that you can change your answer. Click the Next button to move to the next question; click Finish when you're confident that the form's filled out correctly.
Setup... / Settings... / Pizza...	Found less often in pop-up dialog boxes	If you encounter a button with ellipsis dots (. . .) after the word, brace yourself: Selecting that button brings yet another box to the screen. From there, you must choose even more settings, options, or toppings.
Click here to make this your home page / set home page	Found sprinkled nearly everywhere	Windows 98 adopted much of the Internet Web world, where buttons no longer look like buttons. Just about anything can be a button. The clues? When your mouse pointer turns into a little hand, it's hovering over a button. (Little pictures that waver on the screen are telltale signs, too.)

✔ By selecting a command button, you're telling Windows 98 to carry out the command that's written on the button. (Luckily, no command buttons are labeled Explode.)

✔ See how the OK button in Table 5-1 has a slightly darker border than the others? That darker border means that the button is highlighted. Anything in Windows 98 that's highlighted takes effect as soon as you press the Enter key; you don't *have* to select it.

✔ Some command buttons have underlined letters that you don't really notice until you stare at them. An underlined letter tells you that you can press that command button by holding down the Alt key while pressing the underlined letter. (That way you don't have to click or double-click if your mouse is goofing up.)

✔ Instead of scooting your mouse to the Cancel button when you've goofed in a dialog box, just press your Esc key. It does the same thing.

If you've clicked the wrong command button, but *haven't yet lifted your finger from the mouse button,* stop! There's still hope. Command buttons take effect only *after* you've lifted your finger from the mouse button. Press the Escape key while keeping your finger pressed on the button and scoot the mouse pointer away from the button. When the pointer no longer rests on the button, gently lift your finger. Whew! Try *that* trick on any elevator.

Did you stumble across a box that contains a confusing command button or two? Click the question mark in the box's upper-right corner (if there is a question mark, that is). Then, when you click the confusing command button, a helpful comment appears to explain that button's function in life. Also, try merely resting your mouse pointer over the button. Sometimes a helpful caption emerges to explain matters.

Option buttons

Sometimes Windows 98 gets ornery and forces you to choose just a single option. For example, you can elect to *eat* your brussels sprouts or *not* eat your brussels sprouts. You can't choose both, so Windows 98 doesn't let you select both of the options.

Windows 98 handles this situation with an *option button.* When you choose one option, the little dot hops over to it. If you choose the other option, the little dot hops over to it instead. You find option buttons in many dialog boxes. Figure 5-6 shows an example.

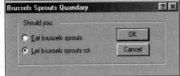

Figure 5-6:
When you
choose an
option, the
black dot
hops to it.

- ✔ Although Windows 98 tempts you with several choices in an option box, it lets you select only one of them. It moves the dot (and little dotted border line) back and forth between the options as your decision wavers. Click the OK button when you've reached a decision. The *dotted* option then takes effect.

- ✔ If you *can* select more than one option, Windows 98 doesn't present you with option buttons. Instead, it offers the more liberal *check boxes,* which are described in the "Check boxes" section, later in this chapter.

- ✔ Option buttons are round. Command buttons, described earlier, are rectangular.

Some old-time computer engineers refer to option buttons as radio buttons, after those push buttons on car radios that switch from station to station, one station at a time.

Minimize/maximize buttons

All the little windows in Windows 98 often cover each other up like teenage fans in the front row of a Pearl Jam concert. To restore order, you need to separate the windows by using their minimize/maximize buttons.

These buttons enable you to enlarge the window you want to play with or shrink all the others so they're out of the way. Here's the scoop.

 The minimize button is one of three buttons in the upper-right corner of almost every window. It looks like that little button in the margin next to this paragraph.

A click on the minimize button makes its window disappear, although its little button still lives on the taskbar along the bottom of your screen. (Click the button to return the window to its normal size.) Keyboard users can press Alt, the spacebar, and then N to minimize a window.

✔ Minimizing a window doesn't destroy its contents; it just transforms the window into a little button on the bar that runs along the bottom of the screen.

✔ To make the button turn back into an on-screen window, click the button. It reverts to a window in the same size and location as before you shrank it. (Keyboard users can press Alt, the spacebar, and then R.)

✔ Closing a window and minimizing a window are two different things. Closing a window purges it from the computer's memory. To reopen it, you need to load it off your hard drive again. Turning a window into an icon keeps it handy, loaded into memory, and ready to be used at an instant's notice.

The maximize button is in the upper-right corner of every window, too. It looks like the one in the margin.

A click on the maximize button makes the window swell up something fierce, taking up as much space on-screen as possible. Keyboard users can press Alt, the spacebar, and then X to maximize their windows.

TECHNICAL STUFF

Don't bother with this Control-menu button stuff

The Control-menu button provides a quick exit from any window: Just give the little ornament a quick double-click. Other than that feature, however, the Control-menu button is pretty useless, redundant, and repetitive.

For example, by clicking the Control-menu button once, you get a pull-down menu with a bunch of options. Choose the Move option, and you can move around the window with the keyboard's arrow keys. (But it's much easier to move a window by using the mouse, as you find out in Chapter 6.)

Choosing the Size option lets you change a window's size. (But that's much easier with a mouse, too, as you find out in Chapter 6.)

Don't bother with the menu's Minimize and Maximize options, either. Those two options have their own dedicated buttons, right in the window's other top corner. Click the minimize button (the button with the little line on it) to minimize the window; click the maximize button (the button with the big square on it) to maximize the window. Simple. You don't need to bumble through a menu for the Minimize and Maximize options when minimize and maximize buttons are already staring you in the face.

The Close option is redundant. You can close the window by double-clicking the Control-menu button in the first place and avoid the hassle of going through a menu. Or click the dedicated Close button once — the button with the X on it in the window's far, upper-right corner.

So don't bother messing with the Control-menu button because it's just a waste of time.

(The Control-menu may come in handy if you lose your laptop's mouse, however. Should this disastrous accident happen to you, press Alt and the spacebar to bring up the Control menu and then press any of the underlined letters to access the function.)

✔ If you're frustrated with all those windows that are overlapping each other, click your current window's maximize button. The window muscles its way to the top, filling the screen like a *real* program.

✔ Immediately after you maximize a window, its little maximize button turns into a *restore button* (described momentarily). The restore button lets you shrink the window back down when you're through giving it the whole playing field.

You don't *have* to click the maximize button to maximize a window. Just double-click its *title bar,* the thick strip along the window's top bearing its name. That double-click does the same thing as clicking the maximize button, and the title bar is much easier to aim for.

In the upper-right corner of every maximized window is the restore button, which looks like the button in the margin.

 After a window is maximized, clicking this button returns the window to the size it was before you maximized it. (Keyboard users can press Alt, the spacebar, and then R.)

✔ Restore buttons appear only in windows that fill the entire screen (which is no great loss because you need a restore button only when the window is maximized).

The Dopey Control-Menu Button

Just as all houses have circuit breakers, all windows have *Control-menu buttons.* These buttons hide in the top-left corner of almost every window, where they look like an inconspicuous hood ornament. (Sharp-eyed readers will notice that the button is actually a miniature icon representing the program.)

That little hood ornament hides a menu full of functions, but they're all pretty dopey, so ignore them all except for this one: Double-click the Control-menu button whenever you want to leave a window.

✔ You can get by without using the Control-menu button at all. Just hold down the Alt key and press the F4 key to close an application and exit the window. Or click the Close button, that button with the X on it in the window's far, upper-right corner.

✔ If you click the Control-menu button, a secret hidden menu appears, but it's pretty useless. So ignore it, skip the technical chatter in the sidebar about the Control-menu button, and move along to the more stimulating dialog boxes that follow.

Dialog Box Stuff (Lots of Gibberish)

Sooner or later, you'll have to sit down and tell Windows 98 something personal — the name of a file to open, for example, or the name of a file to print. To handle this personal chatter, Windows 98 sends out a dialog box.

A *dialog box* is merely another little window. But instead of containing a program, it contains a little form or checklist for you to fill out. These forms can have bunches of different parts, which are discussed in the following sections. Don't bother trying to remember the names of the parts, however. It's more important to figure out how they work.

Text boxes

A *text box* works just like a fill-in-the-blanks test in history class. You can type anything you want into a text box — even numbers. For example, Figure 5-7 shows a dialog box that pops up when you want to search for some words or characters in WordPad.

Figure 5-7:
This dialog box from WordPad contains a text box.

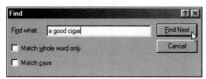

When you type words or characters into this box and press the Enter key, WordPad searches for them. If it finds them, WordPad shows them to you on the page. If it doesn't find them, WordPad sends out a robotic dialog box saying it's finished searching.

✔ Two clues let you know whether a text box is *active* — that is, ready for you to start typing stuff into it: The box's current information is highlighted, or a cursor is blinking inside it. In either case, just start typing the new stuff. (The older, highlighted information disappears as the new stuff replaces it.)

✔ If the text box *isn't* highlighted or there *isn't* a blinking cursor inside it, it's not ready for you to start typing. To announce your presence, click inside it. Then start typing. Or press Tab until the box becomes highlighted or contains a cursor.

✔ If you click inside a text box that already contains words, you must delete the information with the Delete or Backspace key before you can start typing in new information. (Or you can double-click the old information; that way, the incoming text automatically replaces the old text.)

Regular list boxes

Some boxes don't let you type stuff into them. They already contain information. Boxes containing lists of information are called, appropriately enough, *list boxes*. For example, WordPad brings up a list box if you're inspired enough to want to change its font — the way the letters look (see Figure 5-8).

Figure 5-8:
You can select a font from the list box to change the way letters look in WordPad.

✔ See how the Times New Roman font is highlighted? It's the currently selected font. Press Enter (or click the OK command button) and WordPad uses that font in your current paragraph.

✔ See the scroll bars along the side of the list box? They work just as they do anywhere else: Click the little scroll arrows (or press the up or down arrow) to move the list up or down, and you can see any names that don't fit in the box.

✔ Many list boxes have a text box above them. When you click a name in the list box, that name hops into the text box. Sure, you could type the name into the text box yourself, but it wouldn't be nearly as much fun.

✔ When confronted with a bunch of names in a list box, type the first letter of the name you're after. Windows 98 immediately scrolls down the list to the first name beginning with that letter.

TIP

When one just isn't enough

Because Windows 98 can display only one pattern on your desktop at a time, you can select only one pattern from the desktop's list box. Other list boxes, like those in Windows Explorer, let you select a bunch of names simultaneously. Here's how:

✔ To select more than one item, hold down the Ctrl key and click each item you want. Each item stays highlighted.

✔ To select a bunch of adjacent items from a list box, click the first item you want. Then hold down Shift and click the last item you

want. Windows 98 immediately highlights the first item, last item, and every item in between. Pretty sneaky, huh?

✔ Finally, when grabbing bunches of icons, try using the "rubber band" trick: Point at an area of the screen next to one icon, and, while holding down the mouse button, move the mouse until you've drawn a lasso around all the icons. After you've highlighted the icons you want, let go of the mouse button, and they remain highlighted. Fun!

Drop-down list boxes

List boxes are convenient, but they take up a great deal of room. So Windows 98 sometimes hides list boxes, just as it hides pull-down menus. Then, if you click in the right place, the list box appears, ready for your perusal.

So, where's the right place? It's that downward-pointing arrow button, just like the one shown next to the box beside the Font option in Figure 5-9.

Figure 5-10 shows the drop-down list box.

Figure 5-9:
Click the downward-pointing arrow next to the Font box to see a drop-down list box.

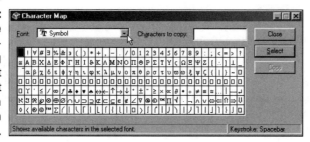

Figure 5-10:
A list box
drops down
to display all
the fonts
that are
available.

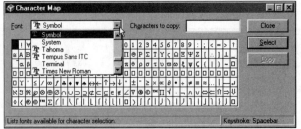

To make a drop-down list box drop down without using a mouse, press the Tab key until you've highlighted the box next to the little arrow. Hold down the Alt key and press the down-arrow key, and the drop-down list starts to dangle.

✔ Unlike regular list boxes, drop-down list boxes don't have a text box above them. That thing that *looks* like a text box just shows the currently selected item from the list; you can't type anything in there.

✔ To scoot around quickly in a drop-down list box, press the first letter of the item you're after. The first item beginning with that letter is instantly highlighted. You can press the up- or down-arrow key to see the words and phrases nearby.

✔ Another way to scoot around quickly in a drop-down list box is to click the scroll bar to its right. (Scroll bars are discussed earlier in this chapter, if you need a refresher.)

✔ You can choose only *one* item from the list of a drop-down list box.

✔ The program in Figure 5-10 is called Character Map, and Windows 98 usually doesn't install that handy little accessory. To slap the hand of Windows 98 and make it install the Character Map, use the Control Panel's Add/Remove Program feature, as described in Chapter 10.

Check boxes

Sometimes you can choose from a whopping number of options in a dialog box. A check box is next to each option, and if you want that option, you click in the box. If you don't want it, you leave the box blank. (Keyboard users can press the up- or down-arrow key until a check box is highlighted and then press the space bar.) For example, with the check boxes in the dialog box shown in Figure 5-11, you pick and choose how the Windows 98 taskbar behaves.

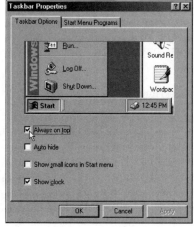

Figure 5-11:
A check
mark
appears in
each check
box you've
chosen.

✔ By clicking in a check box, you change its setting. Clicking in an empty square turns on that option. If the square already has a check mark in it, a click turns off that option, removing the check mark.

✔ You can click next to as many check boxes as you want. With option buttons, those things that look the same but are round, you can select only one option.

Sliding controls

Rich Microsoft programmers, impressed by track lights and sliding light switches in luxurious model homes, added sliding controls to Windows 98 as well. These "virtual" light switches are easy to use and don't wear out nearly as quickly as the real ones do. To slide a control in Windows 98 — to adjust the volume level, for example — just drag and drop the sliding lever, like the one shown in Figure 5-12.

Figure 5-12:
To slide a
lever, point
at it, hold
down the
mouse
button, and
move your
mouse.

Point at the lever with the mouse and, while holding down the mouse button, move the mouse in the direction you want the sliding lever to move. As you move the mouse, the lever moves, too. When you've moved the lever to a comfortable spot, let go of the mouse button, and Windows 98 leaves the lever at its new position. That's it.

✔ Some levers slide to the left and right, others move up and down. None of them move diagonally.

✔ To change the volume in Windows 98, click the little speaker near the clock in the bottom-right corner. A sliding volume control appears, ready to be dragged up or down.

✔ No mouse? Then go buy one. In the meantime, press Tab until a little box appears over the sliding lever; then press your arrow keys in the direction you want the lever to slide.

Changing Your Folder-Viewing Options

Some people store their folders in a fireproof MacMahon Bros. file cabinet and spread them across a finely polished mahogany desk for viewing; others pick them up off the floor and hope the papers don't fall out.

Windows 98 lets you choose three ways of viewing your folders: A "Web page" style, the "classic style," and a customized style combining features of both.

To fiddle with folder viewing, click the Start button and choose Folder Options from the Settings menu. The following three options appear:

Web style

Choose this if you're a died-in-the-wool Internet user, and want to control Windows 98 as if it were a Web page. Your desktop folders and icons will start with a single click, and you can stick Internet items in your Windows wallpaper.

Classic style

The Classic style makes Windows 98 perform like Windows 95: Double-click your desktop folders and icons to open them, for example.

Custom, based on settings you choose

Click the Settings button and a box appears to help fine-tune your folder-viewing needs. The following options appear:

Active Desktop

This offers two options: You can use the Classic, "double-click to see inside a folder" option used by Windows 95. Or you can switch to the new Windows 98 Active Desktop that lets you put Internet buttons, boxes, and sites on your wallpaper. (The complicated Active Desktop gets its coverage in Chapter 21.)

Browse folders as follows

Unless folders sit directly on your desktop, they usually live inside another folder, waiting to be opened. That leaves a big question: When you open a folder, do you want it to leap onto your screen into its own window? Or do you want that new folder's contents to simply replace the existing folder on your screen? Each method has its advantages, as described below:

Open each folder in the same window

Click here, and your newly opened folders replace the old folder. It keeps everything neat and tidy, especially when looking for a folder that's buried deep in other folders: There's always only one open folder on the screen.

Open each folder in its own window

A click over here makes each newly opened folder leap onto the screen in its own window, leaving the old one in its place. This makes it easy to see which folder this new one heralded from, but it leaves a cluttered desktop.

If you open a folder, discover it's the wrong one, and want to go back to the previous folder, here's a quick way to return: Press the Backspace key. Yes, it sounds scary at first, but it doesn't delete anything — it just puts the folder back where it was.

View Web content in folders

These options change how much of the Web's decorating seeps into your folders.

For all folders with HTML content

Click here, and Windows 98 displays a folder as a Web page. You can change font styles, automatically "peek" inside files, use a Web page for that folder's wallpaper, line the folder's menus with Web commands, and perform more Internet-related activities.

Only for folders where I select "as Web page" (View menu)

Holy customization, Batman! Instead of making all your folders behave like Web pages, this option lets you assign that option to specific folders.

Click items as follows

Here's the same single-click versus double-click question that boils down to this: Do you want to start programs and open folders by simply clicking them or clicking them twice in rapid succession (the ol' double-click)?

Single-click to open an item (point to select)

If you choose the single-click option below, you'll find yet two more options: The first one underlines your icon's titles, just like on a Web page. The other option only underlines your icon's titles when you point at them.

Double-click to open an item (single-click to select)

Choose this one, and you double-click an icon to make it leap to life, just like older versions of Windows.

Don't worry if some of these Windows 98 options seem rather confusing or pointless. They are.

- ✔ This stuff is for people who *really* like to fiddle with their computers; chances are, you can avoid it unless your computer forces you to make one of these Internet decisions.

- ✔ If you're comfortable with Windows 95, choose the Classic style. If you're comfortable with the Internet, try the Web-page style. But only choose the Custom settings — and the Active Desktop — if you like to fiddle around with your computer and try new things.

Just Tell Me How to Open a File!

Enough with the labels and terms. Forget the buttons and bars. How do you load a file into a program? This section gives you the scoop. You follow these steps every time you load a file into a program.

Opening a file is a *file-related* activity, so start by finding the word File in the window's menu bar (see Figure 5-13).

Then simply do the following:

1. **Click File (or press Alt and then F) to knock down that word's hidden little menu.**

   Figure 5-14 shows the File pull-down menu.

Figure 5-13:
To open a
file, you
first choose
the word
File in the
window's
menu bar.

Figure 5-14:
When you
choose File,
the File
pull-down
menu
appears.

2. **Click Open (or press O) to bring up the Open dialog box.**

   You can predict that Open will call up a dialog box because of the trailing . . . things beside Open on-screen. (Those . . . things are called an *ellipsis,* or *three dots,* depending on the tightness of your English teacher's hair bun.)

Figure 5-15 shows the Open dialog box that leaps to the front of the screen. In fact, a similar dialog box appears almost any time you mess with the File pull-down menu in any program.

   ✔ If you find your filename listed in the first list box (in this case, the one listing the SHARP.TXT file) you're in luck. Double-click the file's name, and it automatically jumps into the program. Or hold down Alt and press N, type the file's name, and press Enter. Or click the file's name once and press Enter. Or curse Windows 98 for giving you so many options for such a simple procedure.

Figure 5-15:
This Open
dialog box
appears
whenever
you open a
file in any
Windows
program.

✔ If you don't find the file's name, it's probably in a different folder, also known as a *directory*. Click the little box along the top that is labeled Look in, and Windows 98 displays a bunch of other folders to rummage through. Each time you click a different folder, that folder's contents appear in the first list box.

✔ Can't find the right folder or directory? Perhaps that file is on a different drive. Click one of the other drive icons listed in the Look in box to search in a different drive. Drive icons are those little gray box things; folder icons, well, look like folders.

✔ Could the file be named something strange? Click the Files of type drop-down list box (or hold down Alt and press T) to select a different file type. To see *all* the files in a directory, select the All Files (*.*) option. Then all the files in that directory show up.

✔ Don't know what those little icons along the top are supposed to do? Rest your mouse pointer over the one that has you stumped. After a second or so, the increasingly polite Windows 98 brings a box of explanatory information to the screen. For example, rest the mouse pointer over the folder with the explosion in its corner, and Windows 98 tells you that clicking that icon creates a new folder.

✔ Still using a few Windows 3.1 programs? You may still run across the older, Windows 3.1-style boxes for opening files. This wouldn't be a problem, except those oldsters can't handle filenames longer than eight characters — and they simply snip off any name that goes over the edge. Either be careful of Windows 3.1 programs, or avoid them. (Windows 95 programs don't have that problem.)

✔ This stuff is incredibly mind-numbing, of course, if you've never been exposed to directories, drives, folders, wild cards, or other equally painful computer terms. For a more rigorous explanation of this scary file-management stuff, troop to Chapter 11.

✔ Is your Open files box too small to display all your files? Windows 98 lets you change the box's size in many of its programs. Drag and drop its lower-right corner, and the box will expand or contract to match your mouse movements. Windows 95 can't do that!

Hey! When Do I Click, and When Do I Double-Click?

That's certainly a legitimate question, but Microsoft only coughs up a vague answer. Microsoft says that you should *click* when you're *selecting* something in Windows 98 and you should *double-click* when you're *choosing* something. And even that's not for certain. Huh?

Well, you're *selecting* something when you're *highlighting* it. For example, you may select a check box, an option button, or a filename. You click any of the three to *select* it, and then you look at it to make sure that it looks okay. If you're satisfied with your selection, you click the OK button to complete the job.

To *select* something is to set it up for later use.

When you *choose* something, however, the response is more immediate. Choosing a file immediately loads it into your program. Microsoft's "choose" lingo says, "I'm choosing this file, and I want it now, buster."

You *choose* something you want to have carried out immediately.

✔ All right, this explanation is still vague. So always start off by trying a single-click. If clicking once doesn't do the job, try a double-click. It's usually much safer than double-clicking first and asking questions later.

✔ And even this isn't always true. See, Windows 98 can be set up so it chooses files when you perform a single-click *or* a double-click. The software enables you to select a file or program by simply resting your pointer over it, and then clicking to prod it into action. That's the way the Internet's World Wide Web works, so Windows 98 lets you set it up that way, too.

✔ If you accidentally double-click rather than single-click, it usually doesn't matter. You can usually just close a runaway program with a few clicks. But if something terrible happens, hold down the Ctrl key and press the letter Z. You can usually undo any damage.

✔ Like the single-click method? Then choose Folder Options from the Start button's Settings area and choose Web style. Prefer the traditional double-click way? Then go to the Start button's same place and choose Classic style. Want to wade in options? Then choose the third selection, Custom, based on settings you choose.

✔ If Windows 98 keeps mistaking your purposeful double-click as two disjointed single-clicks, head for the section in Chapter 9 on tinkering with the Control Panel. Adjusting Windows 98 so that it recognizes a double-click when you make one is pretty easy.

When Do I Use the Left Mouse Button, and When Do I Use the Right One?

When somebody tells you to "click" something in Windows 98, it almost always means that you should "click with your left mouse button." That's because most Windows 98 users are right-handed, and their index finger hovers over the mouse's left button, making it an easy target.

Windows 98, however, also lets you click your *right* mouse button, and it regards the two actions as completely different.

Pointing at something and clicking the right button often brings up a secret hidden menu with some extra options. Right-click a blank portion of your desktop, for example, and a menu pops up, allowing you to organize your desktop's icons or change the way your display looks. Right-clicking an icon often brings up a hidden menu, as well.

Or hold down your right mouse button while dragging a folder across the desktop. Windows 98 brings up a menu, asking whether you're sure that you want to move the folder over there. If you drag the folder while holding down your left mouse button, Windows 98 doesn't ask; it simply moves the folder there.

✔ The right mouse button is designed more for advanced users, who like to feel that they're doing something sneaky, so clicking the right mouse button often brings up a hidden menu of extra options.

✔ Confused about something on the screen? Try clicking it with your right mouse button, just for kicks. The result may be unexpectedly helpful.

Chapter 6

Moving Windows Around

· ·

· ·

A h, the power of Windows 98. Using separate windows, you can put a spreadsheet, a drawing program, an Internet Web page, and a word processor on-screen *at the same time.*

You can copy a hot-looking graphic from your drawing program and toss it into your memo. Stick a chunk of your spreadsheet into your memo, too. In the background, the Web can display a constantly running news update. And why not? All four windows can be on-screen *at the same time.*

You have only one problem: With so many windows on-screen at the same time, you can't see anything but a confusing jumble of programs.

This chapter shows how to move those darn windows around on-screen so that you can see at least *one* of them.

Moving a Window to the Top of the Pile

Take a good look at the mixture of windows on-screen. Sometimes you can recognize a tiny portion of the window you're after. If so, you're in luck. Move the mouse pointer until it hovers over that tiny portion of the window and click the mouse button. Shazam! Windows 98 immediately brings the clicked-on window to the front of the screen.

That newly enlarged window probably covers up strategic parts of other windows. But at least you'll be able to get some work done, one window at a time.

> 🖊 Windows 98 places a lot of windows on-screen simultaneously. But unless you have two heads, you'll probably use just one window at a time, leaving the remaining programs to wait patiently in the background. The window that's on top, ready to be used, is called the *active* window.
>
> 🖊 The active window is the one with the most lively title bar along its top. The active window's title bar is a brighter color than all the others.
>
> 🖊 The last window you've clicked is the active window. All your subsequent keystrokes and mouse movements will affect that window.
>
> 🖊 Some programs can run in the background, even if they're not in the currently active window. Some communications programs can keep talking to other computers in the background, for example, and some spreadsheets can merrily crunch numbers, unconcerned with whether they're the currently active window. Imagine!

Although many windows may be on-screen, you can enter information into only one of them: the active window. To make a window active, click any part of it. It rises to the top, ready to do your bidding. (The Internet and a computer's TV Card can stick information into background windows, but that's not *you* doing it.)

Another way to move to a window is by clicking on its name in the Windows 98 taskbar. See "The Way-Cool Taskbar" section later in this chapter.

Moving a Window from Here to There

Sometimes you want to move a window to a different place on-screen (known in Windows 98 parlance as the *desktop*). Maybe part of the window hangs off the edge of the desktop, and you want it centered. Or maybe you want to put two windows on-screen side by side so that you can compare their contents.

In either case, you can move a window by grabbing its *title bar,* that thick bar along its top. Put the mouse pointer over the window's title bar and hold down the mouse button. Now use the title bar as the window's handle. When you move the mouse around, you tug the window along with it.

When you've moved the window to where you want it to stay, release the mouse button to release the window. The window stays put and on top of the pile.

✔ The process of holding down the mouse button while moving the mouse is called *dragging*. When you let go of the mouse button, you're *dropping* what you've dragged.

✔ When placing two windows next to each other on-screen, you usually need to change their sizes as well as their locations. The very next section tells how to change a window's size, but don't forget to read "The Way-Cool Taskbar" later in this chapter. It's full of tips and tricks for resizing windows as well as moving them around.

✔ Stuck with a keyboard and no mouse? Press Alt, the spacebar, and M. Then use the arrow keys to move the window around. Press Enter when it's in the right place.

Making a Window Bigger or Smaller

Sometimes, moving the windows around isn't enough. They still cover each other up. Luckily, you don't need any special hardware to make them bigger or smaller. See that thin little border running around the edge of the window? Use the mouse to yank on a window's corner border, and you can change its size.

First, point at the corner with the mouse arrow. When it's positioned over the corner, the arrow turns into a two-headed arrow. Now hold down the mouse button and drag the corner in or out to make the window smaller or bigger. The window's border expands or contracts as you tug on it with the mouse, so you can see what you're doing.

When you're done yanking and the window's border looks about the right size, let go of the mouse button. The window immediately redraws itself, taking the new position.

Here's the procedure, step by step:

1. **Point the mouse pointer at the edge of the corner.**

   It turns into a two-headed arrow, as shown in Figure 6-1.

2. **Hold down the mouse button and move the two-headed arrow in or out to make the window bigger or smaller.**

   Figure 6-2 shows how the new outline takes shape when you pull the corner inward to make the window smaller.

3. **Release the mouse button.**

   The window shapes itself to fit into the border you've just created (see Figure 6-3).

Figure 6-1:
When the mouse points at the window's bottom corner, the arrow grows a second head, as seen in the bottom-right corner.

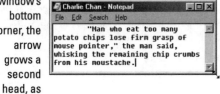

Figure 6-2:
As you move the mouse, the window's border changes to reflect its new shape.

Figure 6-3:
Let go of the mouse button, and the window fills its newly adjusted border.

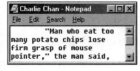

That's it!

- ✔ This procedure may seem vaguely familiar because it is. You're just *dragging and dropping* the window's corner to a new size. That *drag-and-drop* concept works throughout Windows 98. For example, you can *drag and drop* a title bar to move an entire window to a new location on-screen.

- ✔ You can grab the side border of a window and move it in or out to make it fatter or skinnier. You can grab the top or bottom of a window and move it up or down to make it taller or shorter. But grabbing for a corner is always easiest because then you can make a window fatter, skinnier, taller, or shorter, all with one quick flick of the wrist.

If a window is hanging off the edge of the screen, and you can't seem to position it so that all of it fits on screen, try shrinking it first. Grab a visible corner and drag it toward the window's center. Release the mouse button, and the window shrinks itself to fit in its now smaller border. Then grab the window's title bar and hold down the mouse button. When you drag the title bar back toward the center of the screen, you can see the whole window once again.

Making a Window Fill the Whole Screen

Sooner or later, you get tired of all this New Age, multiwindow mumbo jumbo. Why can't you just put *one* huge window on-screen? Well, you can.

To make any window grow as big as it gets, double-click its *title bar,* that topmost bar along the top of the window. The window leaps up to fill the screen, covering up all the other windows.

To bring the pumped-up window back to normal size, double-click its title bar once again. The window shrinks to its former size, and you can see everything that it was covering up.

- ✔ When a window fills the entire screen, it loses its borders. That means that you can no longer change its size by tugging on its title bar or dragging its borders. Those borders just aren't there anymore.

- ✔ If you're morally opposed to double-clicking a window's title bar to expand it, you can expand it another way. Click the window's *maximize button,* the middle-most of the three little boxes in its top-right corner. The window hastily fills the entire screen. At the same time, the maximize button turns into a *restore* button; click the restore button when you want the window to return to its previous size.

- ✔ Refer to Chapter 5 for more information on the maximize, minimize, and restore buttons.

✔ If you don't have a mouse, you can make the window bigger by holding down Alt, pressing the spacebar, and pressing X. But for goodness sake, buy a mouse so that you don't have to try to remember these complicated commands!

✔ DOS programs running in on-screen windows don't usually fill the screen. When you double-click their title bars, they get bigger, but Windows 98 still keeps 'em relatively small. If you take them out of the window, however, they fill the screen completely and shove Windows 98 completely into the background. To take a DOS program out of a window, click the DOS window to make it active and then hold down Alt and press Enter. The DOS program suddenly lunges for the entire screen, and Windows 98 disappears. To bring it back, hold Alt and press Enter again.

Shrinking Windows to the Taskbar

Windows spawn windows. You start with one window to write a letter to Mother. You open another window to check her address, for example, and then yet another to see whether you've forgotten any recent birthdays. Before you know it, four more windows are crowded across the desktop.

To combat the clutter, Windows 98 provides a simple means of window control: You can transform a window from a screen-cluttering square into a tiny button at the bottom of the screen.

See the three buttons lurking in just about every window's top-right corner? Click the *minimize button* — the button with the little line in it. Whoosh! The window disappears, represented by its little button on the bar running along the bottom of your screen. Click that button, and your window hops back onto the screen, ready for action.

The difference can be dramatic. Figure 6-4 shows a desktop with a bunch of open windows.

Figure 6-5 shows that same desktop after all windows but one have been turned into buttons along the taskbar. Those other windows are still readily available, mind you. Just click a window's button from the taskbar along the bottom of the screen, and that window instantly leaps back to its former place on-screen.

Figure 6-4:
A desktop can be distracting with too many windows open simultaneously.

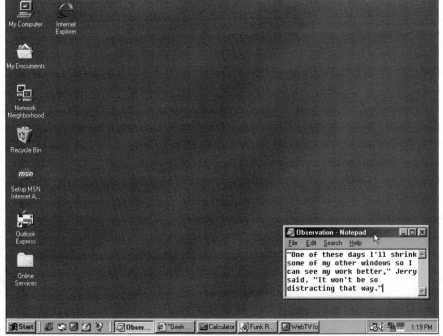

Figure 6-5:
Here's the same desktop that you see in Figure 6-4. Seeing what is going on is easier when the open windows are turned into buttons.

✔ To shrink an open window so that it's out of the way, click the left-most of the three buttons in the window's top-right corner. The window *minimizes* itself into a button and lines itself up on the bar along the bottom of the screen.

✔ The buttons on the taskbar all have a label so that you can tell which program each button represents.

✔ When you minimize a window, you neither destroy its contents nor close it. You merely change its shape. It is still loaded into memory, waiting for you to play with it again.

✔ To put the window back where it was, click its button on the taskbar. It hops back up to the same place it was before.

✔ Whenever you load a program by using the Start button or Explorer, that program's name automatically appears on the taskbar. If one of your open windows ever gets lost on your desktop, click its name on the taskbar. The window immediately jumps to the forefront.

✔ Do you want to shrink all your open windows into buttons, and in a hurry? Click a blank area of your taskbar with your right mouse button and choose Minimize All Windows from the menu that pops up. Slurp. Windows 98 sucks all the open windows off the screen, tidying things up quickly.

✔ Keyboard users can press Alt, the spacebar, and N to minimize a window. Holding down Alt and pressing the Tab key brings up a new window for restoring your minimized programs to their former glory. (That fun little tip gets its own section, titled "The Alt+Tab trick," later in this chapter.)

✔ Using the Windows 98 Active Desktop option to stick Internet windows onto your desktop as wallpaper? Those Internet windows act like wallpaper, so they don't have minimize buttons. They work more like big, permanent stickers. (To turn the Active Desktop on or off, right-click a blank part of your desktop, choose the Active Desktop option from the pop-up menu, and click the View as Web Page option.)

Turning Taskbar Buttons into Windows

To turn a minimized window at the bottom of the screen back into a useful program in the middle of the screen, just click its name on the taskbar. Pretty simple, huh?

✔ If you prefer wading through menus, just click the shrunken window's button with your *right* mouse button. A Control menu shoots out the top of its head. Click the menu's Restore option, and the program leaps back to its former window position.

Keeping your icons straight

Don't be confused by a program's icon on your desktop and a program's button on the taskbar along the bottom of your screen. They're two different things. The button at the bottom of the screen stands for a program that has already been loaded into the computer's memory. It's ready for immediate action. The icon on your desktop or in Windows 98 Explorer stands for a program that is sitting on the computer's hard disk waiting to be loaded.

If you mistakenly click the icon in the Windows Explorer or desktop rather than the button on

the taskbar at the bottom of the screen, you load a second copy of that program. Two versions of the program are loaded: one running as a window and the other running as a taskbar button waiting to be turned back into a window.

Running two versions can cause confusion — especially if you start entering stuff into both versions of the same program. You won't know which window has the *right* version!

✔ In addition to using a click, you can use a few other methods to turn icons back into program windows. The very next section describes one way, and "The Way-Cool Taskbar" section later in this chapter describes another.

Switching from Window to Window

Sometimes switching from window to window is easy. If you can see any part of the window you want — a corner, a bar, or a piece of dust — just click it. That's all it takes to bring that window to the front of the screen, ready for action.

You can also just click that window's button on the taskbar along the bottom of your screen. The following sections give a few extra tricks for switching from window to window to window.

The Alt+Tab trick

This trick is so much fun that Microsoft should have plastered it across the front of the Windows 98 box instead of hiding it in the middle of the manual.

Hold down Alt and press Tab. A most-welcome box pops up in the center of the screen, naming the last program you've touched (see Figure 6-6).

Figure 6-6:
When you
hold down
Alt and
press Tab,
Windows 98
displays the
name of the
last program
you used.

If the program you're after is named, rejoice! And remove your finger from the Alt key. The window named in that box leaps to the screen.

If you're looking for a *different* program, keep your finger on the Alt key and press Tab once again. At each press of Tab, Windows 98 displays the name of another open program. When you see the one you want, release the Alt key, and then hoot and holler. The program leaps to the screen, ready for your working pleasure.

✔ The Alt+Tab trick works even if you're running a DOS program with Windows 98 lurking in the background. The DOS program disappears while the pop-up box has its moment in the sun. (And the DOS program returns when you're done playing around, too.)

✔ The Alt+Tab trick cycles through all the currently open programs, whether the programs are in on-screen windows or living their lives as buttons on the taskbar. When you release the Alt key, the program currently listed in the pop-up window leaps to life.

✔ The first time you press Tab, the little pop-up window lists the name of the program you last accessed. If you prefer to cycle through the program names in the opposite direction, hold down Shift *and* Alt while pressing Tab. If you agree that this is a pretty frivolous option, rub your stomach and pat your head at the same time.

The Alt+Esc trick

The concept is getting kind of stale with this one, but here goes: If you hold down Alt and press Esc, Windows 98 cycles through all the open programs, but in a slightly less efficient way.

Instead of bringing its name to a big box in the middle of the screen, Windows 98 simply highlights the program, whether it's in a window or sitting as a button on the taskbar. Sometimes this method can be handy, but usually it's a little slower.

If Windows 98 is currently cycling through a program on the taskbar, the Alt+Esc trick simply highlights the button at the bottom of the screen. That's not much of a visual indicator, and most of the time it won't even catch your eye.

When you see the window you want, release the Alt key. If it's an open window, it becomes the active window. But if you release the Alt key while a button's name is highlighted, you need to take one more step: You need to click the button or press Enter to get the window on-screen.

The Alt+Esc trick is a little slower and a little less handy than the Alt+Tab trick described in the preceding section.

The Way-Cool Taskbar

This section introduces one of the handiest tricks in Windows 98, so pull your chair in a little closer. Windows 98 comes with a special program that keeps track of all the open programs. Called the *taskbar,* it always knows what programs are running and where they are. Shown in Figure 6-7, the taskbar normally lives along the bottom of your screen, although Chapter 10 shows how to move it to any edge you want. (***Hint:*** Just "drag" it there.)

Figure 6-7:
Always handy, the taskbar lists your currently running programs and lets you bring them to the forefront by clicking their names.

From the taskbar, you can perform powerful magic on your open windows, as shown in the next few sections.

✔ See how the button for Calculator looks "pushed in" in Figure 6-7? That's because Calculator is the currently active window on the desktop. One of your taskbar's buttons always looks "pushed in" unless you close or minimize all the windows on your desktop.

✔ Don't see the taskbar? Then hold down Ctrl and press Esc. Windows 98 instantly brings the taskbar and Start menu to the surface, ready to do your bidding. If the taskbar merely lurks along the edge, grab the visible part with your mouse and drag it toward the center of the screen until the entire taskbar is visible.

Switching to another window

See a window you want to play with listed on the taskbar? Just click its name, and it rises to the surface. Simple. (Especially if you've ever labored under some older versions of Windows.) If the taskbar isn't showing for some reason, pressing Ctrl+Esc calls it to the forefront.

Ending a task

Mad at a program? Then kill it. Click the program's name on the taskbar with your *right* mouse button and then click the word <u>C</u>lose from the menu that pops up (or press C). The highlighted program quits, just as if you'd chosen its Exit command from within its own window. The departing program gives you a chance to save any work before it quits and disappears from the screen.

Cascading and tiling windows

Sometimes those windows are scattered *everywhere.* How can you clean up in a hurry? By using the Cascade and Tile commands. Click a blank spot on the taskbar with the *right* mouse button — the spot on or near the clock is usually good — and the cascade and tile commands appear.

The two commands organize your open windows in drastically different ways. Figure 6-8 shows what your screen looks like when you choose the Cascade command.

Talk about neat and orderly! The taskbar grabs all the windows and deals them out like cards across the desktop. When you choose the taskbar's Ca<u>s</u>cade Windows command, all the open windows are lined up neatly onscreen with their title bars showing.

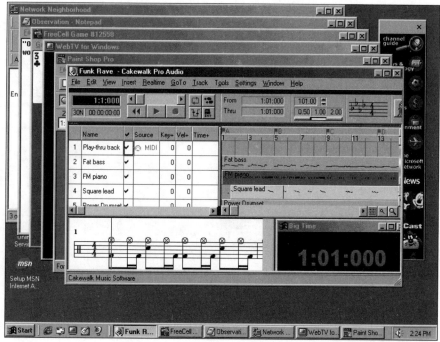

Figure 6-8:
The taskbar's Cascade command piles all the open windows neatly across the screen. It's a favorite command of blackjack players.

The Tile Windows Horizontally and Tile Windows Vertically commands rearrange the windows, too, but in a slightly different way (see Figure 6-9). The tile commands arrange all the currently open windows across the screen, giving each one the same amount of space. This arrangement helps you find a window that has been missing for a few hours.

Note: Both the Tile and Cascade commands arrange only open windows. They don't open up any windows currently shrunken into buttons on the taskbar.

If you have only two open windows, the Tile commands arrange them side by side, making it easy for you to compare their contents. The Tile Windows Vertically command places them side by side *vertically,* which makes them useless for comparing text: You can only see the first few words of each sentence. Choose the Tile Windows Horizontally command if you want to see complete sentences.

Arranging icons on the desktop

The taskbar can be considered a housekeeper of sorts, but it *only* does windows. It arranges the open windows neatly across the screen, but it doesn't touch any icons living on your desktop.

Figure 6-9: The taskbar's Tile commands organize the open windows like tiles on the shower floor. You can see them all, but they're often too small to be of much use.

If the open windows look fine but the desktop's icons look a little shabby, click a blank area of your desktop with your right mouse button. When the menu pops up, click the Arrange Icons command and choose the way you want Windows 98 to line up your icons: by Name, Type, Size, or Date. Or, simply choose the Auto Arrange option from the same menu. Then your desktop's icons always stay in neat, orderly rows.

The taskbar is an easily accessible helper. Take advantage of it often when you're having difficulty finding windows or when you want to clean up the desktop so that you can find things.

Finding the taskbar

Is the taskbar missing from the bottom of your screen? Hold down Ctrl and press Esc, and the taskbar instantly appears. If you'd prefer that the taskbar not disappear sometimes, head for Chapter 10. It explains how to customize your taskbar so that it doesn't bail on you.

Chapter 7

I Can't Find It!

S ooner or later, Windows 98 gives you that head-scratching feeling. "Golly," you say, as you frantically tug on your mouse cord, "that window was *right there* a second ago. Where did it go?"

When Windows 98 starts playing hide-and-seek with your programs, files, windows, or other information, this chapter tells you where to search and how to make it stop playing foolish games. Then when you find your Solitaire window, you can get back to work.

Plucking a Lost Window from the Taskbar

Forget about that huge, 1940s rolltop mahogany desk in the resale shop window. The Windows 98 peewee desktop can't be any bigger than the size of your monitor. (Or two monitors, if you add two another monitor and video card, as described in Chapter 19.)

In a way, Windows 98 works more like those spike memo holders than like an actual desktop. Every time you open a new window, you're tossing another piece of information onto the spike. The window on top is relatively easy to see, but what's lying directly underneath it?

If you can see a window's ragged edge protruding from any part of the pile, click it. The window magically rushes to the top of the pile. But what if you can't see *any* part of the window at all? How do you know it's even on the desktop?

You can solve this mystery by calling up your helpful Windows 98 detective: the taskbar. The taskbar keeps a master list of everything that's happening on your screen (even the invisible stuff).

If the taskbar isn't squatting along one edge of your screen, just hold down your Ctrl key and press Esc. The taskbar pops into action (see Figure 7-1).

Figure 7-1:
Press the
Ctrl key and
Esc key to
retrieve
missing
taskbars.

See the list of programs stamped onto buttons on the taskbar? Your missing window is *somewhere* on the list. When you spot it, click its name, and the taskbar instantly tosses your newfound window to the top of the pile.

- Most of the time, the taskbar performs admirably in tracking down lost windows. If your window isn't on the list, you've probably closed it. Closing a window, also known as *exiting* a window, takes it off your desktop and out of your computer's memory. To get that window back, you need to open it again, using the services of the Start button (see Chapter 10), the Windows Explorer (see Chapter 11), or the My Computer program (also in Chapter 11).

- I lied. Sometimes a window can be running and yet *not* be listed on the taskbar. Some utility programmers figure that people don't *need* to see their programs or their icons. Some screen savers, for example, can be running on your screen and yet not show up on the taskbar. It simply runs in the background.

- Sometimes you see your missing program listed on the taskbar, and you click its name to dredge it from the depths. But even though the taskbar brings the missing program to the top, you *still* can't find it on your desktop. The program may be hanging off the edge of your desktop, so check out the very next section.

Finding a Window That's Off the Edge of the Screen

Even a window at the top of the pile can be nearly invisible. A window can be moved anywhere on the Windows 98 desktop, including off the screen. In fact, you can inadvertently move 99 percent of a window off the screen, leaving just a tiny corner showing (see Figure 7-2). Clicking on the window's name in the taskbar won't be much help in this case, unfortunately. The window's already on top, but it's still too far off the screen to be of any use.

- ✔ If you can see any part of the rogue window's *title bar,* that thick strip along its top, hold the mouse button down and *drag* the traveler back to the center of the screen.

- ✔ Sometimes a window's title bar can be completely off the screen. How can you drag it back into view? Start by clicking on any part of the window that shows. Then hold down your Alt key and press the spacebar. A menu appears from nowhere. Select the word Move, and a mysterious four-headed arrow appears. Press your arrow keys until the window's border moves to a more manageable location and then press Enter. Whew! Don't let it stray that far again!

Figure 7-2: FreeCell is almost completely off the bottom-right corner of the screen, making it difficult to locate.

✔ For an easier way to make Windows 98 not only track down all your criminally hidden windows, but also line them up on the screen in *mug shot* fashion, check out the next two sections.

Cascading Windows (The "Deal All the Windows in Front of Me" Approach)

Are you ready to turn Windows 98 into a personal card dealer who gathers up all your haphazardly tossed windows and deals them out neatly on the desktop in front of you?

Then turn the taskbar into a card dealer. Click a blank area of your taskbar — near the clock is good — with your *right* mouse button, and a menu pops up. Click the Cascade Windows option, and the taskbar gathers all your open windows and deals them out in front of you, just like in a game of blackjack.

Each window's title bar is neatly exposed, ready to be grabbed and reprimanded with a quick click of the mouse.

✔ If the missing window doesn't appear in the stack of neatly dealt windows, perhaps it has been minimized. The Cascade Windows command gathers and deals only the open windows; it leaves the minimized windows resting as buttons along the taskbar. The solution? Click the missing window's button on the taskbar *before* cascading the windows across the screen.

✔ For more about the Cascade Windows command, check out Chapter 6.

Tiling Windows (The "Stick Everything On the Screen at Once" Approach)

Windows 98 can stick all your open windows onto the screen at the same time. You'll finally be able to see all of them — no overlapping corners, edges, or menu flaps. Sound too good to be true? It is. Windows 98 *shrinks* all the windows so that they fit on the screen. And some of the weird-shaped windows still overlap. But, hey, at least you can see most of them.

Click a blank area of the taskbar with your right mouse button and choose Tile Windows Vertically or Tile Windows Horizontally from the pop-up menu.

✔ The Tile command pulls all the open windows onto the screen at the same time. If you have two open windows, each of them takes up half the screen. With three windows, each window gets a third of the screen. If you have 12 windows, each window takes up one-twelfth of the available space. (They're *very* small.)

✔ The Tile Windows Vertically command arranges the windows vertically, like socks hanging from a clothesline. Tile Windows Horizontally arranges the windows horizontally, like a stack of folded sweatshirts. The difference is the most pronounced when you're tiling only a few windows, however.

✔ You can find more information about the Tile command in Chapter 6. The minimize button is covered in Chapter 5.

Finding Lost Files, Folders, or Computers (But Not Misplaced Laptops)

Windows 98 has gotten much better at finding lost files and folders. And it should; after all, it's the one who's hiding the darn things. When one of your files, folders, or programs (or computers, if you're on a network) disappears into the depths of your computer, make Windows 98 do the work in getting the darn thing back.

Click the Start button, choose the Find option, and choose the menu option that describes what you lost. Did you lose a file or folder? Are you trying to find something on the Internet? A coworker's computer on the office network? A friend's phone number from your Address Book?

Choose the option that describes what you've lost, as shown in Figure 7-3.

An incredibly detailed program pops up, letting you search for items meeting the most minute criteria. Best yet, it can simply search for missing things by their names. For example, suppose that your file called HYDRATOR INSPECTION disappeared over the weekend. To make matters worse, you're not even sure you spelled *Hydrator* correctly when saving the file.

What's the solution? Type in any part of the filename you can remember. In this case, type **drat** into the Named box, and click the Find Now button. The Find program lists any file or folder with a name that contains *drat,* as shown in Figure 7-4 — quick and simple.

Figure 7-3:
Windows 98
can search
your com-
puter, a
network,
and the
Internet for
lost files,
folders,
names,
phone
numbers,
and other
information.

Figure 7-4:
Here, the
Windows 98
Find
program
sniffed out a
file with
drat as part
of its name.

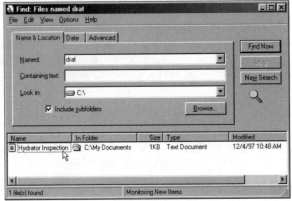

✔ Of course, you don't *have* to keep things quick and simple. For example, the Find program normally searches drive C — your computer's hard drive. If you'd prefer that it search every nook and cranny — all your hard drives and even any floppy disks or CD-ROM drives — click the little downward-pointing arrow near the Look in box. When a menu drops down, click the My Computer setting. That tells the Find program to look *everywhere* on your computer except the Recycle Bin. (Peek inside there yourself.)

✔ Make sure that a check mark appears in the Include subfolders box, as shown in Figure 7-4. If that option's not checked, the Find program searches through only your first layer of folders — it doesn't look inside any folders living inside other folders.

✔ Can't remember what you called a file, but know the time and date you created it? Click the Date tab along the program's top. That step lets you narrow down the search to files created only during certain times. (It's especially handy for finding files you know you created yesterday.)

✔ For a quick peek inside some of the files the Find program turned up, click the file's name with your right mouse button and choose Quick View from the menu that pops up. Windows 98 shows you the file's contents *without* making you load the program that created the file.

✔ The Advanced option lets people search for specific types of files: Bitmap files, Faxes, Configuration settings, and other more complicated options. To be on the safe side, leave the option set for All Files and Folders, so you know that the Find command is searching through *everything*.

✔ Searching for a computer on a network works almost the same way. Click the Start button and choose Computer from the Find menu. Type in part of the computer's name, **yachtclub,** for example, to locate any computer on the network named YachtClub. After the program lists the computer, double-click its icon to begin browsing its files.

✔ If you search for something on the Internet, the Find program brings up Internet Explorer to do your bidding. Likewise, if you click People, Windows 98 brings up your computer's Address Book. (And, if you've been entering information about your friends into the Address Book — part of Outlook Express — you'll be able to find pertinent information about that particular person.)

Finding Snippets of Stored Information

Help! You remember how much Mr. Jennings *loved* that wine during lunch, so you stealthily typed the wine's name into your computer. Now, at Christmas time, you don't remember the name of the file where you saved the wine's name. You don't remember the date you created the file, either, or even the folder where you stashed the file. In fact, the only thing you remember is how you described the wine's biting bouquet when typing it into your computer: "Like an alligator snap from behind a barge."

Luckily, that description is all Windows 98 needs in order to find your file. Click the Start button and choose Files or Folders from the Find menu, shown in Figure 7-3. After the Find program pops up, click in the box marked Containing text, and type **barge,** as shown in Figure 7-5.

Figure 7-5:
The
Windows 98
Find
program
searches
the entire
computer
for a file
containing
the word
barge.

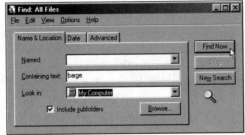

Figure 7-5:
The
Windows 98
Find
program
searches
the entire
computer
for a file
containing
the word
barge.

Just like in the preceding section, the Find program searches the computer, looking for files meeting your specifications. This time, however, it searches inside the files themselves, looking for the information you're after.

- ✔ Feel free to limit your search, using any of the tips and examples discussed in the preceding section; they apply here as well.

- ✔ CD-ROM discs take a *long* time to search. You can speed things up by telling the Find program to limit its search to hard disks. (Just popping the CD out of the drive is one way to keep the Find program from searching it.)

- ✔ When searching for files containing certain words, type in the words *least* likely to turn up in other files. For example, the word *barge* is more unique than *like, an, snap,* or *behind;* therefore, it's more likely to bring up the file you're searching for. And if *barge* doesn't work, try *alligator.*

Peeking into Files Quickly with Quick View

When you open a *real* manila folder, it's easy to separate the food coupons from the letters to a Congressperson; the pieces of paper look completely different. But although Windows 98 sticks titles beneath all the icons in its folders, the icons often look like one big blur, as shown in Figure 7-6. Which icon stands for which file? And where is that letter to the Congressperson, anyway?

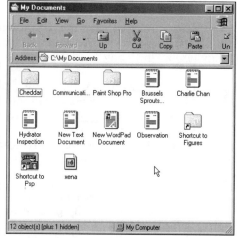

Figure 7-6:
Even with their labels, the icons in Windows 98 are some-times hard to tell apart from each other.

You can double-click an icon to see what file it stands for — a double-click tells Windows 98 to load the file into the program that created it and bring them both to the screen. Or, if you double-click a program, Windows 98 simply loads the program.

But there's a faster way to get a sneak peek of what's inside many Windows 98 icons. Here's how the Quick View feature works:

1. **While pointing at a confusing icon, click your right mouse button.**

   A menu pops up, as shown in Figure 7-7. If Windows 98 recognizes the type of file, you see the Quick View option on the menu.

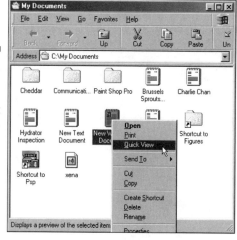

Figure 7-7:
Click an icon with your right mouse button to see if Windows 98 offers the Quick View option.

2. Choose Quick View from the menu.

The Quick View option shows you what's inside the file without taking the time to load the program that created it. The option is a quick way to sort through files with similar-looking icons.

✔ Windows 98 lets you use up to 255 characters when naming files. If you upgrade Windows 98 over Windows 3.1, however, all your old files still have their eight-character filenames. By using Quick View, you can peek into your old files and give them better names. First, peek into the file to see what's inside. When you've decided on a longer, more descriptive name, choose the Rename command. (It's on the same menu as the Quick View command.)

✔ The Quick View command works with a few dozen more popular formats, including Lotus 1-2-3, Bitmap, WordPad, Microsoft Word for Windows, and WordPerfect. (Can't find the Quick View option? Add it by double-clicking the Control Panel's Add/Remove Programs option.)

✔ After you've found the file you're seeking, you can open it easily from within Quick View: Click the little icon in the upper-left corner — the icon beneath the word File. Quick View immediately opens the file for editing.

Chapter 8

That "Cut and Paste" Stuff (Moving Around Words, Pictures, and Sounds)

· ·

In This Chapter

▶ Understanding cutting, copying, and pasting

▶ Highlighting what you need

▶ Cutting, copying, deleting, and pasting what you've highlighted

▶ Making the best use of the Clipboard

▶ Putting scraps on the desktop

▶ Object Linking and Embedding

· ·

*U*ntil Windows came along, IBM-compatible computers had a terrible time sharing anything. Their programs were rigid, egotistical things, with no sense of community. Information created by one program couldn't always be shared with another program. Older versions of programs passed down this selfish system to newer versions, enforcing the segregation with *proprietary file formats* and *compatibility tests.*

To counter this bad trip, Windows programmers created a communal workplace where all the programs could groove together peacefully. In the harmonious tribal village of Windows, programs share their information openly in order to make a more beautiful environment for all.

In the Windows co-op, all the windows can beam their vibes to each other freely, without fear of rejection. Work created by one Windows program is accepted totally and lovingly by any other Windows program. Windows programs treat each other equally, even if one program is wearing some pretty freaky threads or, in some gatherings, *no threads at all.*

This chapter shows you how easily you can move those good vibes from one window to another.

Examining the Cut and Paste Concept (And Copy, Too)

Windows 98 took a tip from the kindergartners and made *cut and paste* an integral part of all its programs. Information can be electronically *cut* from one window and *pasted* into another window with little fuss and even less mess.

Just about any part of a window is up for grabs. You can highlight an exceptionally well-written paragraph in your word processor, for example, or a spreadsheet chart that tracks the value of your Indian-head pennies. After *highlighting* the desired information, you press a button to *copy* or *cut* it from its window.

At the press of the button, the information heads for a special place in Windows 98 called the *Clipboard*. From there, you can paste it into any other open window.

The beauty of Windows 98 is that with all those windows on-screen at the same time, you can easily grab bits and pieces from any of them and paste all the parts into a new window.

✓ Windows programs are designed to work together, so taking information from one window and putting it into another window is easy. Sticking a map onto your party fliers, for example, is *really* easy.

✓ Cutting and pasting works well for the big stuff, like sticking big charts into memos. But don't overlook it for the small stuff, too. For example, copying someone's name and address from your Address Book program is quicker than typing it by hand at the top of your letter. Or, to avoid typographical errors, you can copy an answer from the Windows 98 Calculator and paste it into another program.

✓ Cutting and pasting is different from that *Object Linking and Embedding* stuff you may have seen in the manuals. That more powerful (and, naturally, more confusing) *OLE* stuff gets its own section later in this chapter.

✓ When you cut or copy some information, it immediately appears in a special Windows program called the *Clipboard*. From the Clipboard, it can be pasted into other windows. The Clipboard has its own bag of tricks — including the Clipboard Viewer program — so it gets its own section later in this chapter.

✓ Windows 98 doesn't automatically stick the Clipboard Viewer onto every computer during the installation process. If you're among the left out, head for the Control Panel's Add/Remove Programs icon and tell Windows 98 to copy the Clipboard Viewer systems tool to your hard drive, a process described in Chapter 9. (**Hint:** Clipboard Viewer is under the Systems Tools section of the Windows Setup tab.)

Highlighting the Important Stuff

Before you can grab information from a window, you have to tell the window exactly what parts you want to grab. The easiest way to tell it is to *highlight* the information with a mouse.

You can highlight a single letter, an entire novel, or anything in between. You can highlight pictures of water lilies. You can even highlight sounds so that you can paste belches into other files (see the section, "Looking at Funky Object Linking and Embedding Stuff," later in this chapter).

In most cases, highlighting involves one swift trick with the mouse: Put the mouse arrow or cursor at the beginning of the information you want and hold down the mouse button. Then move the mouse to the end of the information and release the button. That's it! All the stuff lying between where you clicked and released is highlighted. The information usually turns a different color so that you can see what you've grabbed. An example of highlighted text is shown in Figure 8-1.

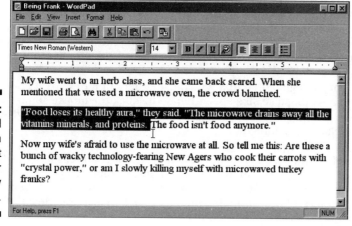

Figure 8-1:
Highlighted text turns a different color for easy visibility.

If you're mouseless, use the arrow keys to put the cursor at the beginning of the stuff you want to grab. Then hold down Shift and press the arrow keys until the cursor is at the end of what you want to grab. You see the stuff on-screen become highlighted as you move the arrow keys. This trick works with almost every Windows 98 program. (If you're after text, hold down Ctrl, too, and the text is highlighted word by word.)

Some programs have a few shortcuts for highlighting parts of their information:

✔ To highlight a single *word* in Notepad, WordPad, or most text boxes, point at it with the mouse and double-click. The word turns black, meaning that it's highlighted. (In WordPad, you can hold down the button on its second click, and then, by moving the mouse around, you can quickly highlight additional text word by word.)

✔ To highlight a single *line* in WordPad, click next to it in the left margin. Keep holding down the mouse button and move the mouse up or down to highlight additional text line by line.

✔ To highlight a *paragraph* in WordPad, double-click next to it in the left margin. Keep holding down the mouse button on the second click and move the mouse to highlight additional text paragraph by paragraph.

✔ To highlight an entire *document* in WordPad, hold down Ctrl and click anywhere in the left margin. (To highlight the entire document in Notepad, press and release Alt and then press E and then A. So much for consistency between Windows 98 programs.)

✔ To highlight a portion of text in just about any Windows 98 program, click at the text's beginning, hold down Shift, and click at the end of the desired text. Everything between those two points becomes highlighted.

✔ To highlight part of a picture or drawing while in Paint, click the little tool button with the dotted lines in a square. (The button is called the Select tool, as Windows 98 informs you if you rest your mouse pointer over the tool for a second.) After clicking the Select tool, hold down the mouse button and slide the mouse over the desired part of the picture.

After you've highlighted text, you must either cut it or copy it *immediately.* If you do anything else, like absentmindedly click the mouse someplace else in your document, all your highlighted text reverts to normal, just like Cinderella after midnight.

Be careful after you highlight a bunch of text. If you press a key — the spacebar, for example — Windows 98 almost always replaces your highlighted text with the character that you type — in this case, a space. To reverse that calamity and bring your highlighted text back to life, hold down Alt and press the Backspace key.

Deleting, Cutting, or Copying What You Highlighted

After you've highlighted some information (which is described in the preceding section, in case you just entered the classroom), you're ready to start playing with it. You can delete it, cut it, or copy it. All three options differ drastically.

Deleting the information

Deleting the information just wipes it out. Zap! It just disappears from the window. To delete highlighted information, just press the Delete or Backspace key.

- ✔ If you've accidentally deleted the wrong thing, panic. Then hold down Ctrl and press the letter Z. Your deletion is graciously undone. Any deleted information pops back up on-screen. Whew!

- ✔ Holding down Alt and pressing Backspace also undoes your last mistake. (Unless you've just said something dumb at a party. In that case, use Ctrl+Z.)

Cutting the information

Cutting the highlighted information wipes it off the screen, just as the Delete command does, but with a big difference: When the information is removed from the window, it is copied to a special Windows 98 storage tank called the *Clipboard.*

When you're looking at the screen, cutting and deleting look identical. In fact, the first few times you try to cut something, you feel panicky, thinking that you may have accidentally deleted it instead. (This feeling never really goes away, either.)

To cut highlighted stuff, hold down Shift and press Delete. Whoosh! The high-lighted text disappears from the window, scoots through the underground tubes of Windows 98, and waits on the Clipboard for further action.

- ✔ One way to tell whether your Cut command actually worked is to paste the information back into your document. If it appears, you know that the command worked, and you can cut it out again right away. If it doesn't appear, you know that something has gone dreadfully wrong. (For the Paste command, discussed a little later, hold down Shift and press Insert.)

- ✔ Microsoft's lawyers kicked butt in the Apple lawsuit, so Windows now uses the same cut keys as the Macintosh. You can hold down Ctrl and press the letter *X* to cut. (Get it? That's an *X*, as in *you're crossing,* or *X-ing, something out.*)

Copying the information

Compared with cutting or deleting, *copying* information is quite anticlimactic. When you cut or delete, the information disappears from the screen. But when you copy information to the Clipboard, the highlighted information just sits there in the window. In fact, it looks as if nothing has happened, so you repeat the Copy command a few times before giving up and just hoping it worked.

To copy highlighted information, hold down Ctrl and press Insert (the 0 on the numeric keypad or Ins on some keyboards). Although nothing seems to happen, that information really does head for the Clipboard.

- ✔ Windows 98 uses the same Copy keys as the Macintosh does. If you don't like the Ctrl+Insert combination, you can hold down Ctrl and press C to copy. This combination is a little easier to remember, actually, because C is the first letter of *copy.*

- ✔ To copy an image of your entire Windows 98 desktop (the *whole screen*) to the Clipboard, press the Print Screen key, which is sometimes labeled PrtScrn or something similar. (Some older keyboards make you hold down Shift simultaneously.) A snapshot of your screen heads for the Clipboard, ready to be pasted someplace else. Computer nerds call this snapshot a *screen shot.* All the pictures of windows in this book are screen shots. (And, no, the information doesn't also head for your printer.)

- ✔ To copy an image of your currently active window (just one window — nothing surrounding it), hold down Alt while you press Print Screen. The window's picture appears on the Clipboard. (You usually don't have to hold down Shift with this one, even for wacky keyboards. But if Alt+Print Screen doesn't work, hey, try holding down Shift anyway.)

Finding out more about cutting, copying, and deleting

Want to know more about cutting, copying, and deleting? Read on (you really should read this stuff).

- ✔ Windows 98 often puts *toolbars* across the tops of its programs. Figure 8-2 shows the toolbar buttons that stand for cutting, copying, and pasting things.

Figure 8-2:
Clicking
these tool-
bar buttons
cuts, copies,
or pastes
highlighted
information.

Cut Paste

Copy

Figure 8-2:
Clicking
these tool-
bar buttons
cuts, copies,
or pastes
highlighted
information.

✔ If you prefer to use menus, the Cut, Copy, and Paste commands tumble down when you select the word Edit on any menu bar.

✔ When you're using the Print Screen key trick to copy a window or the entire screen to the Clipboard (see the preceding section), one important component is left out: The mouse arrow is *not* included in the picture, even if it was in plain sight when you took the picture. (Are you asking yourself how all the little arrows got in this book's pictures? Well, I drew most of 'em in by hand!)

✔ Sometimes figuring out whether the Cut or Copy commands are really working is difficult. To know for sure, keep the Windows Clipboard Viewer showing at the bottom of the screen. Then you can watch the images appear on it when you press the buttons. (The Clipboard Viewer is listed on the Start menu under Accessories, which is listed in the Programs section. Not listed? Head for Chapter 9; you must tell Windows 98 to install the Clipboard Viewer program.)

✔ Don't keep screen shots or large graphics on the Clipboard any longer than necessary. They consume a lot of memory that your other programs could be using. To clear off any memory-hogging detritus, copy a single word to the Clipboard, or call up the Clipboard Viewer and press Delete.

Pasting Information into Another Window

After you've cut or copied information to the special Windows 98 Clipboard storage tank, it's ready for travel. You can *paste* that information into just about any other window.

Pasting is relatively straightforward compared with highlighting, copying, or cutting: Click the mouse anywhere in the destination window and click in the spot where you want the stuff to appear. Then hold down Shift and press Insert (the 0 key on the numeric keypad). Presto! Anything that's sitting on the Clipboard immediately leaps into that window.

✔ Another way to paste stuff is to hold down Ctrl and press V. That combination does the same thing as Shift+Insert. (It also is the command those funny-looking Macintosh computers use to paste stuff.)

✔ You can also choose the Paste command from a window's menu bar. Select the word Edit and then select the word Paste. But don't select the words Paste Special. That command is for the Object Linking and Embedding stuff, which gets its own section later in this chapter.

✔ Some programs have toolbars along their top. Clicking the Paste button, shown in Figure 8-2, pastes the Clipboard's current contents into your document.

✔ The Paste command inserts a *copy* of the information that's sitting on the Clipboard. The information stays on the Clipboard, so you can keep pasting it into other windows if you want. In fact, the Clipboard's contents stay the same until a new Cut or Copy command replaces them with new information.

Using the Clipboard Viewer

Windows 98 employs a special program to let you see all the stuff that's being slung around by cutting and copying. Called the *Clipboard Viewer* (sometimes called the ClipBook Viewer), it's merely a window that displays anything that has been cut or copied to the Clipboard.

To see the Clipboard Viewer, click the Start button and choose Programs from the menu. Choose Accessories from the new menu, followed by System Tools and, finally, Clipboard Viewer. The Clipboard Viewer displays any information you've cut or copied recently. Figures 8-3, 8-4, and 8-5 show some examples.

Figure 8-3: This Clipboard contains a recently copied picture of a chip.

Figure 8-4:
This Clipboard contains text recently copied from a Windows program.

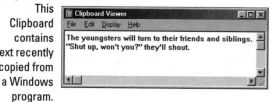

Figure 8-5:
This Clipboard contains a sound copied from the Windows 98 Sound Recorder.

✔ Sometimes the Clipboard Viewer can't show you exactly what you've copied. For example, if you copy a sound from the Windows 98 Sound Recorder, you just see a picture of the Sound Recorder's icon. And, at the risk of getting metaphysical, what does a sound look like anyway?

✔ The Clipboard functions automatically and transparently. Unless you make a special effort, you don't even know it's there. (That's why the Clipboard Viewer is handy — it lets you see what the Clipboard is up to.)

The *Clipboard* is a special area inside memory where Windows 98 keeps track of information that's been cut or copied. The *Clipboard Viewer* is a program that lets you see the information that's currently on the Clipboard.

✔ To better track what's being cut and pasted, some people leave the Clipboard Viewer sitting open at the bottom of the screen. Then they can actually *see* what they've cut or copied.

✔ Most of the time, the Clipboard is used just for temporary operations — a quick cut here, a quick paste there, and then on to the next job. But the Clipboard Viewer lets you save the Clipboard's contents for later use. Choose File from the menu bar and then choose Save As from the pull-down menu. Type in a filename and click the OK command button (or just press Enter).

> ✔ The Clipboard can hold only one thing at a time. Each time you cut or copy something else, you replace the Clipboard's contents with something new. If you want to collect a bunch of *clips* for later pasting, use the Save <u>A</u>s option described in the preceding paragraph. The Clipboard also starts up empty each time you start Windows 98.
>
> ✔ No Clipboard Viewer on your Start menu? Windows 98 doesn't always install it automatically. Head for the Add/Remove Programs section in Chapter 9 for ways to add the Windows accessories that Windows 98 left out.

Looking at Funky Object Linking and Embedding Stuff

Because the concepts of cutting and pasting are so refreshingly simple, Microsoft complicated them considerably with something called *Object Linking and Embedding,* known as *OLE*. It sounds complicated, so I'll start with the simple part: the object.

The *object* is merely the information you want to paste into a window. It can be a sentence, a road map, a sneeze sound, or anything else that you can cut or copy from a window.

TIP

Keeping the Clipboard clear

Whenever you cut or copy something, that information heads for the Clipboard. And it stays there, too, until you cut or copy something else to replace it. But while that information sits there on the Clipboard, it uses up memory.

Windows 98 needs all the memory it can get, or it begins running slowly or balking at opening more windows. Big chunks of text, pictures, and sounds can consume a lot of memory, so clear off the Clipboard when you're through cutting and pasting to return the memory for general Windows use.

To clear off the Clipboard quickly, just copy a single word to the Clipboard: Double-click a word in a text file, hold down Ctrl, and press C.

Or, if the Clipboard Viewer is up on-screen, click it to bring it to the forefront and then press Delete. You clear the Clipboard off, enabling Windows 98 to use the memory for more pressing matters.

Normally, when you paste an object into a window, you're pasting the same kind of information. For example, you paste text into a word processor and pictures into the Windows 98 Paint program. But what if you want to paste a sound into WordPad, the Windows 98 word processor?

That's where Object Linking and Embedding comes in, offering subtle changes to the paste concept. You'll probably never use them, but they can be fun to fiddle around with on cloudy days. Beware, however: OLE awareness is the first step down those ever-spiraling stairs toward computer-nerd certification.

Should you paste, embed, or link your important objects? Here's what to do:

- ✔ Use *Paste* for objects you'll never want to change.
- ✔ *Embed* objects if you want to be able to edit them easily at a later date.
- ✔ Choose the *Link* option if you want several programs to share the same version of a single object.

Leaving Scraps on the Desktop Deliberately

The Clipboard is a handy way to copy information from one place to another, but it has a major limitation: Every time you copy something new to the Clipboard, it replaces what was copied there before. What if you want to copy a *bunch* of things from a document?

If you were cutting and pasting over a real desktop, you could leave little scraps lying everywhere, ready for later use. The same *scraps* concept works with Windows 98: You can move information from window to window, using the desktop as a temporary storage area for your scraps of information.

For example, suppose that you have some paragraphs in a WordPad document you want to copy to some other places. Highlight the first paragraph, drag it out of the WordPad window, and drop it onto the desktop. Poof! A small Scrap icon appears on your desktop. See another interesting paragraph? Drag it onto the desktop, as well: Another Scrap icon appears.

Eventually, you'll have copies of your report's best paragraphs sitting in little scraps on your desktop. To move any of the scraps into another document, just drag them into that other document's window and let go.

Any remaining, unused scraps can be dumped into the Recycle Bin, or simply left on the desktop, adding a nice, comfortable layer of clutter.

To make a scrap, highlight the information you want to move, usually by running the mouse pointer over it while holding down the mouse button. Then, point at the highlighted information and, while holding down the mouse button, point at the desktop. Let go of the mouse button, and a scrap containing that information appears on the desktop.

Note: Not all Windows 98 applications support Scraps. In fact, WordPad is probably the only program in the Windows 98 box that makes good use of Scraps.

Chapter 9

Customizing Windows 98 (Fiddling with the Control Panel and Other Settings)

● ●

In This Chapter

▶ Exploring the Control Panel

▶ Customizing the display

▶ Changing colors

▶ Changing video modes

▶ Changing Desktop Themes

▶ Understanding TrueType fonts

▶ Making Windows 98 recognize your double-click

▶ Setting the computer's time and date

▶ Changing to a different printer

▶ Assigning cool multimedia sounds to your computer's tasks

▶ Installing new computer parts

▶ Installing or removing programs

▶ Avoiding dangerous icons

● ●

*I*n a way, working with Windows 98 is like remodeling a bathroom. You can spend time on the practical things, like calculating the optimum dimensions for piping or choosing the proper brand of caulking to seal the sink and tub. Or you can spend your time on the more aesthetic options, like adding an oak toilet-paper holder, a marble countertop, or a rattan cover for the tissue box.

Windows 98 allows remodeling through its Control Panel, and in just as many ways. On the eminently practical side, you can call up the System icon and check the Read-ahead Optimization of your hard drives.

Or, stick with the decorating options: Change the color of the title bars to teal, for example, or cover the Windows 98 desktop with daisy patterns or pinstripe wallpaper.

This chapter shows you how to transform Windows 98 into that program you've always dreamed of owning someday.

Finding the Control Panel

The Control Panel is the cupboard that holds most of the Windows 98 switches. Flip open the Control Panel, and you can while away an entire work-day adjusting all the various Windows 98 options.

To find the Control Panel, click the Start button, choose <u>S</u>ettings, and click <u>C</u>ontrol Panel. The Control Panel window pops up, as shown in Figure 9-1. Each icon in the window represents a switch that controls part of the computer.

Figure 9-1: Double-click an icon in the Control Panel to reveal hidden switches controlling that particular area.

Everybody's Control Panel looks different because everybody can afford different computer toys. For example, some modem hounds have special icons that control the way their modems collect mail from all their electronic mailboxes. Others have icons that help them agonize over settings for their networks or sound cards. Table 9-1 takes a quick look at some of the icons you may come across in your copy of Windows 98.

Each option is discussed in more glowing detail later in this chapter.

For a quick way to access your Control Panel, double-click the My Computer icon on the corner of your desktop. You can find a Control Panel folder inside, waiting to be opened with a double-click.

Table 9-1	**Deciphering the Control Panel Icons**	
The Icon	*What It Does*	*Chances You'll Use It*
Accessibility Options	Microsoft performed admirably in making Windows 98 accessible to everybody. Options here make the monitor easier to read, add special sonic signals, and customize Windows' controls to work more easily with people with physical limitations.	If you need any of these options, you'll know.
Add New Hardware	Installed that new [insert name of expensive computer gadget here]? Head for this area to summon the Hardware Installation Wizard. The Wizard, a helpful piece of "advice counselor" software, handles the messy chores of introducing Windows 98 to new computer parts.	Every time you install a new part into your computer.
Add/Remove Programs	Bought some expensive new-programs or software? Double-click here and Windows 98 installs it automatically. You can tell Windows 98 to install any optional components, too, like the FreeCell card game or Backup program. (Make sure that your Windows 98 CD is handy, though — you'll need it.) Finally, this icon lets you uninstall software you've grown tired of, provided that the software man-ufacturer listed its program on the uninstallable programs list.	Whenever you install or delete software.

(continued)

Table 9-1 *(continued)*

The Icon	What It Does	Chances You'll Use It
Date/Time	This area lets you change your computer's date, time, and time zone settings.	Rarely. (Windows 98 is smart enough to adjust automatically for daylight savings time.)
Desktop Themes	Microsoft scrounged around its basement, found a few old products — Microsoft Plus!, to be exact — and tossed 'em into the box. Although nothing new, the themes add a distinctive "look" to your computer: underwater themes, groovy colors, and fun sounds.	Most users open this option, choose one theme, then forget about the dozen others waiting to be tested.
Display	Double-click the Display icon to change your screen's wallpaper, color scheme, number of available colors, resolution, screen-saver, and other display-oriented settings. (Double-click a blank part of your desktop to summon the same menu.)	Used often. This icon lets you fine-tune what you'll be staring at all day: your monitor settings.
Fonts	Windows 98 comes with basic fonts like Arial and Courier. If you head back to the software store and buy more, like Lucida Blackletter and Lucida Handwriting, install them by double-clicking this icon. (*Nerdly Note:* This icon is actually a shortcut to the real Fonts setting area. Chapters 3 and 10 cover shortcuts.)	Rarely. Most programs install and maintain their fonts automatically.
Game Controllers	Windows 98 usually spots joysticks and gamepads and installs them automatically. Double-click here for help with problems. Also, here's where you calibrate and test your joystick if you're losing.	Rarely, even by game players.
Infrared	Used mostly for James Bond types with fancy laptops that shoot information to high-tech printers and palmtops.	Rarely.

The Icon	What It Does	Chances You'll Use It
Internet Options	When you're ready to join the Internet and surf the World Wide Web, this icon's waiting for you. It opens a Pandora's box of buttons that let you light your Internet-access pilot light. (Chapter 13 shows how to point and click your way through the Internet.)	Rarely, except when setting everything up for the first time. After your Internet access is set up, everything's pretty low-maintenance.
Keyboard	Here you can change how long the keyboard takes to repeat a letter when you hold down a key. Yawn. Or, if you pack up the computer and move to Sweden, double-click here to switch to the Swedish language format (or Belgian, Finnish, Icelandic, and a bunch of other countries' formats). Finally, here's where you tell Windows 98 whether you've upgraded from an older 83- or 84-key keyboard to a newer 101- or 102-key keyboard — the ones with the numeric keypads.	Rarely. Human nature causes most people to adjust to their existing keyboard — not the other way around. Check out the settings if your keyboard's giving you problems, though.
Modems	Before you can talk to other computers over the phone lines, you need a modem. Double-click here, and Windows 98 tries to figure out what sort of modem you have so that it can boss it around. These menus also let you adjust modem settings.	Rarely. Windows usually detects and installs new modems automatically.
Mouse	Make that mouse scoot faster across the screen, change it from right-handed to left-handed, fine-tune your double-click, choose between brands, and change all sorts of mouse-related behaviors.	Rarely. People with mouse trouble usually aren't experienced enough to know that a mouse can be adjusted by double-clicking here. Plus, dirty mouse balls and rollers — not software settings — cause most mouse problems.

(continued)

Table 9-1 *(continued)*

The Icon	What It Does	Chances You'll Use It
Multimedia	Sound card owners drop by here to tweak their gear settings, adjust playback/record volumes, fiddle with MIDI instruments, and play with other goodies, like video capture cards, as well as their CD- and DVD players.	Mostly used for turning the sound up or down on different computer attachments.
Network	Yech. Let your network folks mess with this one. They're getting paid extra for it. (Or they're buying my *MORE Windows 98 For Dummies* book from IDG Books Worldwide, Inc., to find the basics of getting one up and running.)	Rarely. This stuff is much too complicated.
ODBC Data Sources (32bit)	The Open Data Base Connectivity settings.	Look at this only to see how confusing computers can be.
Passwords	This works with the Users icon to help manage passwords when more than one person uses the same PC.	Rarely; used mostly by network administrators.
PC Card (PCMCIA)	The size of a credit card, these slip into a laptop and commonly house modems, network connections, and other useful computer gadgetry.	Used frequently by laptoppers; rarely by everybody else.
Power Management	On some computers, Windows 98 is very power-conscious. On laptops, for example, a double-click of this icon brings up ways to save battery power. You can make it turn off the screen when you haven't touched the keyboard in a specified number of minutes. Some desktop computers can turn off the hard drives when they haven't been used in a while, too.	Used frequently by laptoppers; occasionally by everybody else.

The Icon	What It Does	Chances You'll Use It
Printers	Come here to tell Windows 98 about your new printer, adjust the settings on your old printer, or choose which printer (or fax card) you want Windows 98 to use. *Technical Note:* This isn't really an icon; it's a shortcut that leads to the Printer setup program.	As often as you buy printers — or permnently change settings on your printer.
Regional Settings	This changes the way Windows 98 displays and sorts numbers, international currency, the date, and the time. (If you've simply changed time zones, just double-click the date/time display on the bottom-right corner of the taskbar, a process described later in this chapter.)	Used mostly by laptoppers with Frequent Flyer cards.
Sounds	The most fun! Make Windows 98 play different sounds for different events. Try out some of the preset settings in the Schemes menu.	Used mostly at homes or small offices where the boss doesn't mind computers that make exploding sounds when they crash.
System	Like race car mechanics, computer gurus can fiddle around in here for hours. Don't play in here unless a nearby computer guru can serve as Safety Patrol. This is scary stuff.	This area's usage increases with the level of the user's experience.
Telephony	I've never used it, actually. But I'm sure that it does something useful.	Never.
Users	Windows can get "personal" with a family of users. When Joe types in his password, for example, Windows replaces Jen's "X-Files" wallpaper with "Packards" photos and assigns football sounds to his mouse clicks.	Creates a personal "feel" when a single computer is used by more than one person.

✔ Don't worry about that overwhelming display of options in the Control Panel; chances are you'll use very few of them. And don't worry if your Control Panel doesn't look identical to the one in this book. Renegade programs often toss their own icons onto the Control Panel.

✔ Many of the Control Panel's menus can be reached *without* calling up the Control Panel. Double-click the taskbar's little clock to summon the Date/Time menu, for example; right-click a blank part of the desktop and choose Properties to bring up the Display's menu.

Customizing the Display

The most-often-used part of the Control Panel is probably the Display icon, which looks like the icon in the margin.

When you open this door, you can change the wallpaper, screen saver, and other visual aspects of the Windows 98 desktop (see Figure 9-2).

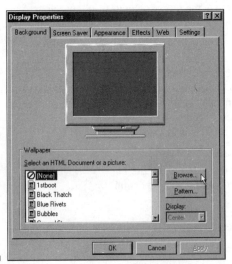

Figure 9-2: The Display icon lets you change your desktop's colors, resolution, wallpaper, screen saver, and other display-oriented options.

Unlike several other switches in the Control Panel, the Display icon doesn't control anything too dangerous. Feel free to fiddle around with all the settings (except the ones that talk about the Internet or the Web). You can't cause any major harm. If you do want to play, however, be sure that you write down any original settings. Then you can always return your display to normal if something looks odd.

TIP

You don't have to root through the Start button and the Control Panel to get to the Display icon's contents. Instead, just click a blank part of your desktop with your right mouse button. When the menu pops up out of nowhere, click Properties. That bypasses the Control Panel and takes you straight to the Display settings area.

The next few sections describe how to customize different parts of your display after you double-click the Control Panel's Display icon.

The display's background

When Windows 98 first installs itself, it paints a boring monotone background across the screen and then starts sprinkling windows and icons over it. Windows 98 *has* to choose that dull color in the beginning, or nobody would think it's a *serious business application.*

However, Microsoft snuck other backgrounds, known as *wallpaper,* into the Windows 98 box. Those pieces of wallpaper are hiding on the hard drive, just waiting to be installed. You can choose a pinstripe pattern that matches your suit. Or you can create your own wallpaper in Paint, the Windows 98 graphics program, and hang your new wallpaper yourself. If you have a digital camera, you can add your own wallpaper to reflect your personality (see Figure 9-3).

Figure 9-3: Windows wallpaper, the backdrop beneath all the windows and icons, can match your mood for the day.

To change the wallpaper, double-click the Display icon from the Control Panel. (Or click a blank spot of your desktop with your right mouse button and choose Properties from the menu that appears from nowhere.)

A rather large dialog box appears (refer to Figure 9-2). Look for the word Wallpaper hovering over a list of names and click one of the names. Click on any name for a preview as to how your selection would look as wallpaper (see Figure 9-4).

To scroll up or down the list of potential wallpaper files, click the little arrows on the bar to the right of the names. If you aren't using a mouse, you can select a listed item by using the arrow keys to highlight the item you want and then pressing Enter. In a long list, you can find a certain name more quickly by pressing the name's first letter.

When you see the name of the wallpaper you want, select it. Then click the Apply button to make Windows 98 install it. Like the way your new wallpaper looks on-screen? Click the OK command button. The dialog box disappears, and you are back at your desktop (with the new wallpaper displayed proudly in the background).

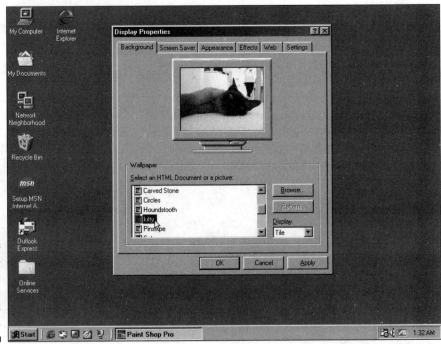

Figure 9-4: Windows 98 displays a small preview of how your selection will look as wallpaper.

✔ Wallpaper can be *tiled* across the screen or *centered.* Small pictures should be *tiled,* or painted repeatedly across the screen. Larger pictures look best when they're centered. Windows 98 adds a *stretch* option, which expands a single picture to fill your screen. Select your preference by selecting it from the Display box.

✔ Wallpaper files are merely bitmaps, or files created in Windows 98 Paint. (Bitmap files end with the letters BMP.) Anything you create in Windows 98 Paint can be used as wallpaper. In fact, you can even use Paint to alter the wallpaper Microsoft provided with Windows 98.

✔ Windows 98 also lets you use Web displays from the Internet known as HTML files. They're pretty but much more complicated than plain old wallpaper.

✔ When using wallpaper, turn off your Active Desktop feature, or Windows might be confused the next time you turn on your computer. To turn it off, right click on your desktop, click the <u>A</u>ctive Desktop, and click View As <u>W</u>eb Page to remove the check mark.

✔ Windows 98 only lists wallpaper that's stored directly in the Windows directory. If you create some potential wallpaper in Paint, you have to move the file to the Windows directory before it shows up in the Desktop dialog box's master list; or you have to choose the file by clicking on the <u>B</u>rowse button. If this concept seems strange, foreign, confusing, or all three, check out Chapter 11 for more information about directories and moving files between them.

✔ Wallpaper looks like a lot of fun, but it may be *too much* fun if your computer doesn't have more than 8MB of RAM. Fancy, colorful wallpaper files can use up a great deal of the computer's memory, consistently slowing Windows 98 down. If you find yourself running out of memory, change the wallpaper to the (None) option. The screen won't look as pretty, but at least Windows 98 works.

✔ Small files that are *tiled* across the screen take up much less memory than large files that are *centered* on-screen. If Windows 98 seems slow or it sends you furtive messages saying that it's running out of memory, try tiling some smaller bits of wallpaper.

✔ Patterns, accessed through the <u>P</u>attern button, are a poor-man's wallpaper. They're only one color, and they don't vary much. If Windows 98 keeps complaining about needing more memory, however, dump your wallpaper and switch to patterns. They don't eat up nearly as much memory.

✔ Did you happen to spot an eye-catching picture while Web surfing with Internet Explorer? Click that Web site's picture with your right mouse button and select the Set as <u>W</u>allpaper option. Sneaky Microsoft copies that picture to your desktop and leaves it on the screen as your new wallpaper. (Just keep the image on your own desktop; don't try to sell it or give it away, or you might run afoul of copyright laws.)

The display's screen saver

In the dinosaur days of computing, computer monitors were permanently damaged when an oft-used program burned its image onto the screen. The program's faint outlines showed up even when the monitor was turned off.

To prevent this *burn-in,* people installed a *screen saver* to jump in when a computer hadn't been used for a while. The screen saver would either blank the screen or fill it with wavy lines to keep the program's display from etching itself into the screen.

Today's monitors don't really have this problem, but people use screen savers anyway — mainly because they look cool.

✔ Windows comes with several screen savers built in, although none of them is activated at first. To set one up, click the Screen Saver tab along the top of the Display Properties dialog box (refer to Figure 9-2). Then click the downward-pointing arrow in the <u>S</u>creen Saver box. Finally, select the screen saver you want.

✔ Immediately after choosing a screen saver, click the Pre<u>v</u>iew command button to see what the screen saver looks like. Wiggle the mouse or press the spacebar to come back to Windows 98.

✔ Fiddlers can click Se<u>t</u>tings for more options. For example, you can control the colors and animation speed.

✔ Click in the <u>P</u>assword protected box to set a password; then when the screen saver kicks in, you won't be able to see the screen again until you type in the password.

✔ Forgot your password? Push your computer's reset button. (Yep, you lose any work you didn't save before the screen saver kicked in.) After Windows 98 returns to life, click the desktop with your right mouse button, choose P<u>r</u>operties from the pop-up menu, and click the Screen Saver tab. Whew! Now, assign a new password before your screen saver kicks in again. (And make this password a little easier to remember.)

✔ Click the up or down arrows next to <u>W</u>ait to tell the screen saver when to kick in. If you set the option to 5, for example, Windows 98 waits until you haven't touched the mouse or keyboard for five minutes before letting the screen saver out of its cage.

✔ Windows 98 comes with more screen savers than it initially installs. To make Windows 98 install *all* its screen savers, use the Control Panel's Add/Remove Programs icon, described later in this chapter, and make Windows 98 install more of itself. (***Hint:*** I like 3D Pipes with a Metal Links texture and Flex tubing.)

TIP

✔ If your monitor's fairly new, click the <u>S</u>ettings button at the bottom of the Screen Saver page. Here, you can tell Windows 98 to turn off your monitor when you haven't used it for a while. That way you never have to remember to turn off your monitor. (Monitors don't like to be left turned on.) Feel free to turn your hard disk off after an hour or so, too, to save wear, tear, and energy.

The display's appearance (getting better colors)

Feeling blue? You can make Windows 98 appear in any color you want by clicking on the tab marked Appearance, found along the top of the Display menu.

The Appearance dialog box opens, enabling you to choose between several Microsoft-designed color schemes or to create your own. (Tell your boss that a more pleasant color scheme will enhance your productivity.) Figure 9-5 shows the Appearance dialog box.

Figure 9-5: Windows 98 lets you personalize your computer by choosing different color schemes.

To choose among previously designed color schemes, click the arrow next to the box beneath <u>S</u>cheme. After the list drops down, click the name of the scheme you want to try out. Each time you select a new color scheme, the sample window shows you how the colors will look.

If you want to change one of the color schemes slightly, go for it: Click the box beneath Item to see a list of areas you can fiddle with. For example, to change the font Windows 98 uses for icon titles, select Icon from the list and select a different font from the ones listed in the Font box.

And, if you want even more choices, you can mix your own colors by choosing Other from the Color menu and clicking on the Define Custom Colors command button.

Feel free to play around with the colors by trying out different schemes or designing your own combinations. Playing with the colors is an easy way to see what names Windows 98 uses for its different components. It's also a fun way to work with dialog boxes. But if you goof something awful, and all the letters suddenly disappear, click the Cancel button. (It's the middle of the three buttons along the bottom.) Letters disappear when they've been changed to white on a white background.

- Color schemes don't refer to color alone; they can change the appearance of Windows 98 in other ways. For example, the Icon Spacing (Horizontal) setting determines how closely your icons sit next to each other. The Scrollbar setting determines the width of the scroll bars and their elevatorlike buttons you click to move around in a document.

- Created an outstanding new color scheme? Click the Save As button and type in a new name for your creation. If you ever grow weary of your creative new color scheme, you can always return to the Windows 98 original colors by selecting Windows Standard.

- Windows 98 continues to display your newly chosen colors until you head back to the Appearance menu and change them again.

- The Appearance menu is pretty boring after you've checked out the Desktop Themes program, also found on the Control Panel. Desktop Themes, discussed later in this chapter, decorates your computer to match your hobbies and interests, from deep-sea diving to plowing fields. (I'm not kidding — check it out!)

- Is all this talk of "dialog boxes," "command buttons," and "funny arrow things" getting you down? Head to Chapter 5 for a field guide to figuring out Windows 98 menus.

Display settings (playing with new video modes)

Just as Windows 98 can print to hundreds of different brands of printers, it can accommodate zillions of different monitors, too. It can even display different *video modes* on the same monitor.

The weird "Effects" and Web tabs

For years, the Display Properties box came with just a few settings to change your wallpaper, choose a screen saver, choose different color schemes, and adjust the settings of your video card.

Sharp-eyed Windows 98 users will notice two other tabs: Effects, and Web. The Effects tab doesn't really do much; if your normal desktop icons like My Computer, Network Neighborhood, and the Recycle Bin suddenly look funny, head back here and click the Default Icon button to restore order.

The Web tab lets you spread little Internet doodads across your desktop. (I think Microsoft's losing interest in the Web tab, actually; it hasn't added a new doodad in more than a year.) Check out Chapter 17 for more information.

For example, Windows 98 can display different numbers of color on-screen, or it can shrink the size of everything, packing more information onto the screen. The number of colors and the size of the information on-screen comprise a *video mode,* or *video resolution.*

Some Windows 98 programs only work in a specific video mode, and those programs casually ask you to switch to that mode. Huh?

Here's what's happening: Monitors plug into a special place on the back of the computer. That special place is an outlet on a *video card* — the gizmo that translates your computer's language into something you can *see* on the monitor. That card handles all the video-mode switches. By making the card switch between modes, you can send more or fewer colors to your monitor or pack more or less information onto the screen.

To make a video card switch to a different video mode, click the Settings tab, one of the four tabs along the top of the Control Panel's Display menu, shown in Figure 9-2. (Can't find the Display menu? Click a blank part of your desktop by using the right mouse button and choose Properties from the menu that springs up.)

As shown in Figure 9-6, the Settings menu lets you select the video mode that you want Windows 98 to display on-screen. (Click the arrow next to the Colors box to change the number of colors Windows 98 is currently displaying; click in the Screen area box to change the current resolution.) Windows 98 gives you a chance to back out if you choose a video mode your computer can't handle, thank goodness.

Figure 9-6:
Windows 98
offers a
preview of
what your
currently
selected
video mode
will look
like. Here,
Windows 98
depicts two
monitors
and two
video cards.

✔ When Windows 98 switches to the new resolution, it gives you 15 seconds to click a button saying that you approve of the change. If your card or monitor can't handle the new resolution, you won't be able to see the button on-screen. Then because you didn't click the button, Windows 98 automatically changes back to the original resolution. Whew!

✔ Monitors and cards can display Windows 98 in different *resolutions*. The higher the resolution, the more information Windows 98 can pack onto the screen. (And the smaller the windows become, too.) Windows 98 refers to resolution as *Desktop area*. For more information about this monitor/card/resolution stuff, troop over to Chapter 2 and read the section about computer parts that I told you to ignore.

✔ To switch to a higher resolution, use your mouse to slide the little bar in the Screen area box. Then watch how the screen changes. The more you slide the bar to the right, the more information Windows 98 can pack onto the screen. Unfortunately, the information also gets smaller. Click the Apply button after you select a new resolution to see it in action.

✔ Earlier versions of Windows made users shut down Windows when changing resolution. Windows 98 isn't nearly as rude. You can change resolution while all your programs are still running. (Make sure that you've saved your work anyway, however. Who *really* trusts their computer to be polite these days?) Also, Windows 98 sometimes still needs to shut down and restart when switching the number of colors it can display. It depends on your particular computer's innards.

✔ Want to change the number of colors Windows 98 can throw onto the screen? Click the little arrow in the Colors box. After the list drops down, select the number of colors you want.

✔ New video cards usually come with a disk that contains special information called a *driver.* If Windows 98 doesn't recognize your breed of video card, it may ask you to insert this disk when you're changing video modes.

✔ The more colors you ask Windows 98 to display, the slower it runs. Usually, it's best to stick with 256 colors unless you have a fancy video card, own a fancy monitor to go with it, and want to look at ultra-realistic photos on-screen.

✔ If you'll be looking at pictures taken with a digital camera, you'll probably want Windows 98 to display as many colors as possible — often 65,000 (16-bit) or 1.6 million (24-bit). Switch back to fewer colors when you're done, however, if Windows 98 starts running too slowly.

✔ Windows 98 can work with two or more monitors simultaneously and display different video resolutions on each monitor. You need a separate PCI video card to power each monitor, however. See the nearby "Two monitors...*at the same time!*" sidebar for more information.

✔ If Windows 98 acts goofy with your video card or monitor — or you've recently installed new ones — head for the "Adding New Hardware" section later in this chapter. Windows 98 probably needs to be formally introduced to your new equipment before it will talk to it.

Two monitors . . . *at the same time!*

Plug a second video card into your computer, plug in a second monitor, and Windows 98 will probably be able to spread its display across both monitors — or even three, if you install another card and monitor.

It sounds frivolous, but this new feature can be kind of handy, actually. For instance, you can run your Internet browser on one monitor, while keeping your desktop handy for other work. Or,

you can spread your work out, making it easy to cut and paste between bunches of open windows.

A few words of caution, however: This two-monitor stuff is new, so not all programs can handle it. Also, TV Viewer cards can only display TV shows on the *primary monitor* — your first monitor. The TV show simply disappears if you try dragging its window to the second monitor.

Adding Fun Desktop Themes and Effects

To add a little life to your computer, double-click the Control Panel's Desktop Themes icon. Here, Windows 98 can decorate your display with a wide variety of sights and sounds. Have a fetish for dangerous animals? Click the Dangerous Creatures option to add a mountain lion for wallpaper (see Figure 9-7); growling noises emerge from clicked icons, and your pointer turns into a killer bee as Windows 98 works in the background.

Figure 9-7:
Desktop
Themes add
fun sounds,
pictures,
and
animation to
your
wallpaper,
clicking
sounds, and
mouse
pointer
shapes.

✔ Don't see the Desktop Themes option on the Control Panel? Double-click the Control Panel's Add/Remove Programs icon, click the Windows Setup tab, and click Desktop Themes from the Components menu. Click the OK button, and Windows 98 will install the Desktop Themes. (It might ask for your original Windows 98 CD, however.)

✔ Curious about the Web tab? It stands for the Active Desktop, and it lets you stick Internet Web effects onto your desktop. It's described in Chapter 21.

✔ For even more display excitement, click the Effects tab. Come here to choose new icons for the desktop, for example, or control their fine adjustments.

Viewing Your Computer's Fonts

Sure, you see the names of the fonts in your word-processing program. But how can you tell what they *look* like before choosing one? To find out, choose the Control Panel's Fonts icon.

There, you see what fonts come with Windows 98; you install additional fonts, and you delete the ugly ones you don't like anymore.

To be on the safe side, don't delete any fonts that come with Windows 98; only delete fonts that you've installed yourself. Windows programs often borrow Windows 98 fonts for menus. If you delete those fonts, your menus mysteriously vanish. And for goodness sake, don't delete any fonts beginning with the letters **MS.** (Don't delete the fonts that have red lettering in their icons, either.)

Double-click any font icon to see what that particular font looks like. For example, if you double-click the icon marked *Impact* font, Windows 98 brings up an eye chart displaying how that font would look on the printed page, as shown in Figure 9-8. (And click the Print button to see what it really looks like on the printed page.)

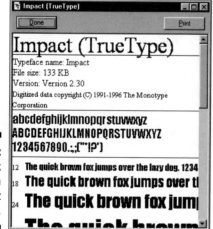

Figure 9-8:
Double-click
a font icon
to see what
it looks like.

✔ Icons marked with the letters "TT" are TrueType fonts, so they'll always look better than the fonts marked with the letter A.

✔ *Note:* You'll probably never need to fiddle with the Fonts icon. Just know that it's there in case you ever want to get fancy and install more fonts on your computer.

Making Windows 98 Recognize Your Double-Click

Clicking twice with a mouse button is called a double-click; most users do a lot of double-clicking in Windows 98. But sometimes you can't click fast enough to satisfy Windows 98. It thinks that your double-clicks are just two single clicks. If you have this problem, head for the Control Panel's Mouse icon.

When you double-click the Mouse icon, the Mouse dialog box pops up (see Figure 9-9). If your mouse dialog box doesn't look like the one in Figure 9-9, the company that made your mouse slipped its own software into the Control Panel. The following instructions may not work for you, but you can generally access the same types of options for any mouse. If your menu looks weird, try pressing F1 for help.

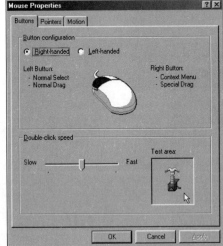

Figure 9-9: Double-click in the Test area box to check your current settings.

To check the double-click speed, double-click in the box marked Test area. Each time Windows 98 recognizes your double-click, a little puppet with water-buffalo horns pops out of the Jack in the Box. Double-click again, and the puppet disappears.

Slide the scroll box toward the words Fast or Slow until Windows 98 successfully recognizes your double-click efforts. Click the OK button when you're through, and you're back in business.

✔ Can't double-click the Mouse icon quickly enough for Windows 98 to open the darn thing up? Just click once, and poke the Enter key with your finger. Or, click once with the right button and choose Open from the menu that shoots out of the Mouse icon's head. Yep, there are a lot of ways to do the same thing in Windows 98.

✔ If you're left-handed, click in the little circle marked Left-handed, shown along the top of Figure 9-9, and click the Apply button. Then you can hold the mouse in your left hand and still click with your index finger.

✔ For a psychedelic experience, click the tab marked Motion along the window's top and then click in the box marked Show pointer trails. Windows 98 makes *ghost arrows* follow the mouse pointer. Laptop users can spot the arrow more easily when ghosts follow it. The more you slide the little box toward the long side of the bar, the longer your trail of mouse ghosts grows.

✔ The mouse arrow doesn't have to move at the same speed as the mouse. To make the arrow *zip* across the screen with just a tiny push, click the Motion tab along the top. Then, in the Pointer speed box, slide the little box toward the side of the scroll bar marked Fast. To slow down the mouse, allowing for more precise pointing, slide the box toward the Slow side.

✔ Some brands of mice come with fancier features and their own different settings page. The Microsoft IntelliMouse, described in the mouse section of Chapter 2, lets you control on-screen action by spinning a wheel embedded in the poor mouse's neck. Laptops with touch-pads and track-balls will find their adjustment areas here, too.

✔ Mouse acting up something fierce? Pointer darting around obstinately like an excited dachshund on a walk? Maybe you need to clean your mouse, a simple maintenance task described in Chapter 14.

Setting the Computer's Time and Date

Many computer users don't bother to set the computer's clock. They just look at their wristwatches to see when it's time to stop working. But they're missing out on an important computing feature: Computers always stamp new files with the current date and time. If the computer doesn't know the correct date, it stamps files with the *wrong* date. Then how can you find the files you created yesterday? Last week?

Also, Windows 98 sometimes does some funny things to the computer's internal clock, so you may want to reset the date and time if you notice that the computer is living in the past (or prematurely jumping to the future).

TIP

To reset the computer's time or date, choose the Control Panel's Date/Time icon.

A double-click the Date/Time icon brings a little calendar to the screen, shown in Figure 9-10. To change the date, just click the correct date as listed on the on-screen calendar. If the date's off by a month or more, click the little arrow next to the currently listed month. A list drops down, letting you choose a different month. To change the year or the hour, click the number you want to change and then click the up or down arrows to make the number bigger or smaller. When the number is correct, click the OK button for Windows 98 to make the changes.

Figure 9-10:
To change
the time,
click the
numbers
beneath the
clock; then
click the
little arrows
next to the
numbers.

✔ Moved to a new time zone? Click the Time Zone tab along the top of the window. Click the downward-pointing arrow next to the currently listed time zone. A *long* list of countries and locations appears; click the one where you're currently hanging your hat.

✔ Windows 98 has a Find program, described in Chapter 7, that can locate files by the time and date they were created, modified, or last accessed — but *only* if you keep your computer's date and time set correctly.

REMEMBER

✔ Most computers have an internal clock that automatically keeps track of the time and date. Nevertheless, those clocks aren't always reliable, especially among laptops with "power-saving" features. Check your $2,000 computer's clock against your $20 wristwatch every few weeks to make sure that the computer is on the mark.

TIP

For an even quicker way to change your computer's time or date, double-click the little clock Windows 98 puts on the taskbar that lives along the edge of the screen. Windows 98 brings up the Date/Time menu, just as if you'd waded through the Control Panel and double-clicked the Date/Time icon.

Fiddling with the Printer

Most of the time, the printer will work fine. Especially after you turn it *on* and try printing again. In fact, most people will never need to read this section.

Occasionally, however, you may need to tweak some printer settings. You'll need to install a new printer or remove an old one that you've sold (so it won't keep cluttering up the list of printers). Either way, start by choosing the Control Panel's Printers icon.

The Printers dialog box surfaces, as shown in Figure 9-11.

Figure 9-11:
Double-clicking the Add Printer icon tells Windows 95 about your new printer.

 Is the My Computer window open? Double-click the Printers icon hiding in there. That step takes you to the same Printers dialog box as the Control Panel does.

If you're installing a new printer, grab the Windows 98 compact disc or floppy disks that came in the box; you'll probably need them during the installation.

1. **To add a new printer, double-click the Control Panel's Printer icon, and click the Add Printers icon.**

   Magic! A Windows 98 Wizard appears, ready to set up your new printer.

2. **Click the Next button and then follow the Wizard's instructions.**

   For example, click whether your printer is physically connected to your printer, or if it's shared with other computers over a network.

3. **Click the Next button and follow the Wizard's instructions.**

   The Add Printer Wizard box lists the names of printer manufacturers on the left; click the name of your printer's manufacturer, and the right side of the box lists the models of printers that manufacturer makes.

4. **Double-click your printer's name when you see it listed. Windows 98 asks you to stick the appropriate setup disks into a drive, and the drive makes some grinding noises.**

   After a moment, you see the new printer listed in the box.

5. **Click the new printer's icon and choose the Set As Default Printer option from the window's File menu.**

   That's it. If you're like most people, your printer will work like a charm. If it doesn't, you may have to wade through the technical stuff in the sidebar (in this chapter) about printer ports and such.

If you have more than one printer attached to your computer, select your most-oft-used printer as the *default* printer. That choice tells Windows 98 to assume that it's printing to that oft-used printer.

- To remove a printer you no longer use, choose Printers from the Start menu's Settings menu. Click its name with your right mouse button, and then click Delete from the menu. That printer's name no longer appears as an option when you try to print from a Windows 98-based program.

- You can change printer options from within many programs. Choose Files in the menu bar and then choose Print Setup. From there, you can often access the same box of printer options as you find in the Control Panel.

- Some printers offer a variety of options. For example, you can print from different paper trays or print at different resolutions. To play with these options, double-click the Control Panel's Printer icon, and right-click your printer's icon. When the menu pops up, choose Properties to change things like paper size, fonts, and types of graphics.

- If your printer isn't listed in the Windows 98 master list, you have to contact the printer's manufacturer for a *driver.* When it comes in the mail or over the Internet, repeat the process for adding a printer, but click the Have Disk button. Windows 98 asks you to stick in the manufacturer's disk so that it can copy the *driver* onto the hard disk. (For more information, check out the section, "Adding New Hardware," later in this chapter.)

- Working with printers can be more complicated than trying to retrieve a stray hamster from under the kitchen cupboards. Feel free to use any of the Help buttons in the dialog boxes. Chances are they'll offer some helpful advice, and some are actually customized for your particular brand of printer. Too bad they can't catch hamsters.

- Windows 98 is a little better at housekeeping than Windows 3.1, especially when it comes to deleting old files. When you delete a printer from the Control Panel, Windows 98 asks if you want to remove the old printer drivers, too. (Click the Yes button, unless you think that you'll be adding that printer back on in the near future.)

Printer ports and configuration nonsense

Windows 98 shoots information to printers through ports (little metal outlets on the computer's rump). Most printers connect to a port called *LPT1:*, or the first *line printer port.*

Always select this option first. If it works, skip the rest of this technical chatter. You've already found success!

Some people, however, insist on plugging printers into a second printer port, or *LPT2:*. (If you meet one of these people, ask them why.) Still, other people buy *serial* printers, which plug into *serial ports* (also known as *COM ports*).

Finally, some people buy network printers, which don't plug into a computer at all. (They probably do this to justify their bigger paychecks as network administrators.) These printers are connected through software-controlled virtual ports. Trust me; leave it to the guy who bought the printer to hook this one up.

Different brands of printers work with Windows 98 in different ways, but here are a few tips. To connect a printer to a different port, click the printer's icon with your right mouse button and choose Properties from the pop-up menu. Click the tab marked Details, and you can select the port you want. Look to see what port you're plugging the printer into, and select that port from the menu. (Computer ports are rarely labeled, so you'll probably have to bribe a computer guru to help you out. Start tossing Cheetos around your chair and desk; computer gurus are attracted by the smell. No Cheetos? Head to Chapter 2 for port pictures.)

If you're connecting a printer to a serial port, you need to do one more little chore: Configure the serial port. Click the Port Settings box, found on that same Details tab page, and make sure that the following numbers and characters appear, in this order: 9600, 8, N, 1, Xon/Xoff.

The printer should be all set. If not, call over a computer guru. At least you only have to go through all this printer hassle once — unless you buy another printer.

Sound and Multimedia

The term *multimedia* means mixing two or more mediums — usually combining sound and pictures. A plain old television, for example, could be called a *multimedia tool,* especially if you're trying to impress somebody.

Windows 98 can mix sound and pictures if you have a *sound card:* a gizmo costing about $100 that slips inside the computer and hooks up to a pair of speakers or a stereo.

Macintosh computers have had sound for years. And for years, Mac owners have been able to *assign sounds to system events.* In lay language, that means having the computer make a professional baseball player's spitting sound when it ejects a floppy disk.

In Windows 98, you can't assign sounds to the floppy drives, but you can assign noises to other *events* by double-clicking the Control Panel's Sounds icon.

The Sounds dialog box appears (see Figure 9-12). Windows 98 automatically plays sounds for several system events. An event can be anything as simple as when a menu pops up or when Windows 98 first starts up in the morning.

Figure 9-12:
Windows 98
can play
back
different
sounds
when
different
things
happen on
your
computer.

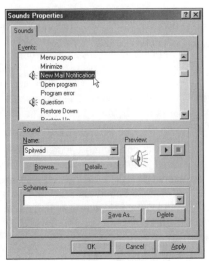

Windows 98 lists the events on the top of the box and lists the possible sounds directly below them in the box called Name. To assign a sound, click the event first and then click the sound you want to hear for that event. In Figure 9-12, for example, Windows 98 is set up to make a spitting sound whenever a new piece of electronic mail comes in over the wire.

 ✔ Are you satisfied with your new choices of sounds? Click in the box marked Save As, and change the words Windows Default to something else, like My Sound Settings. That way you can still change back to the more polite Windows Default sounds when you don't want house guests to hear your computer spit. (You can change back to My Sound Effects after they've left.)

 ✔ For some automatic sound schemes, choose the Desktop Themes icon from the Control Panel. It assigns lots of cutesy sounds automatically to different Windows setups. It's really fun until it becomes annoying.

 ✔ To take advantage of this multimedia feature, your computer needs a sound card. Stuck with an old computer? Buy and install a sound card, and then tell Windows 98 about your new card by clicking the Control Panel's Add New Hardware icon, described later in this chapter.

✔ To hear a sound before you assign it, click its name and then click the Preview button (the little black triangle next to the speaker).

✔ You can record your own sounds through most sound cards. You can probably pick up a cheap microphone at Radio Shack; some sound cards don't include one.

✔ Be forewarned: Sound consumes a *lot* of disk space, so stick with short recordings — short and sweet B.B. King guitar riffs, for example, or the sound of a doorbell ringing.

✔ Sound card not working right? You may have to muddle through the Multimedia icon, described in the dreary technical sidebar "Multimedia setup problems."

Multimedia setup problems

Multimedia gadgetry inevitably brings a multitude of setup problems. There are simply too many file formats and program settings for an easy ride. Although Windows 98 does an excellent job of setting up your computer's hardware automatically, the Control Panel's Multimedia icon lets techno-fiddlers change some of the settings. Because different computers use different parts, the settings listed under the Multimedia icon vary, but here's a general look at what they can do:

Audio: This page controls your sound card's volume settings as well as its recording quality. The better the quality of the recording, the more hard disk space your recordings consume. A quicker way to adjust the volume is to simply click the little speaker in the corner of the taskbar. (If you don't see that taskbar's little speaker control, click the Multimedia icon's Show volume control on the taskbar option.)

Video: This option lets you select the size of your videos. You can force them to play back full-screen, for example, or to consume smaller sizes. (*Hint:* Your best bet is to select Original size from the Window option.)

MIDI: Musicians can tell Windows 98 about new MIDI instruments on this page.

CD Music: Mostly useful for adjusting the volume of headphones that plug into a CD-ROM's headphone jack.

Devices: Here, Windows 98 lists all the multimedia devices attached to your computer (as well as a few devices you may want to add to your computer in the future). By clicking on a device and clicking on the Properties button near the bottom, you can turn a device on or off. If your computer has a game port (found on most sound cards), come here to calibrate your joystick for Windows 98 games.

Adding New Hardware

When you wolf down a sandwich for lunch, you know what you ate. After all, you picked it out at the deli counter, chewed it, swallowed it, and wiped the breadcrumbs away from the corner of your mouth.

But when you add a new part to your computer, it's turned off — Windows 98 is asleep. And when you turn the computer back on and Windows 98 returns to life, it may not notice the surgical handiwork.

Here's the good news, however: If you simply tell Windows 98 to *look* for the new part, it will probably find it. In fact, Windows 98 will not only spot the new part, but it will introduce itself and start a warm and friendly working relationship using the right settings.

The Control Panel's Add New Hardware icon handles the process of introducing Windows 98 to anything you've recently attached to your computer.

Here's how to tell Windows 98 to look for any new computer parts you may have stuffed inside or plugged into your computer:

1. **Double-click the Control Panel's Add New Hardware icon, and click the Next button.**

   The Windows 98 Hardware Installation Wizard pops out of a hat, ready to introduce Windows 98 to whatever part you've stuffed inside your computer.

2. **Click the Next button.**

   Windows 98 looks for any recognizable "Plug and Play" devices installed in your computer.

Here's where things start getting a little different. Did Windows 98 find anything new? If so, click the newly installed part's name from the list, click the Finish button, and follow the rest of the Wizard's instructions.

If the Wizard didn't find anything, though, you need to contact the manufacturer of your new part and ask for a *Windows 98 driver*.

- ✔ Windows 98 comes with a Windows Update program that automatically dials the Internet, looks for new software to keep your computer in shape, and installs it. Chapter 17 has the details.

- ✔ Adding a new modem? Then Windows 98 will want to know your current country and area code, as well as whether you dial a special number (such as a 9) to reach an outside line. If you want to change this stuff later, double-click the Control Panel's Modem icon, which brings you to the same page that the Add New Hardware icon does.

✔ Windows 98 is pretty good about identifying various gadgets that people
have stuffed inside it, especially if your computer is Plug and Play compatible and you're installing a Plug and Play part. You can find more
information about Plug and Play in Chapter 3.

✔ In Windows 3.1, you had to know where you were going in order to get
something done. Windows 98 is much more forgiving, and lots of the
icons' functions are overlapping. If you install a new modem, for example, you can use the Add New Hardware icon or the Modem icon to
introduce it to Windows 98. Adding a new printer? Use either the Add
New Hardware icon or the Printer icon; both take you to the same
place — the spot where you tell Windows 98 about your new printer.

Adding and Removing Programs

By adding an Add/Remove Programs icon to the Control Panel, Windows 98 is
trying to trick you into thinking that it's easier than ever to install a program.
Nope.

Here's how the installation programs work if you're lucky. When you get a
new program, look for a disk marked Install or Installation, and stick the disk
into any disk drive that it fits. If the program came on a compact disc, put the
disc into your compact disc drive.

Next, double-click the Control Panel's Add/Remove Programs icon, click the
Install button, and click Next from the next screen. Windows 98 searches all
your disk drives for a disk containing an installation program; if it finds an
installation program, it runs it, effectively installing the program. If it doesn't
find one, it just gives up.

✔ Programs that live on compact discs often install themselves automatically: Just put them in your disc drive and shut the door.

✔ Add/Remove Programs icon not installing your new program? Then
make a new folder somewhere on your hard drive and copy all the files
from the program's disk to the new folder. Then to load the program,
double-click the program's icon from within that folder. Chapter 11 is
filled with tips on creating folders, copying files, and sticking new programs on the Start menu.

✔ The Add/Remove Programs icon can *uninstall* programs, too. It brings up
a list of installed programs; click on the unwanted program's name, click
the Add/Remove button, and Windows will scrape the program from
your computer's innards.

✔ The Windows Setup tab at the top of the Add/Remove Programs screen lets you add or remove some of the programs that came with Windows 98: programs for laptop users, extra wallpaper and sounds, network utilities, games, The Microsoft Network online service, and a few other goodies. To add one of the programs, click in its check box. To remove one you've installed, click in its check box. (Its check mark disappears, as does the program, when you click the Apply button.)

✔ Most programs that you buy at software stores come with installation programs, so Windows 98 can install them without too much trouble. Some of the smaller shareware programs found on online services don't come with installation programs, unfortunately, so you'll have to install them yourself.

✔ Until the built-in uninstall feature of Windows 98 catches on, the easiest way to remove old or unwanted Windows programs is to buy a third-party *uninstaller* program.

✔ Can't find the Welcome program — a tutorial for new Windows 98 users that's mentioned when Windows 98 first loads itself? From the Start button, click Programs, choose Accessories from the menu, click System Tools, and choose Welcome to Windows from near the menu's bottom.

✔ For safety's sake, make a startup disk — a disk that can still start up your computer if something dreadful happens. Put a blank floppy — or a floppy with destructible information — in drive A and click the StartUp Disk tab from the top of the Add/Remove Programs program. Click the Create Disk button and follow the instructions.

Finding Out Which Icons to Avoid

Unless you have a very pressing reason, avoid these icons in the Control Panel: Network, ODBC Data Sources (32bit), Passwords, Regional Settings, System, Telephony, and Users.

✔ The Network icon controls how Windows 98 talks to other computers through your office's network — those cables meandering from PC to PC. Talk to your network administrator before playing with this icon "just to see what it does."

✔ The Regional Settings icon changes the keyboard layout to the one used by people in other countries. It doesn't make the Windows 98 dialog boxes appear in German (although you can order the German version of Windows 98 from Microsoft). Instead, a foreign keyboard layout makes certain keys produce foreign characters. It also changes the way currency appears and stuff like that.

✔ The information listed in the System icon turns on network hounds and techno-nerds. It's out of the realm of this book.

✔ The Passwords icon is kind of like the switch in fancy cars that can remember different seat- and mirror-adjustment settings for up to four different drivers. By assigning different passwords to different computer users, Windows 98 can switch to a customized desktop setting for each person who logs in.

✔ Nobody really knows what the ODBC Data Sources (32bit) icon does.

✔ Finally, the Telephony and Users icons are for people who enjoy fiddling with their computers — not for people who just want to get their work done and go home.

Part III

Using Windows 98 Applications (And Surfing the Web, Should the Mood Strike)

The 5th Wave   By Rich Tennant

"It still bothers me that I'm paying a lot of REAL dollars to a REAL university so you can get a degree in ARTIFICIAL intelligence."

In this part . . .

Did you know that

- ✔ Rubber bands last longer when refrigerated?
- ✔ A human's eyelashes generally fall off after 5 months?
- ✔ Windows 98 comes with a bunch of free programs that aren't even mentioned on the outside of the box?

This part takes a look at all the stuff you're getting for nothing. Well, for the price on your sales receipt, anyway.

Chapter 10

The Windows 98 Desktop, Start Button, and Taskbar

● ●

In This Chapter

▶ Using the desktop

▶ Making shortcuts

▶ Deleting files, folders, programs, and icons

▶ Retrieving deleted items from the Recycle Bin

▶ Discovering the Start button's reason to live

▶ Putting programs on the Start button menu

▶ Making programs start automatically with Windows

▶ Using the taskbar

▶ Controlling the Print Manager

● ●

*I*n the old days of computing, pale technoweenies typed disgustingly long strings of code words into computers to make the computers do something — anything.

With Windows 98, computers reach the age of modern convenience. To start a program, simply click a button. There's a slight complication, however: The buttons no longer *look* like buttons. In fact, some of the buttons are hidden, revealed only by the push of yet another button (if you're lucky enough to stumble upon the right place to push).

This chapter covers the three main Windows 98 buttonmongers: the desktop, the taskbar, and that mother of all buttons — the Start button.

Rolling Objects along the Windows 98 Desktop

Normally, nobody would think of mounting a desktop sideways. Keeping the pencils from rolling off a normal desk is hard enough.

But in Windows 98, your computer monitor's screen is known as the Windows *desktop,* and it's the area where all your work takes place. When working with Windows 98, you'll be creating files and folders right on your new electronic desktop and arranging those files and folders across the screen.

For example, do you need to write a letter asking the neighbor to return the circular saw she borrowed? Here's how to put the desktop's functions to immediate use.

Point at just about any Windows 98 item and click your right mouse button to see a menu listing the things you're allowed to do with that item.

1. **Click an uncovered area of your desktop with your right mouse button.**

   A menu pops up, as shown in Figure 10-1.

Figure 10-1: Clicking an empty area of your desktop with your right mouse button brings up a list of options.

2. Point at the word New and click WordPad Document from the menu that appears.

Because you're creating something new — a new letter — you should point at the word New. Windows 98 lists the new things you can create on the desktop. Choose WordPad Document, as shown in Figure 10-2.

Figure 10-2:
Point at the
word New
and choose
WordPad
Document
from the
menu.

As your computer fills up with programs, your menu choices change, too. In fact, Microsoft Word often boots WordPad off the menu completely. If you don't have WordPad on your menu, choose Run from the Start menu, type WordPad into the Run box, and press Enter. WordPad opens automatically, ready for action. (Ignore the part in Step 4 about "double-clicking the new icon.")

3. Type a title for your letter and press Enter.

When an icon for a WordPad document appears on the desktop, Windows 98 doesn't want you to lose it. So the first step is to give it a name of up to 255 characters. As soon as you start typing, your new title replaces the old name of New WordPad Document, as shown in Figure 10-3. (Occasionally, Windows 98 frets about your choice of name; if so, try a different name or skip ahead to Chapter 11 to see why Windows is so finicky about names.)

Figure 10-3:
Start typing
to create
the icon's
new name.

4. **Double-click your new icon, write your letter, save it, and print it.**

   Double-clicking the new icon calls up WordPad, the word processor, so you can write the letter requesting the return of your circular saw. Remember, word processors automatically wrap your sentences to the next line for you; don't hit the Enter key when you're nearing the right side of the page. Are you done writing? Then move on to Step 5. (WordPad's letter-writing intuitiveness is addressed more fully in Chapter 12.)

5. **Click Save from the WordPad File menu to save the letter.**

   Used the Start menu to load WordPad? Then now's the time to choose a name for the file.

6. **Head back to the WordPad File menu and choose Print to send the letter to the printer.**

7. **To store the file, drag the icon to a folder. Or to delete it, drag the file to the Recycle Bin.**

   After you've finished writing and printing the letter, you need to decide what to do with the file. You can simply leave its icon on your desk, but that clutters things up. Instead, drag and drop the letter into the My Documents folder that's conveniently located on your desktop. (Dragging and dropping is covered in Chapter 3.)

   If you want to save the letter in your own folder, click the desktop with your right mouse button and choose Folder from the New menu. Windows 98 tosses a new folder onto your desktop, ready for you to drag your letter inside.

   Or, if you want to delete the letter, drag the icon to your Recycle Bin (described in the next section).

✔ Windows 98 is designed for you to work right on top of the desktop. From the desktop, you can create new things like files, folders, sounds, and graphics — just about anything. After working with your new file or folder, you can store it or delete it.

✔ You can store your favorite files and folders right on the desktop. Or, to be more organized, you can drag your files and folders into the folders listed in the My Computer window. (The My Computer program gets a lot more coverage in Chapter 11.)

✔ Are you confused about what something is supposed to do? Click it with your right mouse button, or simply rest the pointer over the confusing spot. Windows 98 often tosses up a menu listing just about everything you can do with that particular object. This trick works on many icons found on your desktop or throughout your programs.

✔ Is your desktop looking rather cluttered? Make Windows 98 line up the icons in orderly rows: Click the desktop with the right mouse button, point at the Arrange Icons option, and choose by Name from the menu.

Using the Recycle Bin

The Recycle Bin, that little wastebasket with green arrows in the upper-left corner of the desktop, is supposed to work like a *real* Recycle Bin — something you can fish the Sunday paper out of if somebody pitched the comics section before you had a chance to read it.

If you want to get rid of something in Windows 98 — a file or folder, for example — simply drag it to the Recycle Bin. Point at the file or folder's icon with the mouse and, while holding down the left mouse button, point at the Recycle Bin. Let go of the mouse button, and your detritus disappears. Windows 98 stuffs it into the Recycle Bin.

But if you want to bypass that cute metaphor, there's another way to delete stuff: Click your unwanted file or folder's icon with the right mouse button and choose <u>D</u>elete from the menu that pops up. Windows 98 asks cautiously if you're *sure* that you want to delete the icon. If you click the <u>Y</u>es button, Windows 98 dumps the icon into the Recycle Bin, just as if you'd dragged it there. Whoosh!

So if you like to "drag and drop," feel free to drag your garbage to the Recycle Bin and let go. If you prefer the menus, click with your right mouse button and choose <u>D</u>elete. Or if you like alternative lifestyles, click the unwanted icon with your left button and push your keyboard's Delete key. All three methods toss the file into the Recycle Bin, where it can be salvaged later or, eventually, purged for good.

Terribly boring desktop trivia

That's right — Windows 98 considers the desktop to be a mammoth folder. That mammoth folder opens across your screen when you start Windows 98, and it closes up when you shut down Windows 98 with the Start button's Sh<u>u</u>t Down command.

The Desktop folder hides inside your Windows folder. But if you want to see inside and poke it with a sharp stick, here's how to make it visible:

1. Open Windows Explorer.

2. From the Explorer's <u>V</u>iew menu, choose Folder <u>O</u>ptions.

3. Click the View tab along the menu's top.

4. Click the Show All Files button under the Hidden Files area.

5. Click the OK button.

6. Go to your Windows folder and look for the Desktop folder.

The once "invisible" files now show up on-screen in a ghostly gray. (And most of these files do Very Important Things, so you don't *really* want to poke them with a sharp stick.)

✔ Want to retrieve something you've deleted? Double-click the Recycle Bin icon, and a window appears, listing deleted items. See the name of your accidentally deleted icon? Then drag it to the desktop, point at the icon's name and, while holding down the left mouse button, point at the desktop. Let go of the mouse button, and the Recycle Bin coughs up the deleted item, good as new.

✔ Sometimes the Recycle Bin can get pretty full. If you're searching fruitlessly for a file you've recently deleted, tell the Recycle Bin to sort the filenames in the order in which they were deleted. Click View, point at Arrange Icons, and choose by Delete Date from the menu that pops out. Instead of listing the deleted files in alphabetical order, Recycle Bin now lists the most recently deleted files at the bottom.

✔ The Recycle Bin icon changes from an empty wastepaper basket to a full one as soon as it's holding a deleted file. You may have to squint a little to notice the pieces of paper sticking out of the trash can's top.

✔ A Recycle Bin can eat up 10 percent (or more) of your hard disk space. To free up some space, cut down on the amount of room it reserves for saving your deleted files. Click the Recycle Bin with your right mouse button and choose Properties from its menu. Normally, Recycle Bin waits until your deleted files consume 10 percent of your hard drive before it begins purging your oldest deleted files. If you want the Recycle Bin to hang on to more deleted files, increase the percentage. If you're a sure-fingered clicker who seldom makes mistakes, decrease the percentage.

Making a shortcut

Some people like to organize their desktop, putting a pencil sharpener on one corner and a box of Kleenex on the other corner. Other people like their Kleenex box in the top desk drawer. Microsoft knew that one desktop design could never please everybody, so Windows 98 lets people customize their desktops to suit individual tastes and needs.

For example, you may find yourself frequently copying files to a floppy disk in drive A. Normally, to perform that operation, you open the My Computer icon and drag your files to the drive A icon living in there. But there's a quicker way, and it's called a Windows 98 *shortcut*. A shortcut is simply a push button — an icon — that stands for something else.

For example, here's how to put a shortcut for drive A on your desktop:

1. **Double-click the desktop's My Computer icon.**

   The My Computer folder opens up, showing the icons for your disk drives as well as folders for your Control Panel and Printer. (My Computer gets more coverage in Chapter 11.)

2. **With your right mouse button, drag the drive A icon to the desktop.**

   Point at the drive A icon and, while holding down your right mouse button, point at the desktop, as shown in Figure 10-4. Let go of your mouse button.

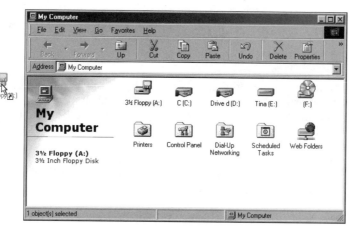

Figure 10-4:
Dragging the drive A icon to the desktop creates a shortcut.

3. **Choose Create Shortcut(s) Here from the menu.**

   Windows 98 puts an icon for drive A on your desktop, but it looks a little different from the drive A icon you dragged. Because it's only a shortcut — not the original icon — it has a little arrow in its corner.

That's it. Now you won't need to root through the My Computer or Explorer folders and programs to access drive A. The drive A shortcut on your desktop works just as well as the _real_ drive A icon found in My Computer and Explorer.

✔ Feel free to create desktop shortcuts for your most commonly accessed programs, files, or disk drives. Shortcuts are a quick way to make Windows 98 easier to use.

✔ If your newly dragged icon doesn't have an arrow in its bottom corner, don't let go of the mouse! You might not be making a shortcut. Instead, you've probably dragged the _real_ program to your desktop, and other programs may not be able to find it. Drag the icon back to where it was and try again. (You probably mistakenly held down the _left_ mouse button instead of the correct button — the _right_ button.)

✔ Have you grown tired of a shortcut? Feel free to delete it. Deleting a shortcut has no effect on the original file, folder, or program that it represents.

✔ You can make as many shortcuts as you'd like. You can even make several shortcuts for the same thing. For example, you can put a shortcut for drive A in _all_ your folders.

> ✔ Windows 98 shortcuts aren't very good at keeping track of moving files. If you create a shortcut to a file or program and then move the file or program to a different spot on your hard drive, the shortcut won't be able to find that file or program anymore.

Uh, what's the difference between a shortcut and an icon?

An icon for a file, folder, or program looks pretty much like a shortcut, except the shortcut has an arrow wedged in its lower reaches. And double-clicking on a shortcut and double-clicking on an icon do pretty much the same thing: start a program or load a file or folder.

But a shortcut is only a servant of sorts. When you double-click the shortcut, it runs over to the program, file, or folder that the shortcut represents and kick-starts that program, file, or folder into action.

You could do the same thing yourself by rummaging through your computer's folders, finding the program, file, or folder you're after, and personally double-clicking on its icon to bring it to life. But it's often more convenient to create a shortcut so that you don't have to rummage so much.

> ✔ If you delete a shortcut — the icon with the little arrow — you're not doing any real harm. You're just firing the servant that fetched things for you, probably creating more work for yourself in the process.
>
> ✔ If you accidentally delete a shortcut, you can pull it out of the Recycle Bin, just like anything else that's deleted in Windows 98.

The Start Button's Reason to Live

The Start button lives on your taskbar, and it's always ready for action. By using the Start button, you can start programs, adjust the Windows 98 settings, find help for sticky situations, or, thankfully, shut down Windows 98 and get away from the computer for a while.

The little Start button is so eager to please, in fact, that it starts shooting out menus full of options as soon as you click it. Just click the button once, and the first layer of menus pops out, as shown in Figure 10-5.

Figure 10-5:
Click the
taskbar's
Start button
to see a list
of options.

The explosive Table 10-1 shows what the different parts of the Start button
do when you point at them.

Table 10-1	The Start Button
This Part	*Does This When You Point at It*
Windows Update	After joining the Internet and registering Windows 98, you can let somebody else play mechanic. Click here and Windows 98 automatically bellies up to a special Microsoft Web site, analyzes itself, and installs any updated software that may help it run better.
Show Desktop	A handy new button for Windows 98: Click here to minimize all your open windows so that you can see your desktop.
Programs	Probably the most-used spot. Point here, and a second menu appears, listing available programs and folders containing related programs.
Favorites	Favorites lists bunches of places Microsoft wants you to visit on the Internet. (Dare I say the word, "Commercial?")
Documents	Point here to see the names of the last 15 files you've played with. Spot one you want to open again? Click its name to reopen it. *Warning:* Some programs shirk their responsibility and don't list their files here.

(continued)

Table 10-1 *(continued)*

This Part	Does This When You Point at It
🔧 Settings ▶	Allows access to the Control Panel and Printer settings, as well as ways to customize the Start button menus and taskbar.
🔍 Find ▶	Lost a program or file? Head here to make Windows 98 search for it.
❓	Clicking here brings up the Windows 98 Help menu.
🏃 Run...	Used mostly by old-school, "stick-shift" computer users, it lets you start a program by typing the program's name and *path*.
🔑 Log Off Andy Rathbone...	Click here if you're nice enough to log off and let somebody else use your computer.
🖥 Shut Down...	Click here to either shut down and restart Windows or shut it down for the day.
▣ Start	Clicking the Start button makes the Start menu shoot out of the button's head.

✔ The Start button menu changes as you add programs to your computer. That change means that the Start button on your friend's computer probably offers slightly different menus than the ones on your own computer.

✔ See the little arrows on the menu next to the words Programs, Documents, Settings, and Find? The arrows mean that when you point at those words, another menu pops up, offering more-detailed options.

✔ Need to open a file yet another time? Before you spend time clicking your way through folders, see if it's listed under the Start button's Documents area. You can often find your past 15 documents listed there, ready to be opened with a click.

Starting a program from the Start button

This one's easy. Click the Start button and when the menu pops out of the button's head, point at the word Programs. Yet another menu pops up, this one listing the names of programs or folders full of programs.

If you see your program listed, click the name. Wham! Windows 98 kicks that program to the screen. If you don't see your program listed, try pointing at the folders listed on the menu. New menus fly out of those folders, listing even more programs.

When you spot your program's name, just click it. In fact, you don't have to click until you see the program's name: The Start button opens and closes all the menus automatically, depending on where the mouse arrow is pointing at the time.

> ✔ Still don't see your program listed by name? Then head for Chapter 7 and find the section on finding lost files and folders. You can tell Windows 98 to find your program for you.
>
> ✔ There's another way to load a program that's not listed — if you know where the program's living on your hard drive. Choose Run from the Start button menu, type the program's name, and press Enter. If Windows 98 finds the program, it runs it. If it can't find the program, though, click the Browse button. Shazam! Yet another box appears, this time listing programs by name. Pick your way through the dialog box until you see your program; then double-click its name and click the OK button to load it.
>
> ✔ If you don't know how to *pick your way through* this particular dialog box, head to the section of Chapter 5 on opening a file. (This particular dialog box rears its head every time you load or save a file or open a program.)

Adding a program to the Start button

The Windows 98 Start button works great — until you're hankering for something that's not listed on the menu. How do you add things to the Start button's menu?

If you're installing a Windows program that comes with its own installation program, breathe a sigh of relief. Those programs automatically put themselves on the Start button menu. But what if your program comes from a simpler household and doesn't have an installation program? Well, it means more work for you, as described here:

1. **Install the program.**

   Install the program, whether you acquired it from the Internet, a compact disc, or a floppy disk. (Double-click the Control Panel's Add/Remove Programs icon to install a program, a process described in Chapter 9.) Hit Chapter 11 if you're a little sketchy about creating folders and copying files.

2. **Click the Start button and then point at Settings.**

   A menu shoots out from the right side of the Start menu.

3. **Click Taskbar & Start Menu and then click the Start Menu Programs tab.**

   The tab lurks along the top, on the right side.

4. **Click the Add button and then click Browse.**

   A new box pops up, as shown in Figure 10-6.

Figure 10-6:
Double-click
a folder, and
the Browse
box lists the
programs
inside that
folder.

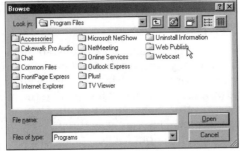

Click the folder where the program and its files live. (The installation program usually mentioned speedily where it was copying the program's files.)

Hint: If you can't find that folder, click the icon of the little folder with the arrow inside, up near the top. That click tells Windows 98 to work its way up the folder listings, eventually showing you a list of your computer's disk drives.

5. **Double-click the icon of the program you want to add.**

   The program's filename appears in the Command line box. (By double-clicking the program's name, you were able to avoid typing the name yourself.)

6. **Click the Next button and then double-click the folder where you want your program to appear on the Start menu.**

   For example, if you want your new program to appear under the Programs heading, simply click the Programs folder.

7. **Type the name that you want to see on the menu for that program and then click the Finish button.**

   Most people just type the program's name. (Just as many people have nicknames, most program's filenames are different from their *real* names. For example, you'd probably want to change WP — the filename — to WordPerfect — the program's real name.)

8. Click the OK button at the bottom of the box.

That click gets rid of the Taskbar Properties box and *really* finishes the job. Now, when you click the Start button, you see your new program listed on the menu.

✔ Windows 98 lets you add programs to the Start menu in several ways. The one I just listed is probably the easiest one to follow step by step.

✔ To get rid of unwanted menu items, follow these steps but click the Remove button rather than the Add button in Step 4.

✔ Just like your Windows 98 desktop, the Start menu is really just a plain old folder. The folder is a directory called Start Menu, and it lives in the folder where Windows 98 is installed, usually Windows on your C drive. Any program shortcuts that you put in the Start Menu folder appear as items on the Start menu. Also, to rearrange the items on the menu, rearrange the folders in the Start Menu folder.

Shutting down Windows 98

Although the big argument used to be about saturated and unsaturated fats, today's generation has found a new source of disagreement: Should a computer be left on all the time or turned off at the end of the day? Both camps have decent arguments, and there's no real answer (except that you should always turn off your monitor when you won't be using it for a half hour or so).

However, if you decide to turn off your computer, don't just head for the off switch. First, you need to tell Windows 98 about your plans.

A quicker but dirtier way to add programs to the Start menu

There's a quicker way to add a program to the Start menu, but it's not as versatile. The steps listed let you add a program's icon anyplace on the menu. But if you simply want the program's icon on the menu *now,* and you don't care about location, try this:

Open the My Computer or Explorer program and find the folder containing your program. Then drag the program's icon over to the Start button and let go. Point at the program and, while holding down the mouse button, point at the Start button. When the icon hovers over the Start button, let go of the mouse button.

Now, when you click the Start button, you see your newly installed program's icon at the very top.

To do that, click the Sh<u>u</u>t Down command from the Start menu and then click the <u>S</u>hut down button from the box that appears. Finally, click the <u>Y</u>es button; that click tells Windows 98 to put away all your programs and to make sure that you've saved all your important files.

After Windows 98 has prepared the computer to be turned off, you see a message on the screen saying that it's okay to reach for the Big Switch.

✔ If Windows 98 is acting weird — or if Windows 98 tells you to shut down and restart your computer — click the Sh<u>u</u>t Down command from the Start menu. However, choose the <u>R</u>estart option from the box. Windows 98 saves all your files, shuts itself down, and comes back to life, ready for more work.

✔ Don't turn off your computer unless you've first used the Sh<u>u</u>t Down command from the Start button. Windows 98 needs to prepare itself for the shutdown, or it may accidentally eat some of your important information.

Making Windows Start Programs Automatically

Many people sit down at a computer, turn it on, and go through the same mechanical process of loading their oft-used programs. Believe it or not, Windows 98 can automate this computerized task.

The solution is the StartUp folder, found lurking in the Start button's <u>P</u>rograms menu. When Windows 98 wakes up, it peeks inside that StartUp folder. If it finds a shortcut lurking, it grabs that shortcut's program and tosses it onto the screen.

Here's how to determine which programs wake up along with Windows 98 and which ones get to sleep in a little.

1. **Click the Start button with your *right* mouse button and choose the <u>O</u>pen option.**

   Feel free to choose the <u>E</u>xplore option if you prefer using Windows Explorer; either program does the trick. Your file comes to the screen and displays part of the goodies in your Start menu.

2. **Double-click the folder named Programs.**

   You see shortcuts and folders for all the programs currently listed in your Start button's <u>P</u>rograms area.

3. **Double-click the folder named StartUp to open it onto your screen.**

4. **Drag and drop any programs you want to start automatically into the StartUp window.**

   Windows 98 automatically turns the program's icons into shortcuts. And whenever you start Windows 98 from scratch, those programs load up right along with it.

✔ Do you find yourself using the StartUp area a lot? Make a Shortcut that points straight toward it and leave the Shortcut on your desktop. A drag and a drop onto your StartUp shortcut puts an oft-used program into the Start menu's automatic StartUp area.

✔ You decide which programs start up when Windows 98 does by dragging and dropping files and shortcuts in and out of the StartUp folder.

✔ Don't want Windows 98 to automatically start one of those programs in the StartUp folder? Then wait until you see the Windows 98 logo on-screen and hold down the Shift key. Keep holding down Shift until Windows 98 finishes loading and let go — the StartUp programs will stay seated.

The Taskbar

Put a second or third window onto the Windows 98 desktop, and you'll immediately see the Big Problem: Windows and programs tend to cover each other up, making them difficult to locate.

The solution is the taskbar. Shown in Figure 10-7, the taskbar is that little bar running along the bottom edge of your screen.

Figure 10-7:
The taskbar
lists the
names
of all your
currently
running
programs
and open
folders.

The taskbar keeps track of all the open folders and currently running programs by listing their names. And, luckily, the taskbar is almost always visible, no matter how cluttered your desktop becomes.

✓ When you want to bring a program, file, or folder to the forefront of the screen, click its name on the taskbar.

✓ If the taskbar *does* manage to disappear, press Ctrl+Esc; that action usually pops it up on the surface.

✓ If you can only see part of the taskbar — it's hanging off the edge of the screen, for example — point at the edge you can see. When the mouse pointer turns into a two-headed arrow, hold down your mouse button and move the mouse to drag the taskbar back into view.

✓ If the taskbar looks too bloated, try the same trick. Point at its edge until the mouse pointer turns into a two-headed arrow and then drag the taskbar's edge inward until it's the right size.

Clicking the taskbar's sensitive areas

Like a crafty card player, the taskbar comes with a few tips and tricks. For one thing, it has the Start button. With a click on the Start button, you can launch programs, change settings, find programs, get help, and order pizza. (Well, you can't order pizza, but you can do all the things mentioned in the Start button section earlier in this chapter.)

But the Start button is only one of the taskbar's tricks; some others are listed in Figure 10-8.

Clicking the Start button brings up the Start menu, described earlier in this chapter. Also, hold the mouse pointer over the clock, and Windows 98 shows the current day and date. Or, if you want to change the time or date, a double-click on the clock summons the Windows 98 time/date change program.

If you have a sound card, click the little speaker to bring up the volume control, as shown in Figure 10-9. Slide the volume knob up for louder sound; slide it down for peace and quiet. (Or click the Mute box to turn the sound off completely.)

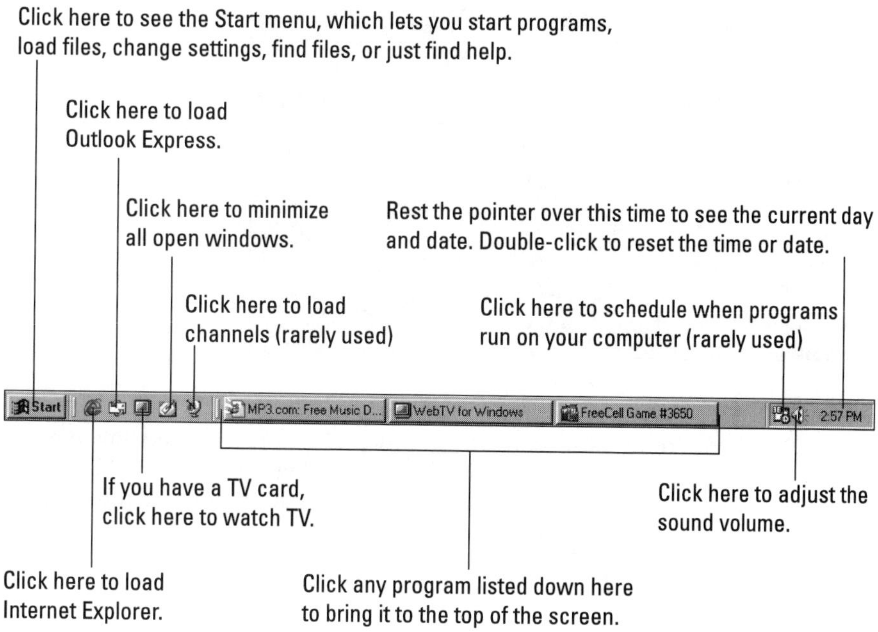

Click here to see the Start menu, which lets you start programs, load files, change settings, find files, or just find help.
Click here to load Outlook Express.
Click here to minimize all open windows.
Rest the pointer over this time to see the current day and date. Double-click to reset the time or date.
Click here to load channels (rarely used)
Click here to schedule when programs run on your computer (rarely used)
Start
MP3.com: Free Music D...
WebTV for Windows
FreeCell Game #3650
2:57 PM
If you have a TV card, click here to watch TV.
Click here to adjust the sound volume.
Click here to load Internet Explorer.
Click any program listed down here to bring it to the top of the screen.

Figure 10-8: Clicking or double-clicking in these areas on the taskbar performs these tasks.

Volume
Mute
Volume
1:53 AM

Figure 10-9: Clicking the little speaker lets you adjust the sound card's volume.

Double-click the little speaker to bring up a more advanced mixer program, as shown in Figure 10-10, if your sound card offers that feature. Mixers let you adjust volume levels for your microphone, line inputs, CD players, and other features.

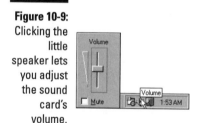

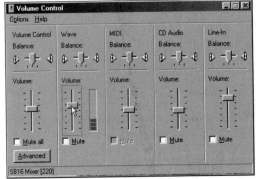

Figure 10-10:
Double-clicking the little speaker brings up a mixer program for the sound card.

If you're running a modem, a tiny picture of two cable-linked computers appears next to the clock, as shown in Figure 10-11. Double-click the picture to see statistics on the amount of data your modem is pushing and pulling over the phone lines.

Figure 10-11:
Double-click the little cable-linked computer picture for statistics on your modem's performance.

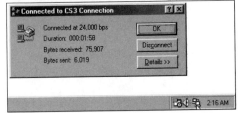

✔ Other icons often appear next to the clock, depending on what Windows 98 is up to. If you're printing, for example, you see a little printer down there. Laptops sometimes show a battery monitor. As with all the other icons, if you double-click the printer or battery monitor, Windows 98 brings up information about the printer's or battery's status.

✔ Want to minimize all your desktop's open windows in a hurry? Click a blank part of the taskbar with your right mouse button and choose the Minimize All Windows option from the pop-up menu. All the programs keep running, but they're now minimized to icons along the taskbar. To bring them back to the screen, just click their names from the taskbar.

✔ To organize your open windows, click a blank part of the taskbar with your right mouse button and choose one of the tile commands. Windows 98 scoops up all your open windows and lays them back down in neat, orderly squares.

Customizing the taskbar

Although Windows 98 starts the taskbar along the bottom of the screen, it doesn't have to stay there. If you prefer that your taskbar hang from the top of your screen like a bat, just drag it there. Point at a blank spot of the taskbar and, while holding down your mouse button, point at the top of the screen. Let go of the mouse button, and the taskbar dangles from the roof, as shown in Figure 10-12.

Do you prefer the taskbar along one side? Drag it there, as shown in Figure 10-13. (The buttons become more difficult to read, however.)

If the taskbar is starting to look too crowded, you can make it wider by dragging its edges outward, as shown in Figure 10-14.

Figure 10-12:
You can move the taskbar to any side of the screen by dragging it there.

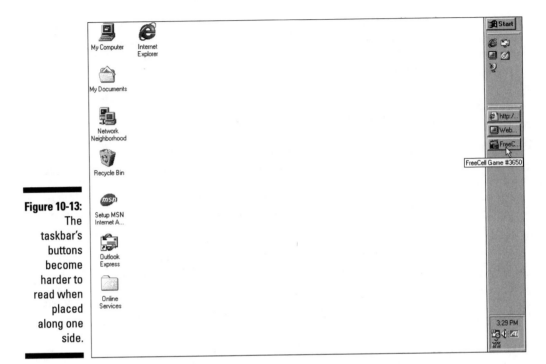

Figure 10-13:
The taskbar's buttons become harder to read when placed along one side.

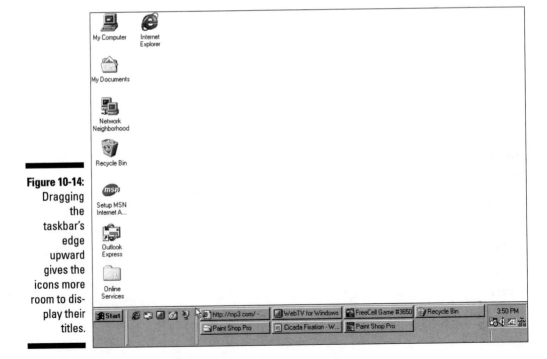

Figure 10-14:
Dragging the taskbar's edge upward gives the icons more room to display their titles.

✔ To change other taskbar options, click a bare taskbar area with your right mouse button and choose Properties from the pop-up menu. From there, you can make the taskbar always stay on top of the current pile of windows, make the taskbar automatically hide itself, hide the clock, and shrink the Start menu icons. Whenever you click an option button, a handy on-screen picture previews the change. If the change looks good, click the OK button to save it.

✔ If you're using two or more monitors with your computer, go wild! You can drag the taskbar to the edge of any of your monitors. It can dangle from the top, line the bottom, or stick to the side of any monitor attached to your computer.

✔ Feel free to experiment with the taskbar, changing its size and position until it looks right for you. It won't break.

Controlling the Printer

Many of the Windows 98 features work in the background. You know that they're there *only* when something is wrong and weird messages start flying around. The Windows 98 print program is one of those programs.

When you choose the Print command in a program, you may see the little Windows 98 printer icon appear at the bottom corner of your screen. When your printer stops spitting out pages, the little printer icon disappears.

Your printer can print only one thing at a time. If you try to print a second memo before the first one is finished, Windows 98 jumps in to help. It intercepts all the requests and lines them up in order, just like a harried diner cook.

To check up on what is being sent to the printer, double-click the taskbar's little printer icon and you see the print program in all its glory, as shown in Figure 10-15.

Figure 10-15:
After telling
a program
to print a file
or two,
double-click
the little
printer icon
along the
bottom edge
of the
taskbar to
see a list of
files waiting
to be
printed.

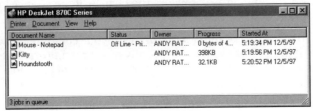

✔ When the printer is through with Mouse, it moves to the second file in the lineup, which, in this case, is Kitty.

✔ Changing the order of the files as they're about to be printed is easy. For example, to scoot Houndstooth ahead of Kitty, click its name and hold down the mouse button. Then *drag* the file up so that it cuts in front of Kitty. Release the button, and the Print Manager changes the printing order. (The printing order is called a *queue,* pronounced *Q.*)

✔ To cancel a print job, click the filename you don't like with your right mouse button and then choose Cancel Printing from the menu that pops up.

✔ If the boss is walking by the printer while you're printing your party flier, choose Document from the menu and select Pause Printing from the menu that drops down. The printer stops. After the boss is out of sight, click Pause Printing again to continue.

✔ If you're on a network (shudder), you may not be able to change the order in which files are being printed. You may not even be able to pause a file.

✔ If your printer is not hooked up, Windows 98 will probably try to send your file to the printer anyway. When it doesn't get a response, it sends you a message that your printer isn't ready. Plug the printer in, turn it on, and try again. Or hit Chapter 14 for more printer troubleshooting tips.

Chapter 11

Those Scary Windows Explorer and My Computer Programs

*T*he Windows Explorer program is where people wake up from the computing dream, clutching a pillow in horror. These people bought a computer to make their work easier to accomplish — to banish that awful filing cabinet with squeaky drawers.

But open Windows 98 Explorer, and that filing cabinet reappears. Folders, dozens of them. And where did that file go? The My Computer program is a little more visually appealing, but it's still awkward.

This chapter explains how to use the Windows Explorer and My Computer programs, and, along the way, it dishes out a big enough dose of Windows file management for you to get your work done. Here you'll find out the wacky Windows way to create folders, put files inside, and move everything around with a mere mouse.

Why Is Windows Explorer So Scary?

Windows Explorer combines two wildly different worlds: A heavy file cabinet and Windows software. It's as if somebody tried to combine an automobile with a bathtub. Everybody's confused when the door opens and water pours out.

To see what the fuss is about, click a folder with your right mouse button and, when the little menu pops out, choose the Explore option.

Everybody organizes his or her computer differently. Some people don't organize their computers at all. So your Windows Explorer window probably looks a little different from the one shown in Figure 11-1.

Figure 11-1:
You use the
Windows
Explorer to
print, copy,
move,
rename, and
delete files.

Like Windows Explorer, the My Computer program, shown in Figure 11-2, lets you sling files around, but in a slightly different way. The My Computer program is a big panel of buttons — sort of an extension of your desktop — and Windows Explorer is a big panel of filenames with buttons on the right. In fact, some people like the Windows Explorer *text-based* system of names better than the My Computer *picture-based* system. (It's that right-brained versus left-brained stuff.)

Figure 11-2:
The My
Computer
program
performs
the same
tasks as
Windows
Explorer, but
in slightly
different
ways.

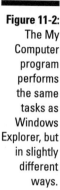

Coming to Windows 98 from Windows 3.1? The icons in the Windows 3.1 Program Manager are just buttons that stand for your programs. Deleting them doesn't harm the actual program. That's not true with the Windows 98 My Computer program. Unless the icon you're deleting has a little arrow lodged in its lower-left side, that icon is an actual program or file. Make sure that you're deleting the icon you want. (And if you goof and delete the wrong one, fish it back out of the Recycle Bin as soon as possible.)

✔ Although they both end in the word Explorer, the *Windows Explorer* program is completely different from the *Internet Explorer* program. Windows Explorer lets you fiddle with the files stored inside your computer. Internet Explorer, on the other hand, lets you connect to other computers through the phone lines, swapping information through the Internet and World Wide Web.

✔ In a way, learning how to deal with files is like learning how to play the piano: Neither is intuitively obvious, and you hit some bad notes with both. Don't be frustrated if you don't seem to be getting the hang of it. Liberace would have hated file management at first, too.

Getting the Lowdown on Folders

This stuff is really boring, but if you don't read it, you'll be just as lost as your files.

A *folder* is a workplace on a disk. Hard drives are divided into many folders to separate your many projects. You can work with a spreadsheet, for example, without having all the word-processing files get in the way.

Any disk can have folders, but hard drives need them the most because they need a way to organize their thousands of files. By dividing a hard drive into little folder compartments, you can more easily see where everything sits.

The Windows Explorer and My Computer programs enable you to probe into different folders and peek at the files you've stuffed inside each one. It's a pretty good organizational scheme, actually. Socks never fall behind a folder and jam the drawer.

Folders used to be called *directories* and *subdirectories*. But some people were getting used to that, so the industry switched to the term *folders*.

✔ Folders can be inside folders to add a deeper level of organization, like adding drawer partitions to sort your socks by color. Each sock color partition is a smaller, organizing folder of the larger sock-drawer folder.

✔ Of course, you can ignore folders and keep all your files right on the Windows 98 desktop. That's like tossing everything into the backseat of the car and pawing around to find your tissue box a month later. Stuff that you organized is a lot easier to find.

✔ If you're eager to create a folder or two (and it's pretty easy), page ahead to this chapter's "Creating a Folder" section.

✔ Windows created several folders when it installed itself on your computer. It created a Windows folder to hold most of its programs and a bunch of folders inside that to hold its internal engine parts.

✔ Just as manila folders come from trees, computer folders use a *tree metaphor,* shown in Figure 11-3, as they branch out from one main folder to several smaller folders.

Figure 11-3:
The structure of folders inside your computer is treelike, with main folders branching out to smaller folders.

What's all this path stuff?

Sometimes Windows 98 can't find a file, even if it's sitting right there on the hard disk. You have to tell Windows where the file is sitting — a process called *browsing* — and to do that, you need to know that file's path.

A path is like the file's address. When heading for your house, a letter moves to your country, state, city, street, and finally, hopefully, your apartment or house number. A computer path does the same thing. It starts with the letter of the disk drive and ends with the name of the file. In between, the path lists all the folders the computer must travel through to reach the file.

For example, look at the Sounds folder in Figure 11-3. For Windows 98 to find a file stored there, it starts from the C:\ folder, travels through the Games folder, and then goes through the Golf folder. Only then does it reach the Sounds folder.

Take a deep breath. Exhale. Quack like a duck, if you like. Now, the C in C:\ stands for disk drive C. (In the path, a disk drive letter is always followed by a colon.) The disk drive letter and colon make up the first part of the path. All the other folders are inside the big C: folder, so they're listed after the C: part. Windows separates these nested folders with something called a backslash, or \. The name of the actual file — let's say GRUNT.WAV — comes last.

C:\GAMES\GOLF\SOUNDS\GRUNT.WAV is what you get when you put it all together, and that's the official path of the GRUNT.WAV file in the Sounds folder.

This stuff can be tricky, so here it is again: The letter for the drive comes first, followed by a colon and a backslash. Then come the names of all the folders, separated by backslashes. Last comes the name of the file (with no backslash after it).

When you click folders, Windows 98 puts together the path for you. Thankfully.

Peering into Your Drives and Folders

Knowing all this folder stuff can impress the people at the computer store. But what counts is knowing how to use the Windows Explorer and My Computer programs to get to a file you want. Never fear. Just read on.

Seeing the files on a disk drive

Like everything else in Windows 98, disk drives are represented by buttons, or icons:

3½ Floppy (A:)   Rhett (C:)   Alice (D:)   (E:)

Those disk drive buttons live in both the Windows Explorer and My Computer programs (although the ones in Windows Explorer are usually smaller). See the little disks above the icons labeled *Floppy?* Those are pictures of the types of floppy disks that fit into those drives. You see a compact disc floating above drive E:. Double-clicking that compact disc icon shows you what's currently in your compact disc drive. Hard drives don't have anything hovering over them except a nagging suspicion that they'll fail horribly at the worst moment.

- ✔ If you're kinda sketchy on those disk drive things, you probably skipped Chapter 2. Trot back there for a refresher.

- ✔ Double-click a drive icon in My Computer, and a window comes up to display the drive's contents. For example, put a disk in drive A and double-click the My Computer's drive A icon. A new window leaps up, showing what files and folders live on the disk in drive A.

- ✔ Click a drive icon in Windows Explorer, and you see the drive contents on the right side of the window.

- ✔ A second window comes in handy when you want to move or copy files from one folder or drive to another, as discussed in the "Copying or Moving a File" section of this chapter.

- ✔ The first two icons stand for the floppy drives, drive A and drive B. If you click a floppy drive icon when no disk is in the drive, Windows 98 stops you gently, suggesting that you insert a disk before proceeding further.

- ✔ Spot an icon called Network Neighborhood? That's a little doorway for peering into other computers linked to your computer — if there are any. You find more network stuff near the end of this chapter.

Seeing what's inside folders

Because folders are really little storage compartments, Windows 98 uses a picture of a little folder to stand for each separate place for storing files.

To see what's inside a folder, in My Computer or on the desktop, just double-click that folder's picture. A new window pops up, showing that folder's contents.

Folder opening works differently in Windows Explorer. In Windows Explorer, folders line up along the left side of a window. One folder, the one you're currently exploring, has a little box around its name.

The files living inside that particular folder appear on the right side of the window. The arrangement looks somewhat like Figure 11-4.

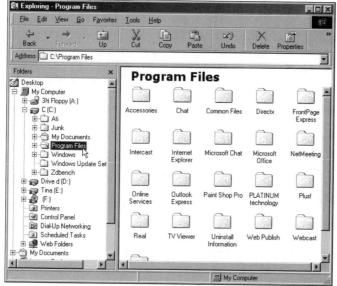

Figure 11-4:
When you
click a
folder on the
left side of
Windows
Explorer,
that folder's
contents
appear on
the right
side of the
window.

To peek inside a folder while in Windows Explorer, click its name on the left side of the window. You see two things: That folder's next level of folders (if it has one) appears beneath it on the left side of the window, and that folder's filenames spill out into the right side of the window.

- ✔ As you keep climbing farther out on a branch and more folders appear, you're moving toward further levels of organization. If you climb back inward, you reach files and folders that have less in common.

- ✔ Yeah, this stuff is really confusing, but keep one thing in mind: Don't be afraid to double-click, or even single-click, a folder just to see what happens. Clicking folders just changes your viewpoint; nothing dreadful happens, and no tax receipts fall onto the floor. You're just opening and closing file cabinet drawers, harmlessly peeking into folders along the way.

- ✔ To climb farther out on the branches of folders, keep double-clicking new folders as they appear.

- ✔ To move back up the branches in Windows Explorer, double-click a folder closer to the left side of the window. Any folders to the right and beneath that folder are now hidden from view.

- ✔ Sometimes a folder contains too many files to fit in the window. To see more files, click that window's scroll bars. What's a scroll bar? Time to whip out your field guide, Chapter 5.

While in Windows Explorer, move the mouse pointer over the bar separating a folder on the left from its filenames on the right. When the pointer turns into a mutant two-headed arrow, hold down the mouse button. Then move the bar to the left to give the filenames more room, or to the right to give the folders on the left more room. Let go of the mouse when the split is adjusted correctly, and the window reshapes itself to the new dimensions.

Using a Microsoft IntelliMouse, the kind with the little wheel embedded in the mouse's neck? Point at the list of folders in Explorer, and spin the little wheel; the list moves up or down as you spin the wheel.

Can't find a file or folder? Instead of rummaging through folders, check out the Find command described in Chapter 7. It's the fastest way to find files and folders that were "there just a moment ago."

Loading a Program or File

A *file* is a collection of information on a disk. Files come in two basic types: program files and data files.

Program files contain instructions that tell the computer to do something: balance the national budget or ferret out a fax number.

Data files contain information created with a program, as opposed to computer instructions. If you write a letter to the grocer complaining about his soggy apricots, you're creating a data file.

To open either kind of file in Windows 98, double-click its name. Double-clicking a program file's name brings the program to life to the screen, whether you found the filename listed in My Computer, Windows Explorer, or even the Find program. If you double-click a data file, Windows 98 loads the file *and* the program that created it. Then it brings both the file and the program to the screen at the same time.

Running Windows 98 in the Web mode? Then a single-click does the trick: Point at the file or program to highlight it and then click it to bring it to life. (If that doesn't bring it to life, try a double-click, because you're not running in Web mode.)

✔ Windows 98 sticks little icons next to filenames so that you know whether they're program or data files. In fact, even folders get their own icons so that you won't confuse them with files. Chapter 20, at the tail end of the book, provides a handy reference for figuring out which icon is which.

Don't bother reading this hidden technical stuff

Sometimes programs store information in a data file. They may need to store information about the way the computer is set up, for example. To keep people from thinking that those files are trash and deleting them, the program hides those files.

You can view the names of these hidden files and folders, however, if you want to play voyeur. Choose View from My Computer or Explorer program's menu bar and then choose Folder

Options from the pull-down menu. Select the View tab from along the menu's top, and click the Show all files button under the Hidden files option.

Click the OK button, and the formerly hidden files appear alongside the other filenames. Be sure not to delete them, however: The programs that created them will gag, possibly damaging other files.

✔ Because of some bizarre New School of Computing mandate, any data file that Windows recognizes is called a *document*. A document doesn't have to contain words; it can have pictures of worms or sounds of hungry animals.

If the program or folder you're after is already highlighted, just give the Enter key a satisfying little pound with your index finger. That not only opens the program or folder, but it also shows you how many different ways Windows 98 lets you do things (which means that you don't need to worry about knowing them all).

Deleting and Undeleting Files and Folders

Sooner or later, you'll want to delete a file that's not important anymore — yesterday's lottery picks, for example, or something you've stumbled on that's too embarrassing to save any longer. But then, hey, suddenly you realize that you've made a mistake and deleted the wrong file. Not to worry: The Windows 98 Recycle Bin can probably resurrect that deleted file if you're quick enough — and your file wasn't on a floppy disk.

Getting rid of a file or folder

To permanently remove a file from the hard drive, click its name. Then press Delete. This surprisingly simple trick works for files and even folders.

The Delete key deletes entire folders, as well as any folders inside them. Make sure that you've selected the right file before you press Delete.

 ✔ When you press Delete, Windows tosses a box in your face, asking whether you're sure. If you are, click the Yes button.

 ✔ Be extra sure that you know what you're doing when deleting any file that has pictures of little "gears" in its icon. These files are sometimes sensitive hidden files, and the computer wants you to leave them alone. (Other than that, they're not particularly exciting, despite the action-oriented gears.)

 ✔ As soon as you find out how to delete files, you'll want to read the very next section, "How to undelete a file."

Deleting a shortcut from the desktop, My Computer, or Windows Explorer just deletes a button that loads a program. You can always put the button back on. Deleting an icon that doesn't have the little shortcut arrow removes that *file* from the hard disk and puts it into the Recycle Bin, where it eventually disappears.

How to undelete a file

Sooner or later, your finger will push the Delete key at the wrong time, and you'll delete the wrong file. A slip of the finger, the wrong nudge of a mouse, or, if you're in southern California, a small earthquake at the wrong time can make a file disappear. Zap!

Scream! When the tremors subside, double-click the Recycle Bin, and the Recycle Bin box drops down from the heavens, as shown in Figure 11-5.

The files listed in the Recycle Bin can be brought back to life simply by dragging them out of the Recycle Bin box: Use the mouse to point at the name of the file you want to retrieve and, while holding down the mouse button, point at the desktop. Then let go of the mouse. Windows 98 moves the once-deleted file out of the Recycle Bin and places the newly revived file onto your desktop.

 ✔ After the file's on your desktop, it's as good as new. Feel free to store it in any other file for safekeeping. Want to return it to its original location? Don't drag it from the Recycle Bin. Instead, right-click on it and choose Restore.

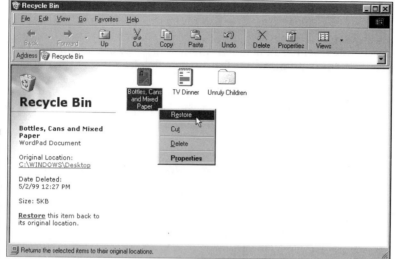

Figure 11-5:
The Recycle
Bin drops
down from
the heavens
to save the
day.

TIP

✔ Unfortunately, the Recycle Bin only holds files deleted by Windows 98 and Windows 95 programs. Windows 3.1 programs delete their files permanently. (Files deleted through the Start button's Run program and through Networked computers bypass the Recycle Bin, too.)

✔ Don't expect to find programs deleted from your floppy disks or computer networks, either. (You can find other programs for undeleting files from disks at the software store, fortunately.)

✔ The Recycle Bin normally holds about 10 percent of your hard disk's space. For example, if your hard drive is 8GB, the Recycle Bin holds onto 800MB of deleted files. When it reaches that limit, it starts deleting the oldest files to make room for the incoming deleted files. (And the old ones are gone for good, too.)

Copying or Moving a File

To copy or move files to different folders on your hard drive, use your mouse to *drag* them there. For example, here's how to move a file to a different folder on your hard drive:

1. **Move the mouse pointer until it hovers over the file you want to move, and then press and hold down the mouse button.**

2. **While holding down the mouse button, use the mouse to point at the folder to which you'd like to move the file.**

The trick is to hold down the mouse button the whole time. When you move the mouse, its arrow drags the file along with it. For example, Figure 11-6 shows how Windows Explorer looks when I drag the Traveler file from the Junk folder on my D drive to my Junk folder on my C drive. (The contents of the D drive's Junk folder are on the right.)

3. **Release the mouse button.**

   When the mouse arrow hovers over the place to which you want to move the file, take your finger off the mouse button.

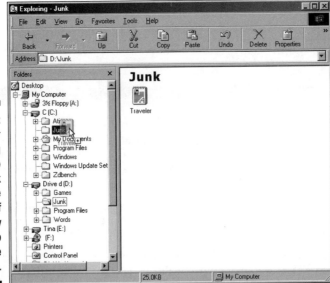

Figure 11-6: The Traveler file is being dragged to the Junk folder on the left side of the window in order to move the file there.

Moving a file by dragging its name is pretty easy, actually. The hard part often comes when you try to put the file and its destination on-screen at the same time. You often need to use both Windows Explorer and My Computer to put two windows on-screen. When you can see the file and its destination, start dragging.

Both Windows Explorer and My Computer do something awfully dumb to confuse people, however: When you drag a file from one folder to another on the same drive, you *move* the file. When you drag a file from one folder to another on a different drive, you *copy* that file.

I swear I didn't make up these rules. And the process gets more complicated: You can click the file and hold down Shift to reverse the rules. Table 11-1 can help you keep these oafish oddities from getting too far out of control.

Table 11-1	Moving Files Around
To Do This . . .	*. . . Do This*
Copy a file to another location on the same disk drive	Hold down Ctrl and drag it.
Copy a file to a different disk drive	Drag it there.
Move a file to another location on the same disk drive	Drag it there.
Move a file to a different disk drive	Hold down Shift and drag it there.
Make a shortcut while dragging a file	Hold down Ctrl+Shift and drag it there.
Remember these obtuse commands	Refer to the handy Cheat Sheet at the front of this book.

Here's an easy way to remember this stuff when this book's not handy: Always drag icons while holding down the *right* mouse button. Windows 98 is then gracious enough to give you a menu of options when you position the icon, and you can choose among moving, copying, or creating a shortcut.

✔ To copy or move files to a floppy disk, drag those files to the icon for that floppy disk, which you should find along the top of the Windows Explorer window.

✔ When you drag a file someplace in Windows 98, look at the icon attached to the mouse pointer. If the document icon has a *plus sign* in it, you're *copying* the file. If the document icon is *blank,* you're *moving* the file. Depending on where you are dragging the file, pressing Ctrl or Shift toggles the plus sign on or off, making it easier to see whether you're currently copying or moving the file.

✔ After you run a program's installation program to put the program on your hard drive, don't move the program around. An installation program often wedges a program into Windows pretty handily; if you move the program, it may not work anymore and you'll have to reinstall it.

Selecting More Than One File or Folder

Windows 98 lets you grab an armful of files and folders at one swipe; you don't always have to piddle around, dragging one item at a time.

To pluck several files and folders from a list, hold down Ctrl when you click the names. Each name stays highlighted when you click the next name.

To gather several files or folders sitting next to each other, click the first one. Then hold down the Shift key as you click the last one. Those two items are highlighted, along with every file and folder between them.

Windows 98 lets you *lasso* files and folders, as well. Point slightly above the first file or folder you want; then, while holding down the mouse button, point at the last file or folder. The mouse creates a lasso to surround your files. Let go of the mouse button, and the lasso disappears, leaving all the surrounded files highlighted.

- ✔ You can drag these armfuls of files in the same way as you drag one.

- ✔ You can delete these armfuls, too.

- ✔ You can't rename an armful of files all at once. To rename them, you have to go back to piddling around with one file at a time.

Renaming a File or Folder

Sick of a file or folder's name? Then change it. Just click the offending icon with your right mouse button and choose Rename from the menu that pops up.

The old filename gets highlighted and then disappears when you start typing the file or folder's new name. Press Enter or click the desktop when you're through, and you're off.

Or, you can click the file or folder's name to select it, wait a second, and click the file's name again. Windows 98 highlights the old name, ready to replace it with your incoming text. (This doesn't work if you've chosen to launch files and programs with a single-click rather than a double-click.)

- ✔ If you rename a file, only its name changes. The contents are still the same, it's still the same size, and it's still in the same place.

- ✔ You can't rename groups of files. The files spit in your face if you even try.

- ✔ Renaming a folder can confuse Windows, however, which often grows accustomed to folder names in the way they're first set up. Don't rename folders that contain programs.

Some icons, like the one for the Recycle Bin, won't let you rename them. How do you know which icons don't let users meddle with their names? Right-click their icon. If you don't see the word Rename on the menu, you won't be able to rename the file. Handy button, that right mouse button.

Using Legal Folder Names and Filenames

Windows is pretty picky about what you can and can't name a file or folder. If you stick to plain old letters and numbers, you're fine. But don't try to stick any of the following characters in there:

```
: / \ * | < > ? "
```

If you use any of those characters, Windows 98 bounces an error message to the screen, and you have to try again.

These names are illegal:

```
1/2 of my Homework
JOB:2
ONE<TWO
He's no "Gentleman"
```

These names are legal:

```
Half of my Term Paper
JOB2
Two is Bigger than One
A #@$%) Scoundrel
```

✔ As long as you remember the characters that you can and can't use for naming files, you'll probably be okay.

✔ Like their predecessors, Windows 98 programs *brand* files with their own three-letter extensions so that Windows 98 knows which program created what file. Normally, Windows 98 hides the extensions so that they're not confusing. But if you happen to spot filenames like SAVVY.DOC, README.TXT, and NUDE.BMP across the hard disk, you'll know that the extensions have been added by the Windows 98 programs WordPad, Notepad, and Paint, respectively. Windows 98 normally keeps the extensions hidden from view, so you just look at the file's icon for heritage clues.

If you really want to see a filename's extension, Choose Folder Options from the folder's View menu, and then click the tab marked View. Finally, click the little box next to the line that says Hide file extensions for known file types. That removes the check mark; when you click the Apply button, files reveal their extensions. (Click the box again to remove the extensions.)

You may see a filename with a weird tilde thing in it, such as WIGWAM~1.TXT. That's the special way that Windows 98 deals with long filenames. Most older programs expect files to have only eight characters; when there's a conflict, Windows 98 whittles down a long filename so that those older programs can use them. When the program's finished, the shorter, weird filename is the file's new name.

Copying a Complete Floppy Disk

To copy files from one disk to another, drag 'em over there, as described a few pages back. To copy an entire floppy disk, however, use the Copy Disk command.

What's the difference? When you're copying files, you're dragging specific filenames. But when you're copying a disk, the Copy Disk command duplicates the disk exactly: It even copies the empty parts! (That's why it takes longer than just dragging the files over.)

The Copy Disk command has two main limitations:

✔ It can copy only floppy disks that are the same *size* or *capacity*. Just as you can't pour a full can of beer into a shot glass, you can't copy one disk's information onto another disk unless they hold the same amount of data.

✔ It can't copy the hard drive or a RAM drive. Luckily, you really have no reason to copy them, even if you know what a RAM drive is.

Here's how to make a copy of a floppy disk:

1. **Put your floppy disk in your disk drive.**

2. **Double-click the My Computer icon.**

3. **Click your floppy disk's icon with your right mouse button.**

4. **Choose Copy Disk from the pop-up menu.**

   A box appears, letting you confirm which disk and disk drive you want to use for your copy.

5. **Click the Start button to begin making the copy and follow the helpful directions.**

✔ All this *capacity* and *size* stuff about disks and drives is slowly digested in Chapter 2.

✔ The Copy Disk command can be handy for making backup copies of your favorite programs.

> ✔ In fact, you should always use the Copy Disk command when making backup copies of programs. Sometimes programs hide secret files onto their floppies; by making a complete copy of the disk with the Copy Disk command, you can be sure that the entire disk gets copied, hidden files and all.

Creating a Folder

To store new information in a file cabinet, you grab a manila folder, scrawl a name across the top, and start stuffing it with information.

To store new information in Windows 98 — a new batch of letters to the hospital billing department, for example — you create a new folder, think up a name for the new folder, and start moving or copying files into it.

New, more organized folders make finding information easier, too. For example, you can clean up a crowded Letters folder by dividing it into two folders: Business and Personal.

Here's how to use Windows Explorer to create a new folder — a folder called Business — that lives in a Letters folder that already exists:

1. **On the left side of the Windows Explorer window, click in the area in which you want the new folder to appear.**

   Click the Letters folder, shown in Figure 11-7, because you want the Business folder to appear in the Letters folder. (No Letters folder? Then create one by clicking on your C drive, and right clicking in its contents displayed on the right side of Explorer. Choose New, select Folder, type Letters, and press the Enter key.)

Figure 11-7: You can organize the Letters folder by creating new folders, such as one each for business and personal letters.

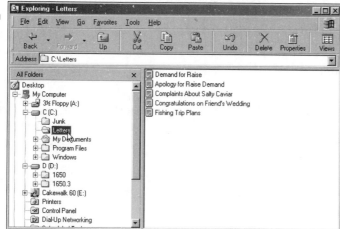

Click the Letters folder, and its current contents spill out into the right side of Windows Explorer.

2. **Click the right side of Windows Explorer with your right mouse button and choose <u>N</u>ew; when the menu appears, choose <u>F</u>older.**

   The My Computer window lets you create a folder when you right-click in any window; Windows Explorer lets you create a folder only when you right-click within its right-hand side. A box pops up and asks you to think of a name for your new folder.

3. **Type the new folder's name and press Enter.**

   Windows 98 can sometimes be picky about names you give to folders and files. For the rules, check out the "Using Legal Folder Names and Filenames" section earlier in this chapter.

After you type the folder's name and press Enter, the new Business folder is complete, ready for you to start moving your business letter files there. For impeccable organization, follow the same steps to create a Personal folder and move your personal files there, using the "dragging" process, as shown in Figure 11-8 (and explained in the "Copying or Moving a File" section in this chapter).

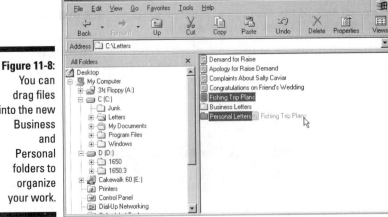

Figure 11-8: You can drag files into the new Business and Personal folders to organize your work.

✔ Want to install a new Windows program that doesn't come with an installation program? Create a new folder for it and copy its files there. Then head to Chapter 10 to see how to put the new program's name in the Start menu for easy clicking.

✔ To move files into a new folder, drag them there. Just follow the directions in the "Copying or Moving a File" section in this chapter.

✔ When copying or moving lots of files, select them all at the same time before dragging them. You can chew on this stuff in the "Selecting More Than One File or Folder" section.

✔ Just as with naming files, you can use only certain characters when naming folders. (Stick with plain old letters and numbers, and you'll be fine.)

Seeing More Information about Files and Folders

Whenever you create a file or folder, Windows 98 scrawls a bunch of secret hidden information on it: its size, the date you created it, and even more trivial stuff. To see what Windows 98 is calling the files and folders behind your back, click on the suspicious file or folder, select <u>V</u>iew from the menu bar, and then choose <u>D</u>etails from the menu.

In fact, you can simply click the arrow next to the right-most button on the toolbar, which lives atop My Computer, Windows Explorer, and most folders. A drop-down menu appears, listing options for arranging icons, as shown in Figure 11-9. (Clicking those options merely changes the way Windows 98 displays the icons — it doesn't do any permanent damage.)

Figure 11-9:
Click this arrow in the toolbar to change the way Windows 98 displays icons in the window.

✔ Is the toolbar not living on top of your window? Put it there by choosing <u>S</u>tandard Buttons from the <u>V</u>iew menu's <u>T</u>oolbars option. That little bar of buttons now appears atop your window like a mantel over a fireplace.

✔ If you can't remember what those little toolbar buttons do, rest your mouse pointer over them and make it look lost. Windows 98 displays a helpful box summing up the button's mission, and a further explanation often appears along the window's bottom.

✔ Although some of the additional file information is handy, it can consume a lot of space, limiting the number of files you can see in the window. Displaying only the filename is often a better idea. Then, if you want to see more information about a file or folder, try the following tip.

✔ Hold down Alt and double-click a file or folder to see its size, date, and other information.

✔ With the Alt+double-click trick (described in the preceding paragraph), you can change a file's attributes, as well. Attributes are too boring to be discussed further, so duck beneath the technical stuff coming up in the sidebar, "Who cares about this stuff, anyway?"

At first, Windows 98 displays filenames sorted alphabetically by name in its Windows Explorer and My Computer windows. But, by right-clicking in a folder and choosing the different sorting methods in the Arrange Icons menu, you display them in a different order. Windows puts the biggest ones at the top of the list, for example, when you choose sort by Size. Or you can choose sort by Type to keep files created by the same application next to each other. Or you can choose sort by Date to keep the most recent files at the top of the list.

Dragging, Dropping, and Running

You can drag files around in Windows 98 to move them or copy them. But there's more: You can drag them outside of the Windows Explorer or My Computer window and drop them into other windows to load them into other files and programs, as shown in Figure 11-10.

Figure 11-10: The mouse pointer changes shape as you drag the Beethoven's Für Elise file into the Media Player window.

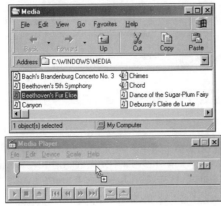

For example, drag the Beethoven's Für Elise file into the Media Player window and let go of the mouse button. Media Player loads the Beethoven's Für Elise file, just as if you'd double-clicked it in the first place.

This feature brings up all sorts of fun ideas. If you have a sound card, you can listen to sounds by dropping sound files into the Sound Recorder windows. You can drop text files into Notepad to load them quickly. Or you can drop WordPad files into WordPad.

✔ Okay, the first thing everybody wants to know is what happens if you drag a sound file into WordPad? Or a WordPad file into Notepad? Or any other combination of files that don't match? Well, Windows 98 either embeds one file into the other — a process described in Chapter 8 — or sends you a box saying that it got indigestion. Just click the OK button, and things return to normal. No harm done, either way.

✔ The second question everybody asks is: Why bother? You can just double-click a file's name to load it. That's true. But this way is more fun and often faster.

✔ You've never dragged and dropped before? Chapter 3 contains complete instructions.

✔ Old-time Windows users will want to know if they can load files by dropping them onto taskbar icons along the screen's bottom. Not anymore — Windows 98 lets you drop things only into *open* windows. But if you drag the object over to the taskbar icon that you're interested in and let the mouse pointer hover over it for awhile, the icon blossoms into an open window, ready to receive the object.

How Do I Make the Network Work?

Windows 98 can connect to bunches of other computers through an office network and, luckily, that makes it pretty easy to grab files from other people's computers. At least it's pretty easy if somebody else has already set up the network. But after the network's running, you'll be running right alongside it. There isn't much new to learn.

See the Network Neighborhood icon on your computer's desktop (and shown in the margin)? That icon is the key to all the computers currently connected to your computer.

Double-click that icon and a window appears, as shown in Figure 11-11. Your windows naturally differ because you have different computers. (And the computers probably have different names, too.)

Figure 11-11:
Double-click
the Network
Neighborhood
icon to
see which
computers
on the
network you
can access.

Double-click the icon of the computer that you want to peek inside and a new window appears, as shown in Figure 11-12, showing that computer's contents.

Figure 11-12:
You can
work with
another
computer's
files through
a network
by using
your
Windows
Explorer or
My
Computer
programs.

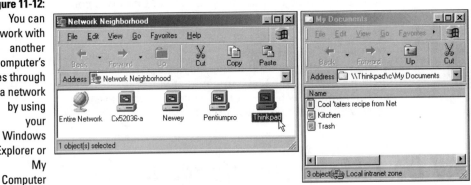

✔ From here, everything works just like the normal Windows Explorer window. Feel free to point and click in the other computer's folders. To copy files back and forth, just drag and drop them to and from your computer's window to the other computer's window.

✔ You can only access the computers that your network administrator has given you access to. Don't get carried away; you're not really getting away with anything.

✔ When you use a network to delete something from another networked computer — or somebody uses the Network to delete a file from *your* computer — it's gone. It doesn't go into the Recycle Bin. Be careful, especially because the network administrator can usually tell who deleted the file.

Who cares about this stuff, anyway?

Windows 98 gives each file four special switches called *attributes.* The computer looks at the way those switches are set before it fiddles with a file.

Read Only: Choosing this attribute allows the file to be read, but not deleted or changed in any way.

Archive: The computer sets this attribute when a file has changed since the last time it was backed up with the Windows 98 Backup program.

Hidden: Setting this attribute makes the file invisible during normal operations.

System: Files required by a computer's operating system have this attribute set.

The Properties box makes it easy — perhaps too easy — to change these attributes. In most cases, you should leave them alone. They're just mentioned here so that you'll know what computer nerds mean when they tell cranky people, "Boy, somebody must have set your attribute wrong when you got out of bed this morning."

> ✔ Networks can be set up in dozens of different ways; sometimes another computer's program will work on your computer, and other times, the program won't. Again, your network administrator should be your guide.

Making My Computer and Windows Explorer List Missing Files

Sometimes Windows 98 snoozes and doesn't keep track of what's *really* on the disk. Oh, it does pretty well with the hard drive, and it works pretty well if you're just running Windows programs. But it can't tell when you stick in a new floppy disk.

If you think that the Windows Explorer or My Computer window is holding out on you, tell it to *refresh,* or take a second look at what's on the floppy disk or hard drive. You can click <u>V</u>iew from the menu bar and choose <u>R</u>efresh from the pull-down menu, but a quicker way is to press the F5 key. (It's a function key along the top or left side of the keyboard.) Either way, the programs take a second look at what they're supposed to be showing and update their lists, if necessary.

Press the F5 key whenever you stick in a different floppy disk and want to see what files are stored on it. Windows 98 then updates the screen to show that *new* floppy's files, not the files from the first disk.

Formatting a New Floppy Disk

New floppy disks don't always work straight out of the box; your computer burps out an error message if you even try to use them fresh. Floppy disks must be formatted, and unless you paid extra for a box of *preformatted* floppy disks, you must format them yourself. The My Computer program handles this particularly boring chore quite easily. It's still boring, though, as you'll discover when repeating the process 10 or 12 times — once for each disk in the box.

Here's the procedure:

1. **Place the new disk into drive A or drive B and close the latch.**

2. **In either Windows Explorer or the My Computer window, click the drive's icon with your right mouse button and choose Format from the menu.**

3. **If you're formatting a *high-capacity* disk in drive A, select the Full setting under Format type and select Start in the top-right corner.**

   Your disk drives whir for several minutes, before announcing it's finished.

4. **Click the Close button when Windows 98 is through.**

   Then remove the floppy disk and return to Step 1 until you've formatted the entire box.

   ✔ You can format disks in your drive B by clicking the drive B icon with your right mouse button. Likewise, you can change a disk's capacity by clicking the little arrow in the Capacity box. You don't know the capacity of your disks? Head for the handy chart in Chapter 2.

   ✔ Don't get your hopes up: The Quick (Erase) option won't speed things up unless your disk has already been formatted once before.

   ✔ If you want to be able to boot your computer from a disk, check the Copy system files option. These System Disks can come in handy if your hard drive ever goes on vacation.

   ✔ In fact, if Windows 98 ever goes on vacation, you should have an emergency disk. The Add/Remove Programs icon in the Windows 98 Control Panel makes one for you.

Chapter 12

The Free Programs!

*W*indows 98 Second Edition, the fanciest version of Windows yet, comes with more free programs than ever. It makes customers happy (and makes the Justice Department members flap their long black robes).

Normally free software is as nice as a free lunch. The problem comes with the Windows 98 menu: The Start button often tosses cutesy, confusing names on-screen without checking to see whether the user flinches.

This chapter explains the easiest-to-use options that spill from the Start button's P̲rograms option, as shown in Figure 12-1.

Remember, Windows 98 doesn't automatically install *all* its possible freebie programs — that would eat up gobs of your hard disk space. Should you find a program here that's indispensable, head to this chapter's last section, "My Version of Windows 98 Doesn't Have the Right Programs!"

Some programs here come only with Windows 98 Second Edition; they're marked accordingly. And one last thing: Describing all these programs in detail would change this book's title to *Windows 98 For Dummies Who Can Lift 10-Pound Books.* No, you'll find the more complicated programs covered in this book's sequel, *MORE Windows 98 For Dummies,* from IDG Books Worldwide, Inc.

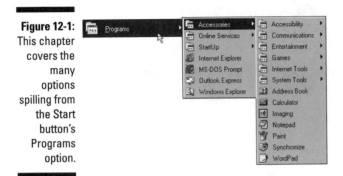

Figure 12-1:
This chapter
covers the
many
options
spilling from
the Start
button's
Programs
option.

Accessories

By far, the bulk of the Windows 98 freebie programs are dumped under the generic menu label "Accessories." Here are programs that make Windows 98 easier to see and hear; they let your computer talk to other computers and the Internet, and they entertain you during slow days. Finally, they let you fiddle with Windows' innards during even slower days.

The rest of this section tackles the programs found in the Accessories menu, accessed through the Start button's Programs button.

Accessibility

The Accessibility Wizard and Microsoft Magnifier help people view the Windows desktop more easily. The Accessibility Wizard leads you through choices of larger font sizes, menus, and icons; you can enlarge window borders, making them easier to click. Sounds can accompany certain actions if you're having difficulty seeing the screen, or if your monitor's growing old.

Having trouble viewing the screen? Let the Accessibility Wizard and Microsoft Magnifier help set up the menus so you can view them easily.

Microsoft Magnifier, shown in Figure 12-2, displays the mouse pointer's current shenanigans in an enlarged window, making small buttons and boxes easier to spot.

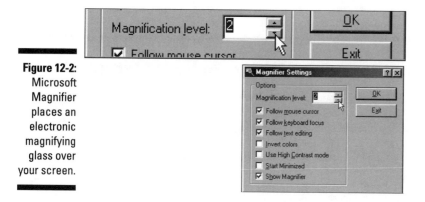

Figure 12-2:
Microsoft
Magnifier
places an
electronic
magnifying
glass over
your screen.

Communications

Much of this stuff applies to the tech-heads, so don't spend too much time here. If you're trying to connect to the Internet, however, head for the Internet Connection Wizard in this section.

Dial-Up Networking

Dial-Up Networking controls how your computer talks to another computer over the phone lines. We're not talking about the Internet here, though; we're talking about hooking up to the computers at work or another location. This stuff gets complicated enough to warrant a thick (but useful) book like Brian Livingston's *Windows 98 Secrets,* published by IDG Books Worldwide, Inc. (And I don't get a kickback, either.)

Direct Cable Connection

Direct Cable Connection swaps information over cables plugged between the two PCs. The program's pretty easy, actually. The hard part is buying the right cables. You need a Parallel File Transfer cable — hopefully rated either ECP or EPP — to connect between the parallel ports of both computers. (Serial File Transfer cables are much slower.) Follow the program's directions, and you've created a sort of mini-network.

Calling other computers with HyperTerminal

An old-school modem program, HyperTerminal, works only with *text-based* online services that are quickly disappearing, such as CompuServe's old formats and computer bulletin boards. It doesn't work with graphics-based bulletin boards, such as those on America Online and the newer portions of CompuServe. And no, you can't use HyperTerminal for looking at cool pictures on the World Wide Web.

Only advanced computer users will use HyperTerminal, and they can find an entire chapter of HyperTerminal madness in this book's more advanced sequel, *MORE Windows 98 For Dummies,* published by IDG Books Worldwide, Inc.

Internet Connection Wizard

If you're thinking of connecting your computer to the Internet, be thankful Microsoft came up with the Internet Connection Wizard. Spruced up for Windows 98 Second Edition, the program helps you and your computer connect to your Internet Service Provider (ISP) so you can Web Surf like the best of them. Here's the checklist to get started:

  ✔ **Find an Internet Service Provider.** This is the company that provides a connection to the Internet. Ask a friend, coworker, or teenager for a recommendation. Don't have one? The Internet Connection Wizard will find one for you that's in your own area.

  ✔ **Look up your user name, password, and phone number for your current Internet Service Provider.** Don't have one? If the Wizard finds you a service provider, it will dish out those things, too.

  ✔ **Find a modem.** Most new computers come with a modem lodged in their innards. To see if one's inside of yours, look for telephone jacks on the back of your computer, near where all the other cables protrude. If a cable modem service is available in your area, go for it. It's zillions times quicker, and you don't need to tie up your phone line. (Plus, you won't need to pay for a second phone line while Web surfing.)

Now you're ready to start the Internet Connection Wizard by following these steps.

In fact, whenever you encounter difficulties in getting your Internet connection "just right," head here and run through the steps in this section. The Wizard displays your current settings and allows you to change them.

1. **Click the Start button, click Programs, choose Accessories, and load the Internet Connection Wizard from the Communications area.**

2. **Choose one of the three options.**

   • **Sign up for a new Internet Account**

   Choose this option if you don't already have an Internet account, and you want to select one. By choosing this, the Wizard dials a number to locate Internet Service Providers in your area and display their rates and options. Chances are, you can sign up with one of several providers, including America Online, Prodigy, AT&T WorldNet Service, and others.

   After you choose a provider, the Wizard makes you fill out your name, address, and credit card information before leaving you at Step 3.

   • **Transfer your existing Internet account to your computer**

   Already have an Internet account from another computer? Click here to set your computer up to access this account. Your modem still dials a number to find local providers in your area. This time, however, it only finds providers who've signed up for Windows 98 Second Edition's new "automatic configuration."

   Chances are, your provider won't be listed. Tell the form your provider isn't listed, and Windows guides you through setting up the Internet connection process manually — the same as the next step.

   • **Set up your existing Internet account manually or through a network**

   Continue along these steps to introduce your computer to your existing Internet account by filling out forms and punching buttons.

3. **Tell Windows 98 whether you connect through a phone line or a network.**

   If you use a network, find a techno-savvy teenager for help or check out this book's sequel, *MORE Windows 98 For Dummies*. That stuff's too complicated for this book.

   If a phone line plugs between the wall and the back of your computer or into a little box near your computer, you're connecting through the phone line and a modem. Choose that option.

4. **Enter the phone number for your Internet Service Provider; click Next and enter your User name and Password.**

   Your provider should have given you these three things. Call them for more information.

5. **Type a name for your Internet provider.**

   Just make up a name for your own reference, or type **My Provider.**

6. **Setup a mail account.**

   On the next page, say you want to set up an Internet mail account. In the coming pages, type your name, your user name, and your e-mail address. This is usually your username, the @ sign, and the name of your provider. If your provider is speedy.com, and your username is josh12, type **josh12@speedo.com.**

   The next page has the most confusing part. Unless your Internet provider tells you otherwise, simply type the word mail in the Incoming mail and Outgoing mail server boxes.

   On the next page, type your account name. Still using the above example, you'd type **josh12**. Then, type your password in the box below. If you want to log on automatically without entering your password each time, check the Remember password box. Because this eliminates a need for a password, however, anybody can read your e-mail.

   Check the Secure Password Authentication box only if your Internet provider asks you to.

7. **Click the Finish button.**

   You're done. Windows 98's latest Internet browser, Internet Explorer 5.0, automatically leaps into action and uses your settings to call your Internet provider.

If everything goes correctly, your modem will dial and you'll soon be logged onto the Internet and ready to browse. Need a place to go for a quick test? Try logging onto www.dummies.com and see what happens. Or head to Chapter 13 for an introduction to the land known as the Internet's World Wide Web.

 Some versions of Windows might not have the Internet Connection Wizard listed on your Start menu. To find it, right-click on your Internet Explorer icon, choose Properties, click the Connections tab, and click the Setup button.

Phone Dialer

The Windows 98 Phone Dialer spiffs up your desktop telephone, even if it's a really cheap one. First, Phone Dialer lets you assign your most frequently dialed phone numbers to push buttons: Just click the button, and Phone Dialer dials the number, as shown in Figure 12-3. Best yet, Phone Dialer keeps track of calls you make using the program.

Figure 12-3:
The Phone
Dialer
automatically
dials num-
bers, and
then keeps
track of the
conversa-
tion's length.

Normally, the program works just like a telephone: You click the buttons to dial the number. After a few seconds, you hear the phone ring and somebody say "Hello?" through your modem's speaker. Pick up your phone and start talking.

The fun part comes from storing the number of your favorite relative, radio station, or pizza delivery service (or whatever) into the Phone Dialer.

1. **Click one of the buttons along the program's right side.**

   The box on the top is probably handiest. A box appears, ready for you to type the name and phone number of the place you're calling.

2. **Type the name of the place you're calling into the Name box; then press Tab, and type the place's phone number into the Number to dial box.**

   Start typing the place's name, and the letters appear in the top box. Press Tab to move the cursor to the second box, where you can type the phone number, as shown in Figure 12-4. You can use the numbers on your keyboard's numeric keypad or the ones along the top of your keyboard, whichever you prefer. (The Function keys won't work, however.)

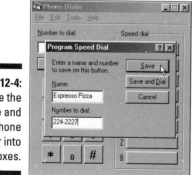

Figure 12-4:
Type the
name and
phone
number into
the boxes.

3. **Click the Save button.**

   The Phone Dialer reappears, showing its newly configured dial button, as shown in Figure 12-5. To dial the number, click the button.

Figure 12-5:
Click the
button to
dial that
particular
number.

~ Can't remember whether you made that important call yesterday morning? Choose Show Log from the Tools menu, and you see a list of the phone numbers you've dialed, when you dialed them, and how long the conversation lasted.

~ The Phone Dialer can be handy for making those complicated long-distance calls with too many digits to remember.

~ The Phone Dialer can dial using a Calling Card number, turn Call Waiting on and off, and dial extra numbers to reach outside lines. Whoopee!

~ Are you using Phone Dialer on your laptop in the hotel room? Phone Dialer automatically sets up your call for dozens of countries, from Albania to Zambia (and Afghanistan and Zimbabwe, too) — lots of international stuff in Windows 98.

~ Now the bad news: If you're using a network modem, cable modem, or a second, dedicated phone line for your modem, Phone Dialer won't work correctly. It only works on the telephone and line that are actually plugged into your modem.

Entertainment

Windows 98 is a bachelor's pad entertainment center, complete with controls for your computer's CD player, DVD player, and TV card. Toss in the free samplers of, you guessed it, Microsoft software, a bag of microwave popcorn, and a modern young couple's plans are set for the evening.

Here's what you'll find in the Windows 98 stereo cabinet of entertainment goodies.

CD Player

Adding a CD-ROM drive to a computer doesn't always add multimedia as much as it adds Bachman-Turner Overdrive to the lunch hour. It's a well-known fact that most multimedia computer owners pop a musical CD into their computer's disk drive now and then.

Media Player, a general-purpose multimedia player, can handle music CDs, but the Windows 98 full-fledged CD Player shown in Figure 12-6 comes with more accessories.

Figure 12-6:
The
Windows 98
CD Player.

The CD Player lets you add song titles to the menu, as well as create your own play lists. If you're feeling random, choose the Random Order setting under Options to make Windows 98 act like a jukebox. Now, if it just came with a pool table.

✔ Music too loud? Just click the little speaker near the end of the taskbar. An easy-to-use sliding bar lets you lower the volume — no more frantic searching to save your ears.

✔ Don't remember what some of those buttons do? Just rest your mouse pointer over them, and Windows 98 sends a message to the screen to help you out. In Figure 12-6, for example, the CD Player says that clicking the big triangle starts playing the CD.

✔ Looking for a certain song, but can't remember which one it is? Choose the Intro Play option under Options. The CD Player automatically plays the first few seconds of every song on the CD until you recognize the one you're after.

✔ See how Figure 12-6 shows the title of the CD and song? You need to enter all that information yourself. Click Edit Play List from the Disc menu, and start typing.

✔ As soon as you insert an audio CD, Windows 98 begins playing it — as long as your CD-ROM drive supports that feature. To stop Windows 98 from immediately playing the CD, hold down Shift while inserting the CD into the CD-ROM drive.

DVD Player

Digital Versatile Discs, once known as Digital Video Discs, are the latest technological spin-off from the compact disc family tree. In fact, they look identical.

A single DVD disc can contain an entire movie, its soundtrack in several languages, a director's voice-over, and all the cool explosion scenes filmed from several directions.

Best yet, your DVD drive also works as a CD-ROM drive, playing your music as well as movies. They work pretty much like the DVD player attached to a regular TV set. In fact, it's usually more fun to watch DVD movies on a regular TV set: The picture is bigger.

Interactive CD Sampler

Yep, it's high-tech junk mail. Microsoft sneaked a flashy product catalog onto the Windows 98 CD in the hopes that every user will stumble across it, think it's important, and install it.

In between happy music and cheery narrators, the program installs "trial versions" of the software you select, letting you try everything from Microsoft Money to Monster Truck Madness. There's even Barney software.

The program and samples eat up lots of hard disk space, so make sure that you uninstall them when you're through. (Double-click on the Control Panel's Add/Remove Programs icon, choose the items from the list, and click the Add/Remove button to give Barney the boot.)

Media Player and Sound Recorder

If your computer has a sound card (speakers are a dead giveaway that your computer is ready to rock), you can play and record sounds with Sound Recorder. It looks and works pretty much like a tape recorder. One warning, however: Don't get carried away when recording particularly long sounds. They take a *lot* of space on the hard drive.

Media Player, updated in Windows 98 Second Edition to handle more formats, still can't record, but it can play back many new types of sound and video. (Yep, it even plays MP3 files. Head to www.mp3.com and check it out.) Musicians can connect Media Player to MIDI keyboards and guitars. Plus, Media Player can play sounds and videos stored on CDs, as well as sounds and videos broadcast over the Internet.

- Windows 98 works with the most popular sound cards. Most computers sold today come with a preinstalled sound card, so there's nothing extra to buy. Hook the sound card up to your home stereo for some real fun.

- Chapter 2 covers sound cards and CD-ROM drives.

- *MORE Windows 98 For Dummies,* a "next-step-up" Dummies Press book, shows you how to use Sound Recorder and Media Player to play and record sounds, listen to compact discs, watch movies, and do more things you're not supposed to do at work.

Trial programs

See the Interactive CD Sampler section earlier in this chapter. This program installs the trial versions of Microsoft programs to your hard drive with the hope that you'll buy them.

WebTV for Windows

It finally happened! You can watch TV on your computer (see Figure 12-7). Best yet, by shrinking the WebTV for Windows into a window, you can watch *Dragnet* reruns while working on Important Business Documents.

Figure 12-7:
With a TV card installed, the Windows 98 WebTV for Windows displays TV channels on your computer screen.

- Don't get excited yet. Windows 98 can't show TV unless your computer has a TV card — which costs from $100–$200. Luckily most TV cards come with a normal video card's circuitry inside, sparing you the expense of two cards.

- WebTV for Windows also comes with a built-in TV guide program. By connecting to the Internet, the program gathers information about the current week's TV shows in your area. It then displays a TV show listing with a search program, letting you ferret out any upcoming favorites.

> ✔ Don't want to miss a show? Rev up the TV guide, search for any upcoming episodes, and click the Remind button. WebTV for Windows will automatically remind you five minutes before the show begins.
>
> ✔ Here's the ugly truth, however, and you heard it here first: The Windows 98 WebTV software is absolutely *awful* compared to the competition. Skip it, and use the TV-viewing program that comes in the box with your TV card. The TV controller in ATI's All-In-Wonder Pro, for instance, is much more reliable, faster, easier to use, and offers many more features. Don't want to miss anything about the stock market on CNN? Tell ATI's card to listen for the word "stock." When the card finds the word, it brings up the TV screen, ready for instant viewing. Now *that's* TV software.

Volume control

Ignore this one — too many menus to wade through. Instead, click the little speaker in the corner of your taskbar. (See it in the bottom-right corner of your screen?) When the control pops up, just slide it up or down to change your volume.

A double-click on that little speaker brings up the master volume, where you control the mix of your computer's media devices. For example, a CD-Player shows up here, as well as general sound (wav), music (MIDI), or peripherals, like TV cards or video capture cards (Line-in).

Games

Playtime! The best way to learn mouse-pushing tactics in Windows 98 is in a low-stress environment. So, Microsoft tossed a few games into the Windows 98 mix. Yes, these games already came packaged with Windows 95; they're nothing new. But then again, card games never get old, do they?

Windows 98 often leaves out the games when it's first installed. To install them, click the Start button, choose Settings, and load Control Panel. Double-click the Add/Remove Programs icon, and click the Windows Setup tab. Double-click the word Accessories from the list and click the box next to Games until a check mark appears.

Click the OK button on the next two screens, and Windows 98 will install the games listed in this section. (You might need to insert your Windows 98 CD.)

FreeCell

Although FreeCell looks a lot like Solitaire, described a few sections later, it plays a lot differently. Shown in Figure 12-8, FreeCell works with double-clicks: Instead of making you drag the cards around, FreeCell simply jumps them into place.

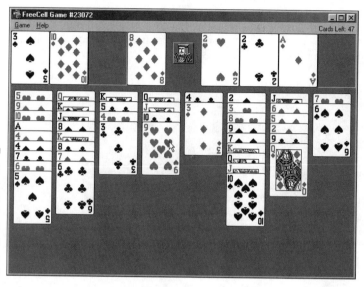

Figure 12-8:
The addict-
ing FreeCell
tracks your
win/loss
statistics as
you play.

FreeCell works just like the card game: Sort the cards in order by suit and number from Ace to King on the four upper-right-hand squares. While moving the cards up there, you can move other cards temporarily to the four *free cells* — temporary card-storage areas — on the left-hand side.

✔ FreeCell comes with 32,000 different games. So far, none of them has been proven unbeatable.

✔ Press F4, and FreeCell reveals your win/loss ratio. To make it look like you win all your games, cheat: Whenever you're about to lose a game, hold down Ctrl and Shift simultaneously, and press F10. A box appears, offering you three options: Abort, but still win the game, Retry and lose the game, or Ignore and pretend you didn't press those keys. Press Abort, double-click on any card, and you automatically win. Sneaky, eh?

✔ Moved the wrong card? Quick — press F10. That's the Undo button, but only if you press it before clicking another card.

✔ After you've won 65,535 games, FreeCell resets your winning streak statistics to zero. Be forewarned.

Hearts

Windows 98 has no shortage of card games, that's for sure. If you're tired of Solitaire and FreeCell, give Hearts a try — especially if you're on a network. It lets you play cards with networked computers all across the office.

The game works just like *real* Hearts, as shown in Figure 12-9. One person tosses a card onto the table, everybody else tosses down a card of the same suit, and the person with the highest card grabs the pile. What's the tricky part? You want the *lowest* score — any card with a heart is one point, and the queen of spades is worth 13 points.

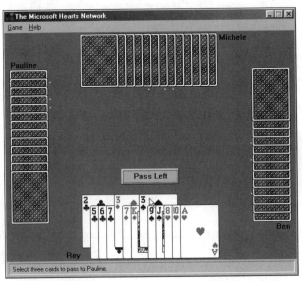

Figure 12-9: Designed for networks, Hearts can substitute computerized opponents if your officemates step out for lunch.

✔ There's a catch: If one player grabs all the hearts and the queen of spades, that player doesn't get any points, and all the other players are penalized 26 points.

✔ If nobody is around at the office network, choose the dealer option, and press F2; the computer fills in for the other three players. You don't need a network to play Hearts.

✔ *Cheat alert:* The computer automatically sorts your cards by suit at the screen's bottom. However, it doesn't sort the cards that represent the other players' hands — the cards around the edges. Therefore, you can't get an idea of what cards the other players have by watching the position of their cards.

✔ If you migrated from Windows for Workgroups, you're probably already used to playing Hearts over the network. Windows 98 keeps Hearts in the mix of games, along with Solitaire.

Solitaire

Windows 98 Solitaire works just like the card game, so here are just a few pointers for the computerized version:

✔ When the boss comes by, click the minimize button, that underscore-looking thing in a box in the upper-right corner. If you can't move the mouse quickly enough, hold down Alt and press the spacebar, followed by the letter N. In either case, Solitaire turns into an icon at the bottom of the screen. Double-click the icon to resume play when the boss passes.

✔ When you're in three-card mode — and Solitaire flips the cards over three at a time — you can cheat to make Solitaire temporarily flip the cards one by one. Just hold down the Ctrl, Alt, and Shift keys simultaneously as you click.

✔ Sharp-eyed players will notice some background fun: The bats flap their wings, the sun sticks out its tongue, and a card slides in and out of a dealer's sleeve. These shenanigans only occur when you play in *timed* mode. To start the fun, choose Options from the Game menu and make sure that you put an X in the Timed Game box.

Minesweeper

Despite the name, Minesweeper does not cause any explosions, even if you accidentally uncover a mine. And it works better on laptops than Solitaire does. Minesweeper is more of a math game than anything else — no jumping little men here.

Start by clicking a random square; some numbers appear in one or more of the little squares. The number says how many mines are hidden in the squares surrounding that square.

Each square is surrounded by eight other squares. (Unless it's on the edge; then there are only five. And only three squares surround corner squares.) If, through the process of elimination, you're sure that a mine exists beneath a certain square, click it with the right mouse button to put a little flag there.

Eventually, through logical deduction (or just mindless pointing and clicking), an accidental click on a mine blows you up, or you mark all the mine squares with flags and win the game.

The object of the game is to win as quickly as you can.

Ready to cheat? To stop the clock, hold down both the left and right mouse buttons and press Escape. To change your high scores, head for your Windows folder and use Notepad to open a file called winmine.ini. Then edit the high score list, changing the names and times to anything you want.

Internet tools

As the Internet becomes increasingly popular during cocktail party conversation, Windows 98's Internet section continues to grow. The following programs appear under the Accessories' Internet Tools area.

FrontPage Express

What it does: When you're ready to create your own Web page, FrontPage Express is ready to help you create it. Make sure that your Internet Service Provider allows you to create your own Web page, however; some don't.

Why bother with it: Unfortunately, FrontPage Express ain't exactly easy to use. That's why it gets its coverage in this book's sequel, *MORE Windows 98 For Dummies*. There you find how to combine text, pictures, and sounds into a Web page, and upload it to your Internet Service Provider.

Internet Connection Wizard

What it does: This program delicately holds your hand when signing up with an Internet provider. It configures your computer to reach the other computer, and begin sending and receiving information.

Why bother with it: You'll want it when first signing up for the Internet or changing Internet Service Providers. It's also helpful when something's not working right: It displays your current settings and allows you to change them. (The program's covered earlier in this chapter in the Communications section, because Windows 98 Second Edition seems to like listing the program there, as well.)

Microsoft Chat

What it does: When Microsoft sees something with potential, it immediately wants to cash in on it by creating its own version. This is Microsoft's version of the oodles of Internet "Chat" areas where people log on and type at each other.

Why bother with it: Don't. There are too many other chat areas out there that are already established. (Besides, Microsoft's Chat program didn't even work right on my computer.) Instead, head to TalkCity at www.talkcity.com or Yahoo Chat at http://chat.yahoo.com/ and start yakking up a storm.

NetMeeting

What it does: Want to see who you're doing business with, even though you're in California and they're in New York? If your computer's set up for it, NetMeeting allows Internet-relayed teleconferences with sound, video, and the sharing of files.

Why bother with it: If you're dealing with other techies, go for it. But you might be marked as a tech-head and blow the deal if you're not sure the other folks are techies, too.

Personal Web Server

What it does: Whereas FrontPage Express lets you create a Web page to be uploaded to another computer — usually for free — Personal Web Server lets you run a Web page server on your own computer — at a cost.

Why bother with it: If you want people dialing into your computer to read your Web page, this is the program. The vast majority of people, however, merely take advantage of the free storage space offered by the company that gives them their e-mail account.

Web Publishing Wizard

What it does: Let's get this straight: FrontPage Express lets you create the Web page, just as if you were creating a word-processed document. Once you've created it, Web Publishing Wizard steps in to upload it to the storage space provided by your Internet account. (It's not like Personal Web Server, which turns your own computer into a Web server for people to dial up.)

Why bother with it: If you're creating a Web page, use this program hand in hand with FrontPage Express to finish your product. Creating a Web page is complicated enough to warrant coverage in this book's sequel, *MORE Windows 98 For Dummies*. (After all, if this book covered everything, it would be too heavy to fit on the lap comfortably.)

System Tools

Windows 98 comes with several technical programs designed to make the nerd feel at home. They're certainly not designed for the normal user. In fact, the Windows 98 installation program doesn't even install all these programs unless you ask.

If any of these programs strikes your fancy — and they're not listed on your System Tools menu — grab your Windows 98 disc and head for Chapter 14. That chapter explains how to use the Control Panel's Add/Remove Programs feature to make Windows 98 toss a few more goodies onto your hard drive.

Meanwhile, the next few sections describe some of the more technical programs in Windows 98.

Backup

What it does: Everybody knows that you're supposed to make backup copies of your computer's information so that you don't lose everything when your computer becomes an embezzler.

Why bother with it: The problem is finding the time to make copies of all your important files. The Microsoft Backup program, shown in Figure 12-10, isn't anything special except in one key area: It can handle long filenames. Because the old-school, pre-Windows 95 era backup programs can only handle eight-character filenames, they can't make reliable backups in Windows 98.

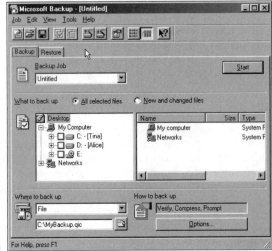

Figure 12-10:
Windows 98 comes with a simple backup program that can handle long filenames.

To keep Windows 98 users from losing data in their old backup programs, Microsoft tossed in a simple backup program with Windows 98. After you tell the backup program which programs to save, it copies them to floppy disks, a tape backup unit, or read/write CD-ROM drives.

If you haven't bought a tape backup unit or read/write CD-ROM drive yet, now may be a good time to put one on your shopping list. They've come way down in price, and copying huge hard drives onto hundreds of floppies is a bore, even if Windows 98 *does* let you play FreeCell while you're doing it.

Character Map (Adding the à in voilà)

What it does: Character Map lets you add weird foreign characters, such as à, £, or even ß, into your document.

Why bother with it: Why? Because Character Map makes it so easy to give your documents that extra shine *à la belle étoile*. A click on the System Tool's Character Map option unleashes a box like the one shown in Figure 12-11, listing every available character and symbol.

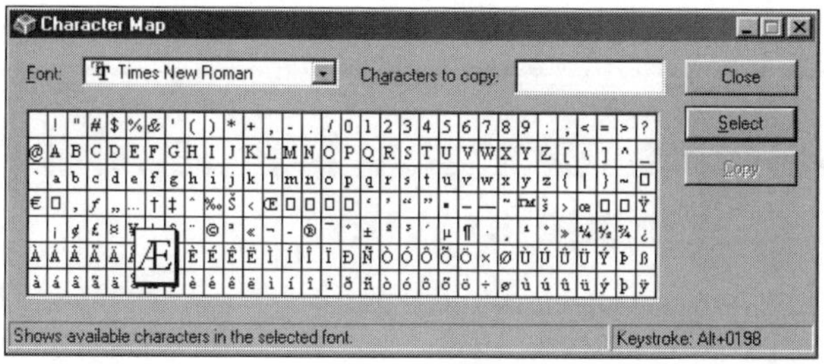

Figure 12-11:
Character
Map finds
foreign
characters
for your font
to place in
your work.

Follow these steps to put a foreign character in your work:

1. **Make sure that the current font — the name for the style of the characters on the page — shows in the Font box.**

   If the current font is not showing, click the down arrow and click the font when it appears in the drop-down list.

2. **Scan the Character Map box until you see the symbol you're after; then pounce on that character with a double-click.**

   The symbol appears in the Characters to Copy box.

3. **Click Copy to send the character to the Clipboard.**

4. **Click the Close button to close the Character Map.**

5. **Click in the document where you want the new symbol or character to appear.**

6. **Press Ctrl+V, and the new character pops right in there.**

   (Give it a second. Sometimes it's slow.)

The symbols in the Character Map box are easier to see if you hold down the mouse button and move the pointer over them.

✔ When working with foreign words, keep the Character Map handy as an icon, ready for consultation.

✔ For some fun symbols like ✎, ▱, ✍, ☛, ☃, 🖥🌙, or ∿, switch to the Wingdings font. It's full of little doodads to spice up your work.

✔ You can grab several characters at a time by double-clicking each of them and then copying them into your work as a chunk. You don't have to keep returning to the Character Map for each one.

That weird Alt+0208 stuff is too trivial to bother with

In the bottom right-hand corner, Character Map flashes numbers after the words Keystroke: Alt+. Those numbers hail back to the stone-tablet days of adding foreign characters when word processing. Back then, people had to look up a character's code number in the back of a boring manual.

If you remember the code numbers for your favorite symbols, however, you can bypass Character Map and add them directly to documents. For example, the code number listed in the bottom corner for é is 0233.

Here's the trick: Press and release Num Lock, hold down Alt, and type 0233 with the numeric keypad. Let go of the Alt key, and the é symbol appears.

If you constantly use one special character, this method may be faster than using Character Map. (Press and release Num Lock after you're finished.)

Clipboard Viewer

What it does: This little window lets you view whatever doodad you've just cut or copied from a file. It makes it very easy to see what you've copied.

Why bother with it: Chapter 8, the "cut and paste" chapter, has the dirt on this handy little program. I keep Clipboard Viewer up and running all the time.

Compression Agent/DriveSpace

What it does: Compresses information so you can pack more programs and software onto your hard drive.

Why bother with it: Don't bother with any disk compression program — buy a bigger hard drive instead. Hard drives are downright cheap right now, and a lot more reliable. Compressed hard drives make it that much more difficult to retrieve stuff when something goes wrong.

Disk Cleanup

What it is: Like the backseat of a car, Windows 98 accumulates junk: Files temporarily grabbed from the Internet to make things run faster; deleted files from the Recycle Bin, and other space-wasters. Disk Cleanup automatically gathers these programs and lets you delete them.

Why bother with it: When you need a little more room on the hard drive in order to install Monster Truck Madness, unleash Disk Cleanup. It's an easy way to purge your system of files you'll never miss.

For best results, delete Temporary Internet Files, the Recycle Bin, and Temporary files. If you've been using Windows 98 Second Edition for a few months and you like it, delete the Windows 98 uninstall information, too.

Disk Defragmenter

What it does: When a computer reads and writes files to and from a hard disk, it's working like a liquor store stock clerk after a Labor Day weekend. It has to reorganize the store, moving all the misplaced beer cans out of the wine aisles. The same disorganization happens with computer files. When the computer moves files around, it tends to break the files into chunks and spread them across your hard drive. The computer can still find all the pieces, but it takes more time. Disk Defragmenter reorganizes the hard drive, making sure that all the files' pieces are next to each other for quick and easy grabbing.

Why bother with it: Your hard drive can grab files more quickly if all the files' pieces are stored next to each other. The Disk Defragmenter organizes the files, speeding up access times. When the program pops up, click the drive you want defragmented. The program looks at the drive and tells you whether the drive needs any work. Take the program's advice. (You probably won't have to use the program more than every couple of months, depending on how often you're using your computer.)

Drive Converter (FAT 32)

What it is: A very techie program that rearranges the virtual shelves on your hard drive.

Why bother with it: Designed for people with hard drives of at least 8 giga-bites, Drive Converter tweaks the packing of information onto your hard drive so it can be reached more efficiently. The bad part? It's comes chock-full of technical warnings, it causes potential conflicts with other programs, and Windows can't "undo" the process once it's been converted. Don't try it unless you're sure you know what you're doing.

DriveSpace

Avoid it. See the earlier section, "Compression Agent/DriveSpace."

Maintenance Wizard

What it does: This offers a chance to automate the Windows 98 mainte-nance/repair tools: ScanDisk, Disk Cleanup, and Disk Defragmenter, plus a few other third-party programs.

Why bother with it: If you make Windows 98 perform all these chores at 3 a.m. while you're snoozing, your computer will automatically run more smoothly.

Net Watcher

What it is: This lets computer snoops play Spy on the network. Net Watcher lets you see who's connected to your computer, and whether they're rooting through your files.

Why bother with it: Not much reason, really. If a network administrator has set up your computer for network access, there's not much you can do about it. Plus, you can usually tell when somebody in another cubicle accesses your computer because its hard drive revs up and makes a pestered sound.

ScanDisk

What it does: Sometimes a computer goofs and loses track of where it has stored information on a hard disk. ScanDisk examines a hard disk for any errors and, if it finds anything suspicious, offers to fix the problem.

Why bother with it: ScanDisk not only finds hard disk errors, but if you click in the Automatically fix errors box, it fixes them.

To bring ScanDisk to work, follow these steps:

1. **From the Start button, choose Programs, Accessories, System Tools, and ScanDisk, in that order.**

2. **Select the drive you want to check.**

3. **Click the Automatically fix errors box.**

   A check mark will appear.

4. **Choose the Standard option, and click the Start button.**

If you still have problems, rerun the program, but choose Thorough instead of Standard in Step 4. That makes ScanDisk work a little harder, but takes its time in the process.

Scheduled Tasks

What it does: Windows 98 can run programs when you're not around to supervise, whether you're sleeping at night or away from the home computer during the day. Scheduled Tasks plans the schedule of your computer's routine, telling it which programs to run, when, and for how long.

Why bother with it: Don't bother, actually, unless you also enjoy programming your VCR. Lots of similarities lurk behind the menus of tedious buttons and options. Plus, most programs that can take advantage of the Scheduled Tasks options sign themselves up automatically.

In fact, you can purge any of those automated tasks by double-clicking the Scheduled Tasks icon in the bottom-right corner of your screen. (The icon is a tiny square with a little clock in one corner and an open book in the other.) Click on the offensive task, press the Delete key, and click the Yes button to send that task to the Recycle Bin.

System Information

What it does: Compiles vast technical charts about your computer's innards.

Why bother with it: Don't. It's a fix-it tool for the mechanics.

System Monitor

What it does: Makes technical charts that reveal performance statistics.

Why bother with it: Don't, unless you just want to see the cool little graphs. Otherwise, it's pretty boring.

System Resource Meter

Yawn. A little meter mumbles something about resources. (This stuff attracts the same crowd who enjoy watching oscilloscopes.)

Welcome to Windows

What it does: As the name implies, this revs up the Welcome to Windows screen that greeted you on your first visit to Windows Land.

Why bother with it: Don't. Nothing new here.

Calculator

Calculator is, well, a calculator. It looks simple enough, and it really is — unless you mistakenly set it for Scientific mode and see some nightmarish logarithmic stuff. To bring the calculator back to normal, choose Standard from the View menu.

To punch in numbers and equations, click the little buttons, just as if it were a normal calculator. When you press the equal sign (=), the answer appears at the top. For an extra measure of handiness, you can copy the answers to the Clipboard by pressing Ctrl+C (holding down the Ctrl key while pressing C). Then click in the window where you want the answer to appear and press Ctrl+V. That method is easier than retyping a number like 2.449489742783.

> ✔ Unlike in other Windows programs, you can't copy the Calculator's answer by running the mouse pointer over the numbers. You have to press Ctrl+C or choose Copy from the Edit menu.

✔ If the mouse action is too slow, press the Num Lock key and punch in numbers with the numeric keypad.

Imaging

You've probably noticed how greeting cards and party fliers are getting increasingly elaborate. It's not just the fancy borders and cartoons, although they've never been more colorful. No, it's the embedded color pictures.

Chances are, a scanner copied that photo and sent it to the computer, where computer software turns the picture information into a file.

Imaging, by Kodak, lets Windows 98 talk to scanners; it then manipulates and saves the image in a variety of file formats. It's a handy program. But chances are, the software that came with your scanner already does a better job.

Notepad

Windows comes with two word processors, WordPad and Notepad. WordPad is for the letters you're sprucing up for other people to see. Notepad is for stuff you're going to keep for yourself.

Notepad is quicker than WordPad. Double-click its icon, and it leaps to the screen more quickly than you can reach for a notepad in your back pocket. You can type some quick words and save them on the fly.

Understanding Notepad's limitations

Notepad's speed comes at a price, however. Notepad stores only words and numbers. It doesn't store any special formatting, such as italicized letters, and you can't paste any pictures into it, as you can with WordPad. Notepad is a quick, throw-together program for your quick, throw-together thoughts.

✔ Unfortunately, Notepad tosses you into instant confusion: All the sentences head right off the edge of the screen. To turn those single-line, runaway sentences into normal paragraphs, turn on the *word wrap* feature by choosing Word Wrap from the Edit menu. (Once you've changed this option the first time, strangely enough, Windows 98 remembers your preference, and uses it each time you use Notepad in the future.)

✔ Notepad prints kind of funny, too: It prints the file's name at the top of every page. To combat this nonsense, choose Page Setup from the File menu. A box appears, with a funny code word in the Header box. Delete the word and click the OK button. If you want to get rid of the automatic page numbering, clear out the Footer box, as well.

✔ Here's another printing problem: Notepad doesn't print exactly what you see on-screen. Instead, it prints according to the margins you set in Page Se<u>t</u>up from the <u>F</u>ile menu. This quirk can lead to unpredictable results.

Turning Notepad into a logbook

Although Notepad leans toward simplicity, it has one fancy feature that not even WordPad can match. Notepad can automatically stamp the current time and date at the bottom of a file whenever you open it. Just type **.LOG** in the very top left-hand corner of a file and save the file. Then, whenever you open that file again, you can jot down some current notes and have Notepad stamp it with the time and date. The result looks similar to what is shown in Figure 12-12.

Figure 12-12:
Add the word .LOG to the top of the file, and Notepad stamps it with the time and date whenever you open it.

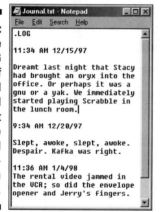

✔ Don't try the .LOG trick by using lowercase letters, and don't omit the period. It doesn't work.

✔ To stick in the date and time manually, press F5. The time and date appear, just as they do in the .LOG trick.

Painting in Paint

Do you love the smell of paint and a fresh canvas? Then you'll hate Paint. After working with real fibers and pigments, you'll find the computerized painting program that comes with Windows 98 to be a little sterile. But at least there's no mess. Paint creates pictures and graphics to stick into other programs. The icon for Paint is a picture of a palette, found in the Accessories menu (which leaps out from the Start menu's <u>P</u>rograms menu).

Paint offers more than just a paintbrush. It has a can of spray paint for that *airbrushed* look, several pencils of different widths, a paint roller for gobbing on a bunch of paint, and an eraser for when things get out of hand. Figure 12-13 was drawn with Paint.

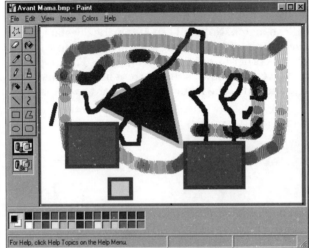

Figure 12-13:
Paint can create exotic art, like this picture my mother drew.

In addition to capturing your artistic flair, Paint can team up with a digital camera or scanner to touch up pictures in your PC. You can create a flashy letterhead to stick into WordPad letters. You can even create maps to paste into your party fliers.

- ✔ Drawings and pictures can be copied from Paint and pasted into just about any other Windows 98 program.

- ✔ Remember that *cut and paste* stuff from Chapter 8? Well, you can cut out or copy chunks of art from the Paint screen using the *select* or *free-form select* tools described later in this section. The art goes onto the Windows 98 Clipboard, where you can grab it and paste it into any other Windows program. (Paint doesn't support "Scraps," covered in Chapter 9.)

- ✔ Paint enables you to add text and numbers to graphics, so you can add street names to maps, put labels inside drawings, or add the vintage year to your wine labels.

Paint replaces Paintbrush from Windows 3.1. Unlike Paintbrush, the Paint program no longer saves files in PCX format. If you used PCX files, you may want to copy your old version of Paintbrush back onto your hard drive. (The old version can also do a few other things that Paint can't, such as erasing in straight lines when you hold down the Shift key.)

Word processing with WordPad

You can find most of the little programs that come with Windows 98 listed under the Accessories section of the Programs menu (which lurks in the menu that leaps up from the Start button). The icon for WordPad looks pretty fancy — a distinguished-looking fountain pen, like the ones that get ink on your hands.

Although the icon is fancy, WordPad isn't quite as fancy as some of the more expensive word processors on the market. You can't create multiple columns, for example, like the ones in newspapers or newsletters, nor can you double-space your reports. But WordPad works fine for letters, simple reports, and other basic documents. You can change the fonts around to get reasonably fancy, too, as shown in Figure 12-14.

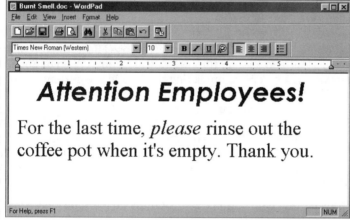

Figure 12-14: WordPad may not have a spell-checker, but it can churn out some fairly fancy pages.

WordPad can also handle the Windows *TrueType fonts* — that font technology that shapes how characters appear on-screen. You can create an elegant document by using some fancy TrueType fonts and mail it on a disk to somebody else. That person can view it in WordPad, just as you did. (Before TrueType, people could see only the fonts they had laboriously installed on their own computers.)

Plus, WordPad can handle all that embedding and linking stuff talked about in Chapter 9.

   ✔ WordPad works well for most word-processing needs: writing letters, reports, or term papers on somber philosophers with weird last names. Unless you're a lousy speller, you'll find WordPad easy to use, and you'll like its excellent price.

✔ If you're ditching your typewriter for Windows, remember this: On an electric typewriter, you have to press the Return key at the end of each line or else you start typing off the edge of the paper. Computers, in contrast, are smart enough to sense when words are about to run off the end of the screen. They automatically drop down a line and continue the sentence. (Hip computer nerds call this phenomenon *word wrap.*)

Press Enter only when you're finished typing a paragraph and want to start a new one. Press Enter twice to leave a blank line between paragraphs.

✔ WordPad replaces the old Write word processor from Windows 3.1, and it does almost everything Write could do. You won't find any way to add headers or footers, however, nor will WordPad let you double-space your documents. Finally, none of the new applications that come with Windows 98 let you search for funny characters, such as Tabs or Paragraph marks.

Opening and saving a file

In a refreshing change of pace, all Windows 98 programs enable you to open and save a file in exactly the same way: Choose File at the top of the program's window, and a menu tumbles down. Choose Open or Save, depending on your whim. A box pops up, listing the files in the current folder. Select the name of the file you want to open (click it) or type the name of a new file. Click Open or Save, and you're through!

✔ If you want to open a file you spot listed in Windows Explorer or the My Computer window, double-click the file's name. Windows 98 yanks the file into the right program and brings both the program and the file to the screen.

✔ You can find more explicit instructions on opening a file in Chapter 5.

✔ Folders and equally mind-numbing concepts are browbeaten in Chapter 11.

✔ When you save a file for the first time, you have to choose a name for it, as well as a folder to put it in. WordPad subsequently remembers the file's name and folder, so you don't have to keep typing them each time you save your current progress.

✔ WordPad can save files in several formats, from plain text to something weird called Unicode. All these formats are covered in the next section.

✔ Sometimes you open a file, change it, and want to save it with a different name or in a different folder. Choose Save As, not Save; WordPad then treats your work as if you were saving it for the first time — it asks you to type in a new name and a location.

✔ Chosen the Save option from WordPad's File menu, but decide to save your masterpiece in a new folder at the last minute? Right-click in the middle of the Save As box, choose New, and create Folder. Your new folder appears, ready for a name and some new files.

Saving a WordPad file in different formats

Just as you can't drop a Ford engine into a Volvo, you can't drop a WordPad file into another company's word processor. All brands of word processors save their information in different ways in order to confuse the competition.

WordPad can read and write in several file formats. As soon as you try to create a new file, WordPad forces you choose between five formats: Word for Windows 6.0, Rich Text Format (RTF), Text Document, Text Document — MS-DOS Format, and Unicode Text Document. Each format meets different needs.

✔ **Word for Windows 6.0:** This format creates files that can be read by Microsoft's *real* (and expensive) word processor, Microsoft Word. Many of the most popular competing word processors can read Word 6 files, too. You'll probably be safe with this format. (In fact, WordPad chooses it automatically if you can't make up your mind on a format and simply press the Enter key.)

✔ **Rich Text Format:** These files can also be read by a wide variety of word processors. Like the Word 6 documents, Rich Text documents can store **boldfaced** and *italicized* words, as well as other special formatting. These files can be *huge,* however. Don't choose this format unless it's the only format your friend's word processor accepts.

✔ **Text Document:** Almost all brands of word processors can read plain old text, making Text Only Document the safest format if you plan on exchanging files with friends. The Text Only document can't have any **boldface** type, *italic* type, columns, or any other fancy stuff, however. ***Nerdly note:*** Text Only files are also called *ASCII* files (pronounced *ASK-ee*).

✔ **Text Document — MS-DOS Format:** Same as Text Document, but a little more basic, if you can believe it.

✔ **Unicode:** Chances are, you'll avoid this one. It works with codes designed to display a variety of foreign languages and technical symbols.

If somebody asks you to save a WordPad file in a different format, choose Save <u>A</u>s from the <u>F</u>ile menu. Click the arrow next to the Save File as <u>T</u>ype box and choose the new format from the drop-down list. Type a new name for the file into the File <u>N</u>ame box and press Enter. *Voilà!* You've saved your file in the new format.

✔ The other word processor that comes with Windows 98, Notepad, can't handle anything but the plainest Text files. Notepad can't load WordPad's Word 6 files, and if it opens the Rich Text Format documents, the files look really weird. (WordPad can easily read Notepad's files, though.) Notepad gets its due earlier in this chapter.

✔ Although most word processors can read and write ASCII files, problems still occur. You lose any formatting, such as italicized words, special indents, or embedded pictures of apples.

✔ ASCII stands for American Standard Code for Information Interchange. A bunch of technoids created it when they got tired of other technoids saving their information in different ways. Today, most programs grudgingly read or write information using the ASCII format. In fact, ASCII files can even be exchanged with computers from different home planets, such as Apple Macintosh and UNIX workstations, with only minor technical glitches.

Other WordPad stuff

✔ A faster way to open a file is to press and release Alt and then press F and then O. If you memorize the keyboard commands, you won't have to trudge through all the menus with the mouse. If you don't remember the key commands, check out the handy chart in Table 12-1. You can find other time-savers listed, as well.

✔ To open a file, feel free to "drag" its name from Windows Explorer or My Computer window and drop the name directly into WordPad's open window. Whoosh! WordPad immediately sucks the file's contents into the open window.

✔ Want to change your page margins? Choose Page Setup from the File menu. The Page Layout dialog box lets you specify top, bottom, and side margins.

✔ Saved a file in WordPad, but now you want to delete it? Head for Windows Explorer or My Computer and delete it there. WordPad is an overly sensitive program; it can only *create* files, not destroy them.

Table 12-1	WordPad Shortcut Keys
To Do This	*Do This*
Open a file	Press Alt, F, and O.
Save a file	Press Alt, F, and S.
Save a file under a new name	Press Alt, F, and A.
Print a file	Press Alt, F, and P.
Select the entire document	Click rapidly three times in the left margin.
Select one word	Double-click it.
Add *italics* to selected text	Hold down Ctrl and press the letter I (press Ctrl+I).
Add **boldface** to selected text	Hold down Ctrl and press the letter B (press Ctrl+B).
Add <u>underline</u> to selected text	Hold down Ctrl and press the letter U (press Ctrl+U).

Internet Explorer and Outlook Express

Internet Explorer, the door to the Internet and its hodgepodge of Web sites, gets its own chapter in Chapter 13. It comes with a handful of other programs for putting together Web pages, sorting e-mail, chatting with other Internet surfers around the world, and performing other Internet-related tricks.

Internet Explorer's companion e-mail program, Outlook Express, gets a run-down in Chapter 13, as well.

The Online Services

Most people have heard about *online services,* where you can hook your computer up to the phone lines and, under the pretense of making direct-deposit payments through your checking account, swap pictures of your cat wearing a beret with newfound friends on the Cat User Group.

The latest version of Windows 98 comes with icons that access a bundle of online services and networks. You can point and click your way to The Microsoft Network, CompuServe, America Online, Prodigy, and AT&T WorldNet. Here's a look at what's what.

America Online, or AOL

America Online uses splashy graphics, easy-to-use buttons, and a huge market-ing campaign to propel its subscription past 17 million people. Unfortunately, many people simply take advantage of its various "trial offers," discover the AOL passageway to the Internet, and bail.

Still, if you're looking for an easy way to try out online services and still have access to the Internet and World Wide Web, America Online may be your best bet.

- ✔ America Online charges a flat fee for providing unlimited access to the Internet.

- ✔ America Online can be a great way to start experiencing online life. It provides a free trial period, and it lets you probe both the advantages of the America Online built-in forums and passageways to the Internet.

AT&T WorldNet

One of the newest entrants to the online service business, AT&T set a new pricing standard when it muscled its way into the Internet Service Provider ring in March 1996. Whereas most companies charged people an hourly rate for Web surfing, AT&T let its long-distance customers access the Internet all they wanted for a flat fee of $19.95.

Everybody else started offering the same deal, so AT&T extended its flat-fee offer to *everyone* — not just its long-distance customers. Since then, it's grown to about 1.5 million users.

- ✔ AT&T WorldNet Service comes with its own Web site offering standard fare: news, weather, entertainment, and convenient passageways to other Internet areas.
- ✔ CompuServe and America Online are *online services,* offering information available only through their own service in addition to the standard Internet fare. The messages on CompuServe's Chess Forum, for example, can only be read by CompuServe members. AT&T WorldNet Service, by contrast, is an *Internet provider,* not an online service. It has no Chess Forum.

CompuServe

One of the earliest and most expensive online services, CompuServe earned a reputation as one of the more "high-quality" services, as well. Because the service cost so much, forum messages stayed short, to the point, and mature. The world's Beavis-and-Butthead types simply couldn't afford to post.

CompuServe switched to the Internet audience today, though, attracting users with low-priced access and vast amounts of information.

- ✔ CompuServe still attracts more than 2 million users.
- ✔ Realizing its need to widen its network, CompuServe now allows its members to surf the Web, as well as send e-mail to and from Internet members.

The Microsoft Network

When Microsoft, always smelling cash, saw people making money through online services, it started an online service of its own. Microsoft called it The Microsoft Network, and it made the service outrageously easy to use: Anytime Windows 98 was installed on a computer, a Microsoft Network icon appeared on the desktop, just a click away.

Talk about free advertising! A curious Windows 98 user merely clicked the MSN icon, and the program took over, slyly grabbing its prey by the arms and telling the user exactly how to install the system and begin enjoying the pleasures of online life.

Needless to say, competing online services were outraged and headed for the courts, claiming unfair competition. Microsoft, eager to keep things from getting *too* ugly, struck a deal: It would put icons for the other online services on a desktop folder, too.

But because proprietary online services — The Microsoft Network included — are dying compared to the Internet, Microsoft has converted The Microsoft Network into a huge Web site, instead. (And, of course, it still costs money to join.)

Prodigy

Yet another online service with a link to the Internet, Prodigy found new investors to bring it back from the bankruptcy trough. Microsoft tosses in a trial kit so you can check it out yourself.

StartUp

Covered in Chapter 10, the StartUp folder lists programs that start automatically when Windows 98 loads itself for a day's work.

MS-DOS Prompt

This remnant lets old-time computer users boss their computers around by typing in a command. It brings up an MS-DOS window, ready to run old DOS programs (and games). In fact, it will even run Windows programs, if you're bored enough to type in the program's name and press the Enter key.

Windows Explorer

Covered completely in Chapter 11, Windows Explorer provides views of files stored on your computer and lets you copy them from one place to another.

My Version of Windows 98 Doesn't Have the Right Programs!

Depending on the buttons you punched when you installed Windows 98, you find different varieties of programs installed on your hard drive. Very few people get all the programs installed. If you feel left out and want some of the optional programs mentioned in this chapter, follow these steps. Beware, however; a few of the programs in this chapter only come with Windows 98 Second Edition.

1. **Double-click the Control Panel's Add/Remove Programs icon.**

   You can load the Control Panel by clicking Settings in the Start menu.

2. **Click the Windows Setup tab.**

   It's the tab in the middle of the three along the top; a box appears show-ing the various components of Windows 98, as well as the amount of space they need to nestle onto your computer's hard drive.

3. **Click in the little box by the programs or accessories you want to add.**

   A check mark appears in the box of the items you select. To select part of a category — a portion of the accessories, for example — click the category's name and click the Details button. Windows 98 lists the items available in that category so that you can select the ones you want. If you clicked the Details button, click the OK button to continue back at the main categories list.

4. **Click the OK button and insert your Windows 98 CD when asked.**

   Windows 98 copies the necessary files from your CD onto your hard drive. You can remove Windows 98 accessories the same way, but by *removing* the check mark from the box next to their name.

Chapter 13

Cruising the Web, Sending E-Mail, and Using Newsgroups

*T*he family photo album is disappearing. A friend of mine visited with his family the other day. He brought his new digital camera and took pictures of the vacation.

Each evening, he used the telephone and his laptop to send the camera's pictures to his Web site, and then he tweaked his Web site's settings to create a daily pictorial journal of the day's events. There's no black photo album in his closet; he's sharing his life with anybody who cares to look.

Other Web sites go to even more extremes. A cab driver in New York has a digital camera hooked up to a cellular phone; every few minutes, the camera takes a picture of the bustling streets, and automatically sends the photo to the cabbie's Web site.

You needn't be as elaborate with your own Web site. In fact, you don't need to have one at all. This chapter shows how to peek at all the other ones out there, though, should you get the urge.

What's the Difference Between the Internet, the World Wide Web, and a Web Browser?

The *Internet* is a rapidly growing collection of computers linked around the globe through wires and satellites. Millions of people of all ages swap information with other computers through the Internet.

The *World Wide Web* (known as "The Web," to be cool) runs on the Internet to let computers display *Web sites* — electronic, interactive software that resembles magazine pages with pretty pictures.

A *Web browser* lets you flip through a Web site's different pages, just like flipping a magazine. Best yet, the Web browser lets you jump from Web site to Web site, reading newspapers at one site, and ordering books or take-out food at another.

Internet Explorer, Windows 98's Web browser, makes the Web look like a kiosk in a hotel or airport lobby. There, you push different areas of the screen to find the right rental car.

Internet Explorer tosses similar "kiosklike" menus onto your computer screen. You point and click the on-screen buttons to view things like museums, beach cameras, pizza menus, guitar shops, city maps, and more. (You can even find the right rental car.)

- ✔ Just as television's channel surfers flip from channel to channel sampling the wares, Web surfers move from page to page, sampling the vast and esoteric piles of information.

- ✔ Just about anybody can set up a Web site, but doing so usually involves some programming skills using a language called *HTML* (HyperText Markup Language). Surfing across the pages is much easier than building the wave itself. That's why most people remain Web surfers.

- ✔ Because setting up a Web site on the Internet is fairly easy for programmers, thousands of just plain wacky sites exist. If you're agog over gargoyles, for example, head for `ils.unc.edu/garg/whatis1.html` to see pictures and read the history of these funky critters. Another fellow displays a puzzle game involving that wondrous can of mystery flesh, Spam (`www.rowan.edu/~hess/spam.html`).

Who Can Use the Internet and World Wide Web?

Gosh, everybody who *doesn't* use the Internet is forced to see everybody else talk about it at parties, on TV commercials, and read it in magazines, newspapers, and billboards.

Here are a few of the Internet's most enthusiastic subscribers:

- ✔ Universities, corporations, government entities, and millions of plain ol' normal folk use the Internet every day. Many simply send messages back and forth — *electronic mail* or *e-mail*. Other users swap programs, pictures, or sounds — anything that can be stored as data inside a computer.

- ✔ The United States government loves the Internet. The FBI posts pictures of its ten most wanted criminals (`www.fbi.gov`) for public viewing, for example, and the Internal Revenue Service (`www.irs.ustreas.gov/prod/cover.html`) lets Internet users make free copies of tax forms 24 hours a day.

- ✔ Universities, too, love the network. Departments can file grant forms more quickly than ever. Worried about the goo coagulating in the center of your bromeliads? The Internet's famed botanical (`www.botany.net/IDB`) allows researchers to move quickly from 24 Canoe Plants of Ancient Hawaii to the Zoosporic Fungi database.

- ✔ Many computer companies support their products on the Internet. Callers correspond with repairmen, hopefully figuring out why their latest computer doodads aren't working. After posting messages back and forth, callers can often download a software cure or patch to fix the problem.

- ✔ Businesses, spotting a new way to advertise, quickly jumped aboard the Web. Some vintage guitar dealers (`www.choiceguitar.com/guitars.html`), for example, display photos of their classic guitars, like the one shown in Figure 13-1, hoping to snag potential buyers. Some sites even let you click a picture to hear the howl of a '67 Stratocaster.

- ✔ Curious about Volkswagen's camper vans? Head for Volkswagen's special spot (`www.vw.com`) and start flipping the pages to see its latest "point and clickable" brochure on the camper van. (See Figure 13-2.)

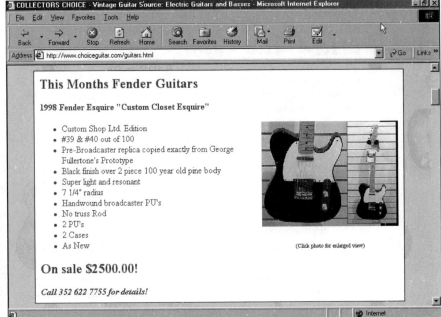

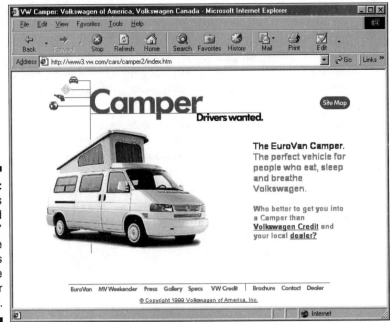

What's an ISP and Do I Need One?

Signals for television channels come wafting through the air to your TV set for free. Unless you're paying for cable or satellite TV, you can watch *Dawson's Creek* for free.

The Internet ain't free, though. You need to pay for Internet signals, just like you pay for gas and electricity. For the privilege of surfing the Web, you do business with an *Internet Service Provider* or *ISP.* You pay the ISP for a password and phone number to call. When your computer's modem dials the number and connects to your ISP's network, you type your password and grab your surfboard: You've entered the Web.

> ✔ Some ISPs charge for each minute you're connected; others provide a flat fee for unlimited service. The going rate seems to be stabilizing at around $20 a month for unlimited service. Make sure that you find out your rate before hopping aboard, or you may be surprised at the end of the month.

> ✔ If you're computer-inclined, some ISPs provide hard disk space on their computers so you can create *your* own Web pages for other Internet members to visit. Show the world pictures of your kids and cats! Share favorite recipes! Talk about your favorite car waxes! Swap tips on constructing fishing flies!

> ✔ Different ISPs let you connect in different ways. The slowest connect through the phone lines with a modem. Faster still are special ISDN lines provided from some phone companies. Some ISPs send their signal through satellites; some of the fastest come from your cable TV company.

What Do I Need to Access the World Wide Web?

A first-timer needs a computer, Internet browser software, a modem, and an ISP to connect to the Web. You have the computer, and the Internet Explorer Web browser comes wedged into almost every menu and crevice of Windows 98. (Click the little Windows symbol in the upper-right corner of nearly every folder, and Internet Explorer dashes to the forefront, ready to connect to the Web.)

How does an online service differ from the Internet?

Big corporations started following the government's lead on computer networks years ago. H&R Block, eager to get some use out of its huge computer network when it wasn't tax time, set up an online service company called CompuServe. People paid hourly fees to dial CompuServe and swap information, join discussion forums with people of similar interests, and download free software — all within the CompuServe community of networked computers.

As computers and modems grew more popular, other online services grew, too. America Online, Prodigy, Sierra Online, and other companies set up networks for people to call.

But as the World Wide Web grew in popularity, online services dwindled, mainly because they were too self-contained. The Web simply offered more information, and in most cases, at a better price.

Today, most online services offer access to the Internet to keep their customers from leaving. Windows 98 comes with free programs to access many online services; they're described in Chapter 12.

You can find an ISP listed in your community's Yellow Pages under *Computers — Online Services & Internet or Telecommunications.* Or, ask your local computer dealer for names and numbers. Also, many computer stores sell software called *Internet in a Box* that contains the software and the phone number you need to begin. You might even find offers in your mailbox.

- ✔ Blatant Endorsement Department: If you use the Internet a lot, please check with your cable department to see if it offers cable modem service. No more thumb-twiddling: Pictures, graphics and animation simply pop onto the screen. I love mine.

- ✔ Because techies created the Internet, it's often cumbersome to enter and navigate. Sometimes your computer can slip in as easily as a crooked politician. Other times, your computer makes you fill out many forms and enter a lot of numbers before it can use the Internet. Don't be afraid to ask a friend for help when connecting to your ISP for the first time.

- ✔ Don't be afraid to bug your ISP, too. The best ones come with technical support lines, where somebody can talk you through the installation process.

Should I connect to the Web through an ISP or an online service?

Both an online service and an Internet Service Provider let you connect to the Internet and begin pointing and clicking your way around the world. Both have their advantages.

Online services offer their own personalized banks of information for their customers that are inaccessible to other Web users. Only CompuServe members can access CompuServe's many product support forums, for example.

Plus, online services usually offer toll-free phone numbers to call from around the world (or at least around the United States). If you travel a great deal, this feature can be a valuable way to connect to the Internet from hotel rooms. Some ISPs also offer nationwide access, however — check before signing up.

What are the disadvantages? Online services tend to have slower connections to the Internet, and their phone numbers are often busy.

If you don't travel much and want a fast, steady connection to the Internet, you may be best off going straight through an Internet Service Provider.

- ✔ Life rolls along much easier once you're aboard the Internet. The Web is *enormous,* but it contains speedy indexes known as *search engines* that ferret out your favorite goodies. Type in a subject, and the search engine spits out bunches of applicable places to visit.

- ✔ Because Windows 98 can run so many things in the background, forgetting that you're connected to the Internet is an easy thing to do. If you're being charged by the hour, keep a wary eye on your Internet browser and make sure you log off when you no longer need to access the service.

What Is a Web Browser?

Your Web browser is your Internet surfboard — your transportation between the computers strewn along the Web. Internet Explorer 5.0 comes free with Windows 98 Second Edition. Some people use a competing browser called Netscape.

Both browsers work basically the same way. Every Web page comes with a specific address, just like houses do. When you type that address into the browser, the browser takes you there like a veteran cabby — unless you make a typo when typing in the address.

To avoid typing laborious addresses (those www things), Web browsers allow for lazy flipping through the Web's pages. They use *hypertext,* or *Web links.* Web page owners embed addresses of other Web pages into their own Web page. For example, the Web Museum Network in Paris (sunsite.unc.edu/louvre/) lets you visit museums from Australia to Singapore by simply clicking the museums' names.

Today's Web browsers come with little add-on bits of software for spicing things up. They can handle animated cartoons, voices, sounds, music, scrolling marquees, and other flashy goodies. If you kind of squint — and your computer's powerful enough — it looks like your computer's turning more and more into a TV.

- ✓ You don't like that new Web page you just clicked your way into? Click the big Back button at the top of your Web browser (on the top-left corner of Internet Explorer). Your Web browser immediately scurries back to your last location.

- ✓ Many places set up their own Web sites as simply collections of links to certain hobby areas, such as growing vegetables, weaving, or making cigars.

- ✓ Web sites come with hyperlinks. Highlighted words or buttons are linked to certain addresses of other computers on the Web. Click the button or highlighted word — usually underlined or a different color — and your Web browser takes you to the Web page with that address.

- ✓ Web site addresses look pretty strange. They usually start with the letters www and end with something even more weird-looking, like winespectator.com. Now you know what all those strange-looking words in parenthesis mean throughout this chapter.

How Do I Navigate the Web with Microsoft Internet Explorer?

After you've chosen and set up your Internet Service Provider — either by choosing The Microsoft Network, CompuServe, America Online, AT&T WorldNet, Prodigy, or somebody *not* included in the Windows 98 Online Services folder — you're ready to cruise the Internet.

Although Windows 98 Second Edition makes it easier than ever to hook up with an Internet provider, tweaking the settings can be a drag. First, try using the Internet Connection Wizard using the step-by-step process outlined in Chapter 12. That cures most of the basic problems.

If you're still having trouble getting your computer set up for the Internet, or you need more customized settings, a book like *The Internet For Dummies,* 6th Edition may help (published by IDG Books Worldwide, Inc.).

After you bring Internet Explorer to the screen, shown in Figure 13-3, you can put it to work. The next few sections show how.

Figure 13-3: Internet Explorer puts a Web page on the screen surrounded by navigational buttons.

What's a Home page?

Just as your television set always shows some channel when you turn it on, your Web browser automatically displays a certain portion of the ever-running Internet when loaded.

This first Web page you see when a Web browser comes to life is called your *Home page.* Your browser's Home page is simply a Web page that always appears whenever the browser is first loaded. It's always the same Web site.

A Web site's Home page, however, is a little different. It's like the cover of a magazine that lists the contents. Whenever you jump to a new Web site, you usually jump to that page's Home page.

From there, you can move around the Internet, searching for topics by look-ing in indexes or simply pointing and clicking from topic to topic.

- ✔ Most Web browsers come with their own home page preinstalled. When you install Internet Explorer and first log on to the Web, for example, you're whisked away to the Microsoft home page. The competing company's browser, Netscape Navigator, takes you to the Netscape home page.

- ✔ When you're bored with those Home pages, you can turn *any* Web site into a home page. While viewing the page you'd like to assign as your new home page, choose Internet Options from the Internet Explorer Tools menu. Click the General tab (that page usually opens automati-cally), and click the Use Current button. (It's the top-left button.)

- ✔ To return to your Home page quickly, whenever you're connected to the Internet, click the Home button along the top of Internet Explorer. (See the button in Figure 13-3, between the Refresh and Search buttons?)

How do I move around between Web pages?

Internet Explorer lets you move from page to page in three different ways:

- ✔ Pointing and clicking a button or link that automatically whisks you away to another page

- ✔ Typing a complicated string of code words into the browser's Address box and pressing Enter

- ✔ Clicking the navigation buttons along a browser's menu

The first way is the easiest. Look for a page's *links* — highlighted words or pictures — and click them. See the list of topics along the right side of Figure 13-3? Clicking "Favorite Wine Links" takes you to the Web page where Robin Garr shares his favorite Web sites with information about wine. See how the adjacent text in Figure 13-3 contains underlined words? Those are also links; click the underlined words to see Web pages with more information about them.

Buttons won't help if a friend gives you a napkin with a cool Web page's address written on it, however. In that case, you need to type the Web site's address yourself. That's fairly easy, as long as you don't misspell anything. See the Web site address for the Wine page along the top of Figure 13-3? I typed www.wine-lovers-page.com into the Address box and pressed Enter; Internet Explorer scooted me to Robin Garr's Wine Lovers Page. To head for the Volkswagen Web site, type in www.vw.com and press Enter. By pointing and clicking your way to that site's page with pictures of cars, you see the site in Figure 13-2.

Finally, you can maneuver through the Internet by clicking various parts of Internet Explorer itself. Clicking the F<u>a</u>vorites button along the top reveals a folder where you can stash buttons leading to your favorite Web sites. Click Go from the top-most menu for some other navigational menus.

Feel free to explore the Internet by simply clicking the buttons. You really can't get into any trouble; if you get stuck, you can always click the Home button along the top to move back into safety.

✔ The easiest way to start surfing the Internet is to be a button pusher, so remember this bit o' wisdom: Watch how your mouse pointer changes shape as you move it over a Web page. When the pointer changes into a little hand, you're hovering over a button that aches to be pressed.

✔ Why the caution over buttons? Because Web page manufacturers get mighty creative these days, and it's often hard to tell where to point and click. Some buttons look like sturdy elevator buttons; others look more like fuzzy dice or vegetables. But when you click a button, the browser takes you to the page relating to that button. Clicking the fuzzy dice may bring up a betting odds sheet for local casinos, for example.

✔ Pointed and clicked yourself into a dead end? Click the Back button along the top, left-hand corner to head for the last Web page you visited. If you click the Back button long enough, you'll wind up back at the Home page, where you started.

✔ Visited a Web site in the past few weeks, but can't remember which one? Click the History button from along the program's top to see links to all the sites you've visited in the past few weeks.

✔ Text can be grabbed, too. Slide your cursor over the text while holding down the mouse button, just as if you were in a word-processing program. When Internet Explorer highlights the text, press Ctrl+C to copy the text to the Clipboard.

How can I revisit my favorite places?

Sooner or later, you'll stumble across a Web page that's indescribably delicious. To make sure that you can visit it later, add it to your favorite places folder. Click the folder marked Favorites from the top of the Internet Explorer menu and choose the <u>A</u>dd to Favorites option. That effort deposits a link to your current page into the folder.

To return to the page, click the Favorites folder along the top of the screen again, and click the name of the link you want to revisit.

What's an index or search engine?

Just as it is nearly impossible to find a book in a library without a card catalog, it is nearly impossible to find a Web site on the Internet without a good index. Luckily, several exist.

To find one, click the Internet Explorer Search button along the top of the menu. The Internet Explorer Search page appears, as shown in Figure 13-4.

Type the name of the subject you're searching for — Cher, in this case — into the search box on the left, and click the Search button. After a few seconds, Internet Explorer brings up a list of Web sites dealing with that subject.

✔ Don't like dealing with that awkward search box on the left? Close it with a click on the X in its upper right corner. Then use the search box at the top of the remaining page.

✔ That particular page lets you choose from dozens of different search engines. Each engine searches for applicable material in a different way, using different databases.

✔ If you don't like what one index is coming up with, click another one and try again.

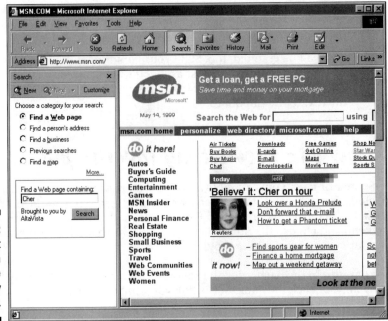

Figure 13-4:
Internet
Explorer can
search the
Web for any
subject.

✔ AltaVista is a personal favorite, as is Infoseek and Yahoo!

 ✔ Searches usually come up with hundreds, or even thousands, of hits relating to your subject. If you come up with too many, try again, but be more specific.

How Does Windows 98 Improve Internet Access?

Windows 98 doesn't improve Internet access as much as it makes it more accessible by piling it onto menus. It includes a free Web browser — Internet Explorer — in addition to bunches of free programs for chatting and video-conferencing over the Net, faster video access, more secure online transaction, and other exciting technojabber.

Want the Internet to work behind your back? Fire up the Active Desktop, and you can put a little stock ticker in the corner of your screen.

Windows and the Internet understand each other better. For example, if you're typing in a long-and-laborious HTTP address — one you just typed in last night — Windows 98 recognizes the address and types it in for you.

While many of these goodies are already available to Windows 95 users through a few handfuls of upgrades, Windows 98 provides an all-in-one package that's bound to be the standard.

It Doesn't Work!

Don't feel bad. The Internet's been around for a while, but this whole Web thing is relatively new, and quickly becoming overburdened. It's not supposed to work smoothly. Here are some of the most common problems and some possible solutions.

I can't get it to install!

Installing Internet Explorer isn't all that difficult; the hard part is telling Internet Explorer how to connect to your Internet Service Provider — the company that's providing the phone connection to the Internet.

Check out the Internet Connection Wizard described in Chapter 12. It displays your current settings, and allows you to change them if needed.

Because the ISPs all use slightly different ways to connect, your best bet is to call the tech support number and ask for help.

Yeah, installation is a pain, but remember — you only have to install the thing once. After Internet Explorer is installed, you can simply click a button to make it dial up the connection and start surfing.

I keep getting busy signals!

This problem means that your Internet Service Provider is probably offering a great deal — unlimited access to the Internet for one low price. Unfortunately, a bargain means that many people are going to be calling at the same time as you, leading to busy signals.

What's the answer? Reassess your priorities. Are you looking to save money or find a reliable connection to the Internet? You may be able to find a better deal with a different provider.

The Web page says it needs [insert name of weird plug-in thing here]!

Computer programmers abandoned their boring old TV sets and turned to their exciting new computers for entertainment. Now, they're trying to turn their computers back into TV sets. They're using a fancy programming techniques called *Java*, *Shockwave*, *Frames*, and other goodies that add animation and other gizmos to the Internet.

They're also adding little software tidbits called "plug-ins" that increase your computer's capability to display flashy advertisements along the top of your screen.

What's the problem? New versions of these plug-ins follow the seasons. If your computer says it needs a plug-in or its latest version, click the Web page's button that takes you to its downgrade area.

Close down all your software (except for the Web browser), download the software, and install it. The next time you open your Web browser, the advertisements will have never looked better.

The Web page says that it's optimized for Navigator, not Explorer!

Many Web surfers use Netscape Navigator, not Internet Explorer. So, many programmers optimize their Web pages for the Navigator program.

Usually, this doesn't matter. Internet Explorer can usually display the page just as well as Netscape Navigator. Other times, the differences won't even be noticeable. You might not see the animation of a cockroach crawling across the screen, for example.

I can't figure any of this stuff out!

The Internet and its World Wide Web can be rough for beginners to figure out — and it's much too complex to be stuffed into a single chapter of this book. To pick up more information on the Internet, head for the bookstore and pick up a copy of *The Internet For Dummies,* 6th Edition, published by IDG Books Worldwide, Inc.

Managing E-Mail With Outlook Express

Internet Explorer merely flips through the Web pages stuffed onto the Internet, letting you jump from page to page.

Outlook Express, on the other hand, uses the Internet as a Post Office, letting you send letters and files to anybody with an Internet account. Best yet, the recipients of your e-mail don't have to use Outlook Express to view and respond to them: Almost any e-mail program can talk to almost any other one. (Some e-mail programs can't receive files well — or at all — but that's another story.)

This section guides you through setting up Outlook Express, writing a letter, sending it, and reading the responses.

Setting up Outlook Express 5.0

The outlook for Outlook Express isn't always good. See, Outlook Express is designed to work with an industry-standard Internet Service Provider that pipes the Internet signal to your computer without an online service getting in the way.

That means Outlook Express 5, the version included with Windows 98 Second Edition, doesn't work with online services like CompuServe and America Online (AOL). Those online services come with built-in e-mail programs that process mail differently than Outlook Express does. So if you're using America Online or CompuServe, don't bother reading this section. You won't be using Outlook Express 5.0.

If you're using a plain old Internet Service Provider, however, you're in luck. Chances are, Windows 98 Second Edition's newly improved Internet Connection Wizard has already configured Outlook Express to send and receive your mail. (Outlook Express sends and receives mail through the same service you're using to access Web sites.)

Can't get any e-mail, or is your account acting weird? Head back to Chapter 12 and check out Step 6 of the Internet Connection Wizard. You'll need the username, phone number, and password given to you by your ISP.

To call up Outlook Express for the first time, click on its desktop icon: An envelope surrounded by twirling blue arrows. Or click on the tiny version of that icon next to your Start button. Or click the Start button and choose Outlook Express from Programs. Or . . . well, you get the idea. No matter which button you push, Outlook Express pops onto the screen, looking like Figure 13-5.

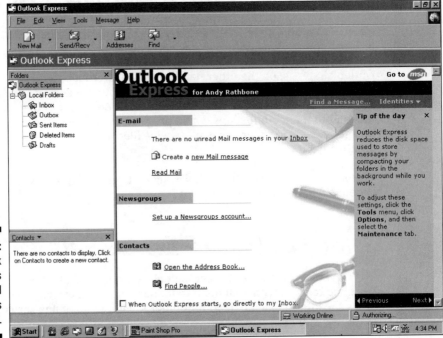

Figure 13-5: Outlook Express sends and receives e-mail.

If Outlook Express asks for a password, head back to Chapter 12 and run the Internet Connection Wizard, making sure to type your password into the correct box. You gotta have that password, or you can't read your mail. (Nobody else can read it, either — the password protects your e-mail from prying eyes, no matter how gross that metaphor sounds.)

America Online and CompuServe users can't use Outlook Express 5.0 on their own computers to send e-mail. However, they can still accept e-mail from somebody using Outlook Express 5.0, or any other e-mail program.

The screen consists of three main parts: Folders, where you store your e-mail; Contacts, which displays address book entries; and the work screen, where you choose whether you'll be looking at e-mail or newsgroups. (More on newsgroups later.)

Getting ready to send e-mail

To send e-mail to a friend or enemy you need three things:

✔ **A properly configured Outlook Express**

The Internet Connection Wizard automatically configures Outlook Express when it sets up Internet Explorer 5.0.

✔ **Your friend or enemy's e-mail address**

You need to find out your friend's e-mail address by simply asking them. There's no way to guess. It consists of a user name (which isn't always their real name), followed by the @ sign, followed by the name of their Internet Service Provider, be it America Online, Juno, or any of the thousands of other ISPs. The e-mail address of somebody with the user name of Jeff9435 who subscribes to America Online would be jeff9435@aol.com.

✔ **Your message**

Here's where the fun part starts: Typing your letter. When you've typed in the e-mail address and the letter, you're ready to send your message along its merry way.

You can find e-mail addresses on business cards, Web sites, and even return addresses: Whenever anybody sends you some e-mail, you can see their e-mail address for responding.

It doesn't matter if you capitalize part of an e-mail address or not. It will still get there.

Composing a letter

Ready to send your first letter? Follow these steps to compose your letter and drop it into the electronic mailbox, sending it through virtual space to your friend's electronic mailbox.

New Mail

1. **Click the New Mail icon in the upper-left corner of Outlook Express.**

   A New Message window appears, as shown in Figure 13-6.

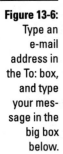
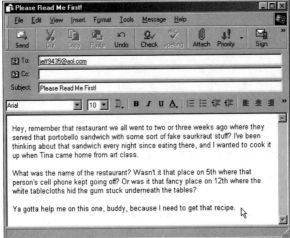

Figure 13-6:
Type an
e-mail
address in
the To: box,
and type
your mes-
sage in the
big box
below.

2. **Type your friend's e-mail address into the To: box.**

   Type or whatever the person's e-mail happens to be.

3. **Fill in the Subject: box.**

   This one's optional, but it helps your friend know what your e-mail is about. That way they can choose to respond right away, or file it in the "I'll respond when I get around to it" box.

4. **Type your message in the large box at the box's bottom.**

   Type whatever you want, and for as long as you want. There's very little limit on the size of a text file.

5. Click the Send button in the box's top, left corner.

Whoosh! Outlook Express whisks your message through the Internet pipelines where it will appear in your recipient's mailbox. Depending on the speed of the Internet connections, the mail will arrive anywhere within 15 seconds to 5 days, with a few minutes being the average.

Not too good of a speler? Then click the spell check button from the icons along the top. Or, click on Tools and choose Spelling from the menu that appears. Or push your F7 key. Or grab a dictionary off the shelf. (Pressing F7 is quicker.)

Want to attach a file to your message? After completing Step 4, click the paperclip icon. Windows 98 brings up a box straight out of My Computer. Navigate through the folders to reach the file you'd like to send, and then double-click on its name. When you click the Send button in Step 5, Outlook Express will send your message — and the attached file — to your friend. (Files usually can't be larger than about 4MB, though.)

Reading a received letter

If you keep Outlook Express running 24 hours a day, you'll know when a new letter drops into your mailbox. Most computers make a breezy little sound to notify you of its arrival. You'll also spot a tiny Outlook Express icon sitting in the bottom-right corner of your desktop, right next to the digital clock.

To check for any new mail if Outlook Express isn't running, load it from the Start menu, toolbar, or any other way that's convenient.

Then follow these steps to read your letter and either respond or file it away into one of Outlook Express' convenient folders.

1. Open Outlook Express.

When Outlook Express fills the screen, it says you have an unread mail message in your Inbox, as seen in Figure 13-7.

2. Click on the words *Read Mail* to read your new message.

The new message appears, as shown in Figure 13-8, ready for reading.

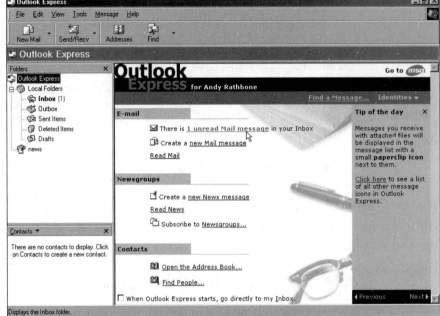

Figure 13-7: Click in Outlook Express to read your unread message.

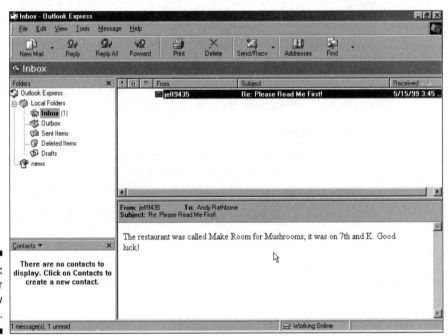

Figure 13-8: Read your new message.

From here, Outlook Express leaves you with many options, each described below.

- ✔ You can do nothing. This leaves the message in your Inbox folder, where it will stay until deleted.

- ✔ You can respond to the message. Click the Reply icon along the top of Outlook Express, and a new box appears, ready for you to type in a message. The box is just like the one that appears when you first compose a message, but there's a big difference: This one is preaddressed with the recipient's name and the subject.

- ✔ You can file the message. See the Folders window on the left? Right-click on Local Folders, choose New Folder, and type a name like Personal or Business into the Folder name box. See your newly created folder listed beneath Local Folders? Drag and drop the message into that folder for organized safekeeping.

- ✔ You can print the message. Click the Print icon along the menu's top, and Outlook Express shoots your message to the printer to make a paper copy.

- ✔ Outlook Express can handle more complicated tasks, but these basic steps allow you to send and receive e-mail to your friends and congressional leaders.

What does the "News" area do?

Thousands of people with similar interests yak it up on the Internet through something called *Newsgroups*. Newsgroups work sort of like mail that everybody gets to read.

A Newsgroup is like a public bulletin board. One person posts a message, then everybody can read it and post their own reply, which spawns more replies.

To keep them on track, Newsgroups are divided by subject — usually more than 30,000 of them — and Outlook Express can display all the subjects onto your screen when you double-click on the word News or choose Subscribe to Newsgroups on the main window, as shown in Figure 13-9.

Outlook Express then searches for names of all the newsgroups carried by your Internet Service Provider and displays them on the screen. Collecting the names and descriptions of thousands of Newsgroups takes some time, as shown in Figure 13-10, so play FreeCell for awhile. Luckily, Outlook only searches for the Newsgroups once, and then it remembers them all.

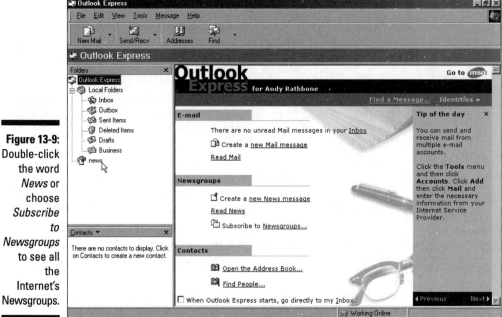

Figure 13-9:
Double-click
the word
News or
choose
*Subscribe
to
Newsgroups*
to see all
the
Internet's
Newsgroups.

Figure 13-10:
Outlook
Express
must track
down all the
Newsgroups'
names and
descriptions
so you can
look at
them.

Finding and reading a Newsgroup

With many thousands of Newsgroups, how can you find the right one? Well, start by making Outlook Express find it for you. For example, here's how to find and subscribe to a Newsgroup with discussions on recipes.

1. **Make Outlook Express gather a list of Newsgroup names.**

   Discussed in the preceding section, the searching for Newsgroup names must only be conducted once. (Thank goodness, because it can take a l-o-n-g time.)

2. **Type recipe into the box named Display newsgroups which contain.**

   That's the word `recipe` – nothing else. As soon as you begin to type, Outlook Express begins weeding out Newsgroups that don't contain the letters of the word *recipe.* Eventually, only the Newsgroups that deal with recipes will remain on your screen.

3. **Search through the findings.**

   In this case, a dozen or so Newsgroups deal with recipes. Click on the scroll bar to the right of the Newsgroup box to view all the findings.

4. **Subscribe to the Newsgroup you want.**

   Click a Newsgroup name that looks interesting and then click the Subscribe button to the right. A little icon appears beside the name, letting you know you've subscribed. Subscribe to as many or as few Newsgroups as you want.

5. **After subscribing to your chosen Newsgroups, click the OK button.**

   Your newly chosen Newsgroups now appear at the very bottom of the folders on the left side of the Outlook Express window.

6. **Click one of your recently subscribed names.**

   A list of postings in that particular Newsgroup appears on the right side of the screen, as shown in Figure 13-11.

7. **Finally, click one of the postings to see what that person has written about the topic.**

   In Figure 13-11, for example, you click on WANTED PICKLED MANGO RECIPE!!!! or any of the other postings, and Outlook Express brings up the message in a window, just as if it were e-mail.

That's it; you've subscribed to the wacky world of Newsgroups, where you can find people chatting about nearly every subject imaginable — and some unimaginable ones, as well.

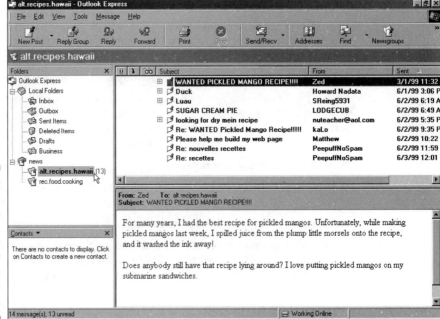

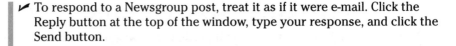

Figure 13-11:
After sub-
scribing to
Newsgroups,
click on one
of their
names to
see the
postings.

✔ To respond to a Newsgroup post, treat it as if it were e-mail. Click the Reply button at the top of the window, type your response, and click the Send button.

✔ Newsgroups are public information, as opposed to e-mail, which is private. Don't say anything on a Newsgroup that might hurt your chances for public office. (And don't write anything that you wouldn't want your parents, spouse, boss, or next-door neighbor to read.)

✔ Some of the information on Newsgroups deals with very adult-oriented content. Make sure you know what Newsgroups your kids are reading.

✔ Newsgroups can be a valuable source of computer help. If your monitor isn't working correctly, look for a Newsgroup dealing with monitor issues. You might even find a Newsgroup dealing with your specific brand of monitor. Post your question, and see if anybody's had a similar problem and, best yet, found a solution.

✔ Many people who hang out on Newsgroups view themselves as "old-timers" who resent any encroachment on their territory. Before posting, spend some time "lurking" on a Newsgroup to get a taste of its particular flavor and decorum.

Part IV
Help!

The 5th Wave   By Rich Tennant

©RICHTENNANT

"IT'S A MEMO FROM SOFTWARE DOCUMENTATION. IT'S EITHER AN EXPLANATION OF HOW THE NEW SATELLITE COMMUNICATIONS NETWORK FUNCTIONS, OR DIRECTIONS FOR REPLACING BATTERIES IN THE SMOKE DETECTORS."

In this part . . .

Windows 98 can do hundreds of tasks in dozens of ways. This means that approximately one million things can fail at any given time.

Some problems are easy to fix. For example, one misplaced pair of clicks in the taskbar makes all your programs disappear. Yet one more click in the right place puts them all back.

Other problems are far more complex, requiring teams of computer surgeons to diagnose, remedy, and bill accordingly.

This part helps you separate the big problems from the little ones. You'll know whether you can fix it yourself with a few clicks and a kick. If your situation's worse, you'll know when it's time to call in the surgeons.

Chapter 14

The Case of the Broken Window

In This Chapter

▶ How to make an emergency startup disk

▶ How to fix a haggard mouse

▶ What to do if you're stuck in Menu Land

▶ How to install a new "driver" for a new computer gizmo

▶ How to install other parts of Windows 98

▶ What to do when you click the wrong button

▶ What to do when your computer freezes

▶ What to do when your printer is not working correctly

▶ Some of Windows' files don't work right

▶ How to change double-clicks to single-clicks and vice versa

Sometimes you just have a sense that something's wrong. The computer makes quiet grumbling noises, or Windows 98 starts running more slowly than Congress. Other times something's obviously wrong. Pressing any key just gives you a beeping noise, menus keep shooting at you, or Windows 98 greets you with a cheery error message when you first turn it on.

Many of the biggest-looking problems are solved by the smallest-looking solutions. Hopefully, this chapter points you to the right one.

Making a Startup Disk

Unless you grab a spare floppy right now, this information won't do you any good. See, Windows 98 can make a startup disk for emergencies. When Windows 98 refuses to load, you can pop the disk into your computer's mouth, push the reset button, and a bare-bones version of Windows 98 comes to the screen. That bare-bones version may be enough to get you started. At the very least, it can make it easier for a computer guru friend to get your computer started.

So grab a floppy disk that's blank or doesn't have important information on it. This procedure erases the disk's contents and there's no turning back.

1. **Double-click the Control Panel's Add/Remove Programs icon.**

   You can load the Control Panel by clicking Settings in the Start menu.

2. **Click the Windows Startup Disk tab.**

   It's the right-most tab of the three along the top.

3. **Click the Create Disk button.**

   After grunting a little bit, Windows 98 tells you to insert a disk into drive A. Before pushing the disk into the drive, grab a felt-tip pen and write Emergency Startup Disk on the floppy disk's label.

4. **Insert a blank disk into drive A when told; then click the OK button.**

   Windows 98 formats the blank disk and copies special files onto it, allowing it to start your computer in the worst of situations. Put the disk in a safe place and hope you never have to use it.

   - In an emergency, put the disk in drive A and push your computer's reset button — that "last resort" button that's one step shy of turning the power switch on and off. The computer "boots" off the floppy disk; that is, the computer comes to life, even though its hard drive isn't working.

   - When loaded from the floppy disk, Windows 98 comes up in "DOS prompt" mode. It won't look anything like the real Windows 98, but a computer guru may be able to use the DOS prompt as a doorway to fix whatever's gone wrong.

My Mouse Doesn't Work Right

Sometimes the mouse doesn't work at all; other times the mouse pointer hops across the screen like a flea. Here are a few things to look for:

✔ If no mouse arrow is on the screen when you start Windows, make sure that the mouse's tail is plugged snugly into the computer's rump. Then exit and restart Windows 98.

✔ If the mouse arrow is on-screen, but won't move, Windows may be mistaking your brand of mouse for a different brand. You can make sure that Windows 98 recognizes the correct type of mouse by following the steps on adding new hardware, as described in Chapter 9.

TIP

✔ A mouse pointer can jump around on-screen if it's dirty. First, turn the mouse upside-down and clean off any visible dirt stuck to the bottom. Then twist the little round cover until the mouse ball pops out. Wipe off any crud and blow any dust out of the hole. Pull any stray hairs and dust off the little rollers and stick the ball back inside the mouse. If you wear wool sweaters (or have a cat that sleeps on the mouse pad), you may have to clean the ball every week or so.

✔ If the mouse was working fine and now the buttons seem to be reversed, you've probably changed the right- or left-handed button configuration setting in the Control Panel. Double-click the Control Panel's Mouse icon and make sure that the configuration is set up to match your needs. (That's covered in Chapter 9, by the way.)

I'm Stuck in Menu Land

If your keystrokes don't appear in your work but instead make a bunch of menus shoot out from the top of the window, you're stuck in Menu Land. Somehow you've pressed and released Alt, an innocent-looking key that's easy to hit accidentally.

When you press and release Alt, Windows turns its attention away from your work and toward the menus along the top of the window.

To get back to work, press and release Alt one more time. Alternatively, press Esc. One or the other is your ticket out of Menu Land.

I'm Supposed to Install a New Driver

When you buy a new toy for the computer, it usually comes with a piece of software called a *driver*. A driver is a sort of translator that lets Windows know how to boss around the new toy. If you buy a new keyboard, sound card, compact disc player, printer, mouse, monitor, or almost any other computer toy, you need to install its driver in Windows. Luckily, it's a fairly painless process covered in the section on adding new hardware in Chapter 9.

✔ Companies constantly update drivers, fixing problems or making the drivers perform better. If the computer device is misbehaving, a newer driver may calm it down. Call the manufacturer and ask for the latest version. Or, if you've entered the world of the Internet, fire up your modem and head for the manufacturer's Web page so that you can make a free copy.

✔ To find the company's Web page, rev up Internet Explorer, head to the Yahoo.com web site and type the company's name. Chances are, Yahoo! can dig it up and let you head there with a mouse click.

✔ Not all computer toys work with Windows 98. In fact, some games don't even work with some sound cards, and some software won't work with certain CD-ROM drives. Bring a list of your computer's parts to the store and check them with the requirements listed on the side of a computer toy's box before setting down the cash.

✔ To get a list of your computer's parts, right-click the My Computer icon and click the Device Manager tab. Click the Pri<u>n</u>t button and click OK. You might not be able to make sense of the detailed computer information, but the folks at the store can decipher the numbers.

✔ After you've registered Windows 98, a program called Windows Update handles many chores for keeping Windows 98 up to date. Windows Update dials a special place on the Internet and downloads updated information your computer might need.

His Version of Windows 98 Has More Programs Than Mine!

Windows 98 installs itself differently on different types of computers. As it copies itself over to a hard drive, it brings different files with it. If installed on a laptop, for example, Windows 98 brings along programs that help a laptop transfer files and keep track of its battery life.

Computers with smaller hard drives will probably get the minimum files Windows 98 needs to run. Chapter 12 describes some of the programs and accessories Windows 98 comes with; here's how to copy them to your computer if Windows 98 left them off the first time.

1. **Double-click the Control Panel's Add/Remove Programs icon.**

   You can load the Control Panel by clicking <u>S</u>ettings in the Start menu.

2. **Click the Windows Setup tab.**

   It's the tab in the middle of the three along the top; after a moment of thumb-twiddling, a box appears that shows the various components of Windows 98, as well as the amount of space they need to nestle onto your computer's hard drive.

3. **Click in the little box by the programs or accessories you want to add.**

   A check mark appears in the box of the items you've selected. To select part of a category — a portion of the accessories, for example — click the category's name and click the <u>D</u>etails button. Windows 98 lists the items available in that category, so you can only click the ones you want. If you clicked the <u>D</u>etails button, click the OK button to continue back at the main categories list.

4. **Click the OK button and insert your installation disks when asked.**

Windows 98 copies the necessary files from your installation disks onto your hard drive. You can remove Windows 98 accessories by *removing* the check mark from the box next to their name.

Windows 98 comes with some pretty weird stuff, so don't get carried away and copy *all* of it over — especially stuff that you're not even going to use.

I Clicked the Wrong Button (But Haven't Lifted My Finger Yet)

Clicking the mouse takes two steps: a push and a release. If you click the wrong button on-screen and haven't lifted your finger yet, press the Esc button and slowly slide the mouse pointer off the button on-screen. Then take your finger off the mouse.

The screen button pops back up, and Windows 98 pretends nothing happened. Thankfully.

My Computer Is Frozen Up Solid

Every once in a while, Windows just drops the ball and wanders off somewhere to sit under a tree. You're left looking at a computer that just looks back. Panicked clicks don't do anything. Pressing every key on the keyboard doesn't do anything — or worse yet, the computer starts to beep at every key press.

When nothing on-screen moves except the mouse pointer, the computer is frozen up solid. Try the following approaches, in the following order, to correct the problem:

Approach 1: Press Esc twice.

That action usually doesn't work, but give it a shot anyway.

Approach 2: Press Ctrl, Alt, and Delete all at the same time.

If you're lucky, Windows flashes an error message saying that you've discovered an "unresponsive application" and lists the names of currently running programs — including the one that's not responding. Click the name of the program that's causing the mess and click the End Task button. You lose any unsaved work in it, of course, but you should be used to that. (If you somehow stumbled onto the Ctrl+Alt+Delete combination by accident, press Esc at the unresponsive-application message to return to Windows.)

If that still doesn't do the trick, try clicking the Shut Down button that's next to the End Task button (pressing Ctrl+Esc, then U and S), or pressing Ctrl+Alt+Delete again. That shuts down your computer and lets you start over.

Approach 3: If the preceding approaches don't work, push the computer's reset button.

The screen is cleared, and the computer acts like you turned it off and on again. When the dust settles, Windows 98 should return to life.

Approach 4: If not even the reset button works, turn the computer off, wait 30 seconds, and then turn it back on again.

Don't ever flip the computer off and on again quickly. Doing so can damage its internal organs.

If your computer's *really* acting up, it's time for heavy duty action. As the computer starts up, press your F8 key. Instead of loading itself, Windows will toss a menu onto the screen. Tell Windows to load in "Safe" mode. Windows will come to life with a minimum set of drivers: bare-bones color and screen size, no network support, and no CD-ROM drive. But at least you'll be able to access your files.

The Printer Isn't Working Right

If the printer's not working right, start with the simplest solution first: Make sure that it's plugged into the wall and turned on. Surprisingly, this step fixes about half the problems with printers. Next, make sure that the printer cable is snugly nestled in the ports on both the printer and the computer. Then check to make sure that it has enough paper — and that the paper isn't jammed in the mechanism.

Then try printing from different programs, such as WordPad and Notepad, to see whether the problem's with the printer, Windows 98, or a particular Windows program. Try printing the document by using different fonts. All these chores help pinpoint the culprit.

The Windows Help program can also pitch in; click Help from the Start menu, click the Index tab, and type the word **printers** into the box. Press Enter to find the printers help section, then choose the printer's troubleshooting program to figure out why the printer's goofing off.

If you don't have access to the Internet, call the printer's manufacturer and ask for a new Windows driver. When the disk comes in the mail, follow the instructions in the printer section of Chapter 9.

If you can get on the Internet, head to the printer manufacturer's Web site and look for the latest driver. Chances are, you'll find the manufacturer listed at Yahoo.com, a huge Internet search engine that's particularly efficient at finding businesses.

Some of Windows' Files Don't Work Right

Windows 98 comes with some built-in sleuths for tracking down damaged parts of itself and helping you repair them. Follow these steps to put Windows 98 up on the jacks and make it wear its own mechanic's overalls.

1. **Click the Start button, point at Programs, and choose Accessories.**

2. **From the Accessories area, click on System Tools and load the System Information program.**

3. **Click Tools and choose System File Checker from the menu that tumbles down.**

4. **Make sure that the Scan for altered files button is checked and choose Start.**

Windows 98 kicks the tires of all the files it came with. If any of the files are damaged or altered, it asks you to insert your original Windows 98 CD so it can copy the good versions back onto your hard drive.

This trick comes in handy if Windows 98 sends messages upon startup that a file is missing or damaged.

My Double-Clicks Are Now Single-Clicks!

In an effort to make things easier, Windows 98 lets people choose whether a single-click or a double-click should open a file or folder.

But if you're not satisfied with the click method Windows 98 uses, here's how to change it:

1. **Click the Start button, point at Settings and choose Folders Options.**

2. **If you want the traditional, double-click look — the one where your entire computer doesn't act like a Web page — click the Classic style button. To make the computer behave more like a Web page — where you activate programs by clicking them once — click the Web style button.**

3. **If you want a combination of the Web-page look plus your own choice of single or double-clicks, choose Custom, based on settings you choose option; then click the OK button to put your choices into action.**

Chapter 15

Error Messages (What You Did Does Not Compute)

● ●

In This Chapter

▶ Not enough memory

▶ A:\ is not accessible. The device is not ready.

▶ Destination disk drive is full

▶ The file or folder that this shortcut refers to cannot be found

▶ This filename is not valid

▶ There is no viewer capable of viewing WordPad document files

▶ Deleting this file will make it impossible to run this program

▶ Open with . . .

▶ You must type a filename

▶ Cannot open Internet address; connection to server could not be established

▶ Windows 98 was not properly shut down

● ●

*M*ost people don't have any trouble understanding error messages. A car's pleasant beeping tone means that you've left your keys in the ignition. A terrible jumping sound from the stereo means that the compact disc has a scratch.

Things are different with Windows 98, however. The error messages in Windows 98 could have been written by a Senate subcommittee, if only they weren't so brief. When Windows 98 tosses an error message your way, it's usually just a single sentence. Windows 98 rarely describes what you did to cause the error, and even worse, hardly ever tells you how to make the error go away for good.

Here are some of the words that you'll find in the most common error messages Windows 98 throws in your face. This chapter explains what Windows 98 is trying to say, why it's saying it, and just what the heck it expects you to do about it.

Not Enough Memory

Meaning: Windows 98 is running out of the room it needs to operate.

Probable cause: You have too many windows simultaneously opened on the screen.

Solutions: A short-term solution is to close some of the windows. Also, make sure that you're not using any large color pictures of peacocks for wallpaper. It takes much less memory to tile small pictures across the screen (see Chapter 9 for information about tiling windows). If Windows 98 still acts sluggish, click the Start button, choose Sh<u>u</u>t Down, and choose the <u>R</u>estart the Computer option.

For a long-term solution, make sure that you have plenty of empty space on your hard drive so that Windows has room to read and write information. Delete any files or programs you don't use anymore.

The DiskClean program, described in Chapter 12, rummages through your hard drive and automatically clears it of file detritus.

Finally, consider buying some more memory. Windows works much better with 16MB of memory than with 8MB of memory. And 32MB of memory is better still. Today, people are walking out the door with 64MB of memory in their laptops, and nobody's laughing. In fact, the oldsters are crying because memory costs about one-tenth of what it did five years ago.

Whenever you cut or copy a large amount of information to the Clipboard, that information stays there, taking up memory — even after you've pasted it into another application. To clear out the Clipboard after a large paste operation, copy a single word to the Clipboard. Doing so replaces the earlier, memory-hogging chunk, freeing some memory for other programs.

A: Is Not Accessible. The Device Is Not Ready.

Meaning: Windows can't find a floppy disk in drive A.

Probable cause: No floppy disk is in there.

Solution: Slide a disk in and wish all errors were this easy to fix.

Destination Disk Drive Is Full

Meaning: Windows 98 has run out of room on a floppy disk or on the hard drive to store something.

Probable cause: Windows 98 tried saving something to a disk file, but ran out of space.

Solution: Clear more room on that disk before saving your work. Delete any junk files on the hard disk. Try running the DiskClean program described in Chapter 12. Also, delete any programs you don't use anymore using the Control Panel's Add/Remove Programs feature.

Also, in this era when the Microsoft Monster Truck Madness game consumes 100MB of hard drive space for a rowdy race, it may be time to upgrade to a larger hard drive.

The File or Folder That This Shortcut Refers to Can't Be Found

Meaning: Windows 98 can't find the program that's supposed to be attached to a Shortcut icon.

Probable cause: One of the programs has moved, renamed, or deleted a file after a shortcut was attached to it.

Solution: Try using the Windows 98 Find program, described in Chapter 7. If the Find program can't find it, double-click the Recycle Bin to see if it's in there and can be salvaged.

This Filename Is Not Valid

Meaning: Windows 98 refuses to accept your choice of filename.

Probable cause: You've tried to name a file by using one or more of the forbidden characters.

Solution: Turn to the section about renaming a file in Chapter 11 and make sure that you're not naming a file something you shouldn't.

There Is No Viewer Capable of Viewing WordPad Document Files

Meaning: Windows 98 can't show you what's in that file using Quick View.

Probable cause: You're probably trying to view a word-processor file using Quick View, and that file probably ends in the hidden letters DOC. Therefore, Windows 98 thinks that it's about to see a WordPad file and gets confused by another word processor's format.

Solution: Quick View simply can't view this file, unfortunately. To see inside the file, you must load it into the word processor that created it.

Try opening WordPad and dragging and dropping this file into the WordPad document. Sometimes that's enough to crack it open.

Deleting This File Will Make It Impossible to Run This Program and May Make It Impossible for You to Edit Some Documents

Meaning: You're trying to delete a file containing a program.

Probable cause: You're clearing off some hard disk space to make room for incoming programs.

Solution: Just make sure that you know what program you're deleting before you delete it. And make sure that you have the program sitting on the shelf so you can reinstall it if you decide you need it after all.

Open with . . .

Meaning: Windows 98 doesn't know what program created the file that you've double-clicked, so it's asking *you* to figure it out. Windows 98 then sticks a list of programs on the screen and asks you to choose the right one to open the file with. (The Microsoft programmers can get away with ending sentences with prepositions.)

Probable cause: Windows 98 usually sticks secret hidden codes, known as *file extensions,* onto the ends of filenames. Notepad, for example, uses the letters TXT. When you double-click the Notepad icon, Windows 98 spots the secret, hidden TXT letters and uses the Notepad program to open the file.

Solution: This problem's a little rough, so you may have to experiment. First, find the Open With window's box marked Always <u>u</u>se this program to open this file and click in the box to turn off that option. Next, try double-clicking Notepad from the Open With window's vast list of programs. If your screen fills with legible text, you're saved! Close Notepad and double-click the mischievous file again. This time, however, leave the Always <u>u</u>se this program to open this file box checked so that Windows 98 learns that Notepad should automatically open that file.

You Must Type a Filename

Meaning: Windows 98 insists that you type a filename into the box.

Probable cause: You've chosen (accidentally or otherwise) the Rena<u>m</u>e command from a menu or clicked an icon's title in *just the right way.*

Solution: Type in a new filename — consisting of mostly numbers and letters — to describe the file, and you'll be fine. Or, if you're just trying to get out of the filename box, press Esc, and the Rename box dissipates.

Cannot open Internet . . . A connection to the server could not be established.

Meaning: Your Internet browser can't connect to your Internet Service Provider.

Probable cause: Your Internet Service Provider might be turned off temporarily, but most likely your Internet Browser's settings are probably configured incorrectly.

Solution: Use the Internet Connection Wizard described in Chapter 12.

My Computer Keeps Saying Windows 98 Wasn't Properly Shut Down!

Meaning: You probably turned your computer off without giving Windows time to "brace itself."

Probable cause: If your computer complains that it wasn't properly shut down when you first turn it on to begin work, that usually means you succumbed to temptation: You just flipped the computer's Off switch when you were done working. That's a Compu-No-No.

Solution: When you want to turn off your computer, click the Start button and choose Shut Down from the menu that shoots up. When Windows 98 says it's okay to turn off your computer, it's okay to reach for the Off switch.

Chapter 16

Help on the Windows 98 Help System

*J*ust about everybody's written a bizarre computer command (like Alt+F4) on a stick-on note and slapped it on the side of the monitor.

Windows 98 comes with its *own* set of stick-on notes built right in. You can pop them up on-screen and leave them there for easy access. In fact, they're often virtually real stick-on notes because they can never escape from inside the computer. Actually, it's probably better than the real thing: You'll never find a "How to Change Wallpaper" stick-on note on the bottom of your shoe.

This chapter covers the Windows 98 built-in Help system. When you raise your hand in just the right way, Windows 98 walks over and offers you some help.

Get Me Some Help, and Fast!

Don't bother plowing through this whole chapter if you don't need to: Here are the quickest ways to make Windows 98 dish out helpful information when you're stumped. Each tip is explained more fully later in this chapter.

Press F1

When you're confused in Windows 98, press the F1 key or choose <u>H</u>elp from the Start button's menu. That key always stands for "Help!" Most of the time, Windows 98 checks to see what program you're using and fetches some helpful information about that particular program or your current situation. In fact, pressing F1 usually brings up a huge Help program, which gets its own section later in this chapter.

Click the right mouse button on the confusing part

Windows 98 constantly flings confusing questions onto the screen, expecting you to come up with an answer. If you know where to tickle the program, however, you can often shake loose some helpful chunks of information.

When a particular button, setting, box, or menu item has your creativity stifled, click it with your right (the opposite of left) mouse button. A <u>W</u>hat's This? box often appears, as shown in Figure 16-1, letting you know that Windows 98 can offer help about that particular area. Click the <u>W</u>hat's This? box, and Windows 98 tosses extra information onto the screen, shown in Figure 16-2, explaining the confusing area you clicked on.

Figure 16-1: Click a confusing button with the right mouse button, and click the <u>W</u>hat's This? button.

When confused about something on-screen, make Windows 98 explain it: Click the confusing item with your right mouse button and click the <u>W</u>hat's This? box that pops up.

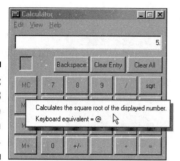

Figure 16-2:
Windows 98
tosses more
information
your way.

Choose Help from the main menu

If pressing F1 doesn't get you anywhere, look for the word Help in the menu along the top of the confusing program. Click Help, and a menu drops down, usually listing two words: Help Topics and About. Click Help Topics to make the Windows 98 Help program leap to the screen and bring assistance to your dilemma. (Clicking About just brings a version number to the screen, which can be dangerously irritating when you're looking for something a little more helpful.)

Sending in the Troubleshooters

Sometimes the Windows 98 Help program scores big: It tells you exactly how to solve your particular problem. Unfortunately, however, the Help program occasionally says you need to load a *different* program to solve your problem. (Don't get grumpy, though: Save your real angst for long touch-tone menus.)

To let Windows 98 fix its own problems, follow the steps below:

1. **Click Help from the Start button.**

2. **Click Troubleshooting from the Contents tab's drop-down menu.**

3. **Choose Windows 98 Troubleshooters from the drop-down menu, as shown in Figure 16-3.**

    A torrent of computer subjects tumbles from the menu, from Print to Hardware Conflict.

4. **Click the subject that troubles you.**

    Click Print, for example, if your printer is bugging you, and a chart pops up, similar to the one shown in Figure 16-4.

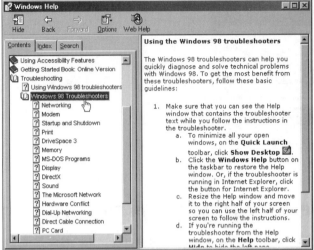

Figure 16-3:
Click
Trouble-
shooting,
and then
choose
Windows 98
Trouble-
shooters to
unleash the
Windows 98
friendly
"mechanic"
programs.

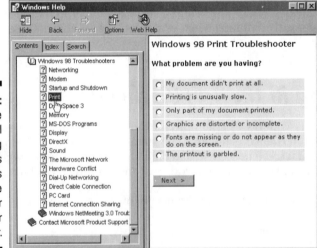

Figure 16-4:
Answer the
clinical
questioning
as Windows
98 attempts
to diagnose
and repair
your
computer.

Click the little leaping arrow, and Windows 98 automatically takes you to that other program you need to use. Yep, it's refreshingly helpful. As you answer the questions, Windows narrows down your problem until it decides whether it can fix things itself, or whether the situation requires outside intervention. (In which case, you need to beg assistance from the computer store or manufacturer, the computer guy at work, or a neighboring 12-year-old.)

Consulting the Windows 98 Built-In Computer Guru

Almost every Windows program has the word Help in its top menu. Click Help, and the Windows 98 built-in computer guru rushes to your aid. For example, click Help in Paint, and you see the menu shown in Figure 16-5.

Figure 16-5:
Click Help
when you
need
"Help!"

To pick the computer guru's brain, click Help Topics, and Windows 98 pops up the box shown in Figure 16-6. This box is the table of contents for all the help information Windows 98 can offer on the Paint program.

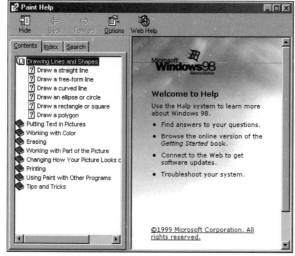

Figure 16-6:
Help Topics
lists a quick
table of con-
tents of
helpful
subjects.

See any subject covering what you're confused about? Then choose it. For example, if Erasing has you stumped, choose the word *Erasing;* the Help program then shows what additional help it can offer, as shown in Figure 16-7.

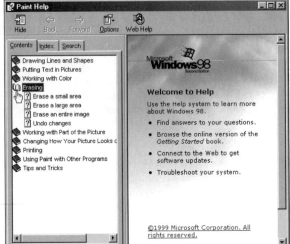

Figure 16-7:
Choose a topic to see more specific help areas.

Want to see more information on erasing small areas? Click that listed subject, and a new window pops up, as shown in Figure 16-8, bringing even more detailed information to the screen.

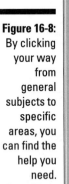

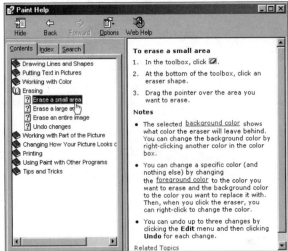

Figure 16-8:
By clicking your way from general subjects to specific areas, you can find the help you need.

Windows 98 can offer help with any underlined topic. As the mouse pointer nears an underlined topic, the pointer turns into a little hand. When the hand points at the phrase that has you stumped, click the mouse button. For example, click background color in the Paint Help box, and Windows 98 displays more help on what background colors are supposed to mean, as shown in Figure 16-9.

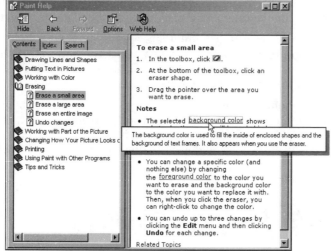

Figure 16-9:
Click under-
lined words
and phrases
to see quick
definitions.

The Windows 98 Help system is sometimes a lot of work, forcing you to wade through increasingly detailed menus to find specific information. Still, it can be much faster than paging through the chunky, awkward Windows 98 manual. And it's often much faster than tracking down the newly pocket-protected neighbor who's just announced himself to be a "computer expert."

✔ The quickest way to find help in any Windows 98 program is to press F1. Windows automatically jumps to the table of contents page for the help information it has for the current program.

✔ Does the Help program look sort of like a Web page? It should: It's been redesigned using the same technology that creates Web pages for the Internet.

✔ Windows 98 packs a lot of information into its Help boxes; some of the words usually scroll off the bottom of the window. To see them, click the scroll bar (described in Chapter 5) or press PgDn.

✔ Sometimes you click the wrong topic and Windows 98 brings up something really dumb. Click the <u>C</u>ontents button at the top of the window, and Windows 98 scoots back to the contents page. From there, click a different topic to move in a different direction.

✔ Underlined phrases and words appear throughout the Windows 98 Help system. Whenever you click something that's underlined, Windows 98 brings up a definition or jumps to a spot that has information about that subject. Click the <u>H</u>elp Topics or Back button to return to where you jumped from.

✔ If you're impressed with a particularly helpful page, send it to the printer: Click the right mouse button and choose <u>P</u>rint Topic from the menu that appears. Windows 98 shoots that page to the printer so you can keep it handy until you lose it.

✔ Actually, to keep from losing that helpful page, read about sticking an electronic bookmark on that page, as described later in this chapter.

✔ If you find a particularly helpful reference in the Help system, minimize the window to an icon on the taskbar: Click the button with the tiny bar near the window's upper-right corner. Then you can just double-click the taskbar's Help icon to see that page again.

✔ To grab a help message and stick it in your own work, highlight the text with your mouse and choose Copy from the menu. Windows then lets you highlight the helpful words you want to copy to the Clipboard. I dunno why anybody would want to do this, but you can do it, just the same.

Finding Help for Your Problem

If you don't see your problem listed in the particular table of contents page you've accessed, there's another way to find help (although it takes a little more time and effort). Click the Index tab at the top of any help window; the box shown in Figure 16-10 leaps to the screen. Type a few words describing your problem. When you type them, Windows 98 shows any matches in the box below it.

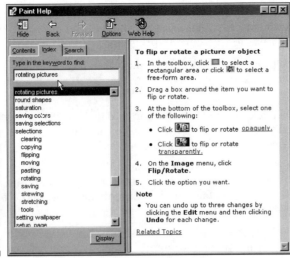

Figure 16-10: Windows 98 lets you perform more detailed searches in the index.

If Windows matches what you type with an appropriate topic, click the topic that looks the most pertinent and then click the Display button. Windows jumps to the page of information that describes that particular subject the best.

A quicker way to find help is to click the scroll bar or press PgUp and PgDn to see what subjects Windows is willing to explain. If you see a subject that even remotely resembles what you're confused about, double-click it. Windows 98 brings up that page of help information.

From there, you can jump around by clicking underlined words and phrases. Sooner or later, you stumble onto the right page of information.

✔ Windows searches alphabetically and, unfortunately, isn't very smart. So, if you're looking for help on margins, for example, don't type **adding margins** or **changing margins**. Instead, type **margins** so that Windows jumps to the words beginning with M.

✔ In fact, if you have trouble finding help for your specific problem, use the Find command, described in the next section. Instead of forcing you to type the right words in the right order, the Find command roots through every word in the Help file and brings back every match.

Finding Help on Specific Problems

When you're looking for help on a specific problem, it's sometimes hard to be a casual pointer and clicker. You want help *now!*

For people who want to make sure that they wring every ounce of help from the Windows 98 Help system, Microsoft included a special Search program: You can tell the Help program to make an index of every word contained in its help libraries. That way, you can type **PCMCIA,** for example, and know you'll see every paragraph in the Help system that contains the word *PCMCIA*. You won't have that nagging suspicion that Windows 98 didn't give you help because you didn't type **32-bit PCMCIA** or some other sneaky computer gibberish.

Why doesn't Windows 98 come with the Find index already set up and ready to go? Because the Find index can eat up a lot of hard drive space. Here's how to make Windows 98 perform the master search:

1. **From within any program, press F1 to bring up its Help program and then click the Find Search tab.**

   The Find Search tab is along the top of the window, toward the right side.

2. **Type your confusing word into the box and press Enter.**

   If you're confused about how to rotate pictures, for example, type the word **rotate**. Windows 98 displays a list of the subjects containing information on rotation.

3. Double-click the information that answers your question.

Hopefully, Windows 98 has found the solution to your dilemma.

✔ After you create an index, clicking the Find tab brings you straight to the search area. Type the word you're looking for, and, if it's mentioned in the Help system, Windows 98 brings up that nugget of helpful information.

✔ The Search feature often serves as a quick way to find answers to distressing problems. Just keep clicking on related subjects until you (hopefully) find the right answer.

✔ See the words "Related Topics" along the bottom of a help page? Try clicking those to find other helpful bits of information.

Finding Help on the Web

The Help system built into Windows 98 is better than ever, and finding help for a particular trouble is relatively painless. Now, however, the Help system has grown past windows and programs. In fact, it's grown past your computer. A Web Help icon rests atop each Help window, offering to pitch in with dilemma-solving suggestions from the Internet.

This has pros and cons. Pros: The Web site will always be up-to-date and available to Internet subscribers. You'll find information on the site that's only a day or two old. Cons: It changes often, meaning the rest of this section might be slightly out of date by the time you read it.

To find help for Windows 98, choose <u>H</u>elp from the Start menu. When the Help window appears, give the Web Help icon a click, and Windows 98 brings up a page of chatter and then asks you to begin your Internet search by clicking the highlighted words *Support Online*.

Clicking on the words *Support Online* brings up the Highlights for Windows 98 Web page, shown in Figure 16-11.

The Web page offers help in several ways, each described below and rated on a Helpfulness Scale of 1 to 10.

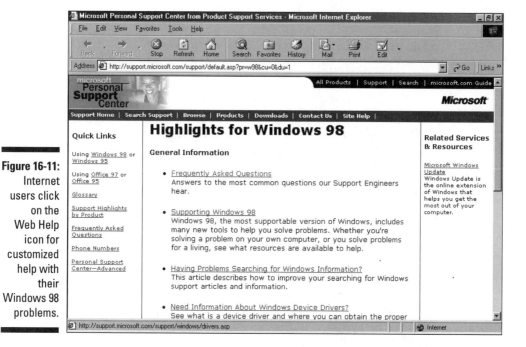

Figure 16-11:
Internet
users click
on the
Web Help
icon for
customized
help with
their
Windows 98
problems.

Frequently asked questions

Helpfulness Rating: 7

Click here to bring up SAM, the Automated Personal Support Assistant from Microsoft. Type your question, using plain English. (SAM even offers to check your spelling.) Click the Ask button, and SAM brings up a handful or two of similar questions. Choose the question that's closest to your problem, click the Ask button again, and SAM answers the question.

For a computer, it's relatively smart at understanding a beginner's question. Unfortunately, the answers are usually involve procedures and language that only a techie can understand.

Supporting Windows 98

Helpfulness Rating: 7

After you've connected to the Internet, this site turns you right back to Windows 98: It explains the troubleshooting and diagnostic programs included with Windows, mostly in the System Tools area found under the Start Menu's Accessories area (which is found in the Programs area).

About 50 percent of the programs are valuable for beginners; the rest exist for the techies — and the techie types probably don't need the Internet to tell them about Windows 98's built-in help programs.

Still, it's worth a gander.

Having problems searching for Windows information?

Helpfulness Rating: 5

Click here for an academic lecture on the correct way to phrase questions when asking Microsoft's Internet robots for advice. There's no help for your programs here, just help on how to talk to Microsoft's automated Internet Help databases.

Need information about Windows device drivers?

Helpfulness Rating: 6

You probably won't find information about specific problems here, either. Microsoft defines the term "driver," just like Chapter 3 in this book. Then it shows how to get software created by Microsoft for Windows 98. You don't need Microsoft's stuff nearly as often as you need drivers written by other companies for your computer's parts.

Click the words "Search the Internet" and type the brand name of your failing computer part. The Web Help page will try to find the Web site of that manufacturer so you can seek an updated driver.

Finally, check out the Hardware Compatibility List section to see if your computer's ready to run Windows 98. It also lists on-the-shelf parts that can and can't work with Windows 98. You can also download kits to see if your computer can run certain things — a USB gadget like a USB digital camera, for instance.

The How-To guide

Helpfulness Rating: 8

Some of the information included in other Web Help sections appears in this section — a list of How-To articles. Although it can be technical at times, it's definitely worth a try.

Training

Helpfulness Rating: 2

Don't go here unless you want to be a certified computer technician. Seriously.

Before you install

Helpfulness Rating: 5

More software and hardware compatibility lists lurk here, as well as technical information on how to install Windows 98. Yawn.

Need help troubleshooting a problem?

Helpfulness Rating: 9

If your problem appears under these "Troubleshooters," you're in luck. Windows 98 guides you through several possible solutions. It's interactive, sending you on a tree of possible solutions. When it gets a clue as to a possible solution, it sends you on that path.

If no Troubleshooters appear for your particular problem, however, you're completely out of luck.

Don't have an Internet connection? Many of these Troubleshooters already exist on your computer, as discussed earlier in this chapter. Choose Help from the Start button and choose Troubleshooting from the window that appears.

Need help using the Windows update Web site?

Helpfulness Rating: 4

Windows Update, when activated from the Start button, forces your computer to automatically call Microsoft's Windows Update Web site, search for any new Windows patches or programs, and automatically download and install them.

If it doesn't work, head here for help. The site is useful, but because it only deals with a single program, it's very limited in scope.

More Windows 95 Support Options

Helpfulness Rating: 0

Uh, since this book deals with Windows 98, you probably don't need help with Windows 95. If you have a second computer running Windows 95, and if you stumble upon this paragraph, head here for some helpful Windows 95 information.

Part V
The Part of Tens

The 5th Wave   By Rich Tennant

THUD SOFTWARE

"GENTLEMEN, I SAY RATHER THAN FIX THE 'BUGS,' WE CHANGE THE
DOCUMENTATION AND CALL THEM 'FEATURES.'"

In this part . . .

*E*verybody likes to read top tens in magazines —
especially in the grocery store checkout aisle when
you're stuck behind someone who's just pulled a rubber
band off a thick stack of double coupons and the checker
can't find the right validation stamp.

Unlike the reading material at the grocery store, the chapters in this part of the book don't list ten new aerobic
bounces or ten ways to stop your kids from making explo-
sives with kitchen cleansers. Instead, you find lists of
ways to make Windows 98 more efficient — or at least not
as hostile. You find a few tips, tricks, and explanations of
Windows 98 icons and what they do.

Some lists have more than ten items; others have fewer.
But who's counting, besides the guy wading through all
those double coupons?

Chapter 17

Ten Exciting Windows 98 Features Worth Checking Out

· ·

In This Chapter

▶ Windows 98 Second Edition's new improvements

▶ Watching television on your monitor

▶ Turning your desktop into a "Web page"

▶ Using up to eight monitors *at the same time!*

▶ Keeping Windows 98 up-to-date with the Windows Update site

▶ Using the right (not just the left) mouse button

▶ Peeking inside files with Quick View

▶ Using long filenames

▶ Using the Recycle Bin

▶ Highlighting icons with a "lasso"

▶ Using the Windows 98 Wizards

▶ Jumping to the right place in Help

· ·

*L*ike a new car model, Windows 98 adds several improvements over the older Windows versions. Some of the changes are cosmetic, like the fancy new fish tank screen saver. Other changes are more useful, like the way that you can use an Internet Web page as your wallpaper. And some changes, like the ones in Windows 98 Second Edition, lie mostly beneath the surface.

Consider this chapter a pamphlet that explains some of the best features Windows 98 has to offer. (You'll also find a few tasty features from Windows 95, just in case you're updating from Windows 3.1.)

The New Stuff in Windows 98 Second Edition

Windows 98 Second Edition comes preinstalled on new computers these days, and it's sold in the computer stores for about $80, replacing the older, first edition of Windows 98. Already running the first edition of Windows 98? An upgrade to the second edition costs about $20.

But contrary to Microsoft's Marketing Machinery, there's nothing really exciting about the Second Edition of Windows 98. In fact, most people won't notice the difference.

The Second Edition sprinkles several new goodies onto Windows 98, all discussed in the following list:

- **Internet Explorer 5.0 and Microsoft Outlook:** The latest version of Microsoft's Web browser and e-mail program team up to saturate your computer with even more ways to access the Internet. (You can download this for free at the downloads area.)

- **Fixes and patches:** Dubbed Service Pack 1, this collection of utilities smooths Windows 98's rough edges. It increases security, fixes problems with the 2000-year rollover known as Y2K, and fixes problems discovered since the first release of Windows 98. (You can also download this for free at the downloads area.)

- **Internet Connection Sharing:** Here's the big one: Computers on a network can share a single modem to access the Internet simultaneously. Home network users with a fast cable, ISDN, or ASDL connection will benefit the most.

- **Better Security:** The USA copies of Windows 98 Second Edition receive 128-bit encryption on Dial-Up Networking and Virtual Private Networking. What does that mean? The information shared between two computers on the Internet or other networks can now be made more secure at a cheaper cost.

- **DeviceBay Support:** For years, computer parts plugged into different areas of your computer; each required a different method of configuration — a laborious process. Computers will soon come with Intel's DeviceBay slots: hard drives, CD and DVD drives, modems, network cards, and other gizmos can simply be slid in and turned on. Windows 98 Second Edition now supports the technology.

- **TV Tuner Card Support:** Windows 98 never worked well with all TV Tuner cards. Now it supports a lot more. (I still prefer ATI's All-In-Wonder Pro card and ATI's bundled software over Microsoft's stuff.)

✔ **NetMeeting 3.0:** A tidbit for toy-hungry executives, this lets people connect a microphone and video camera to their computer; when they connect to other people with the same setup over the Internet, everybody can see each other while talking.

✔ **Euro Support:** Remember when Europe adopted a new currency? Windows 98 SE now comes with fonts that support the Euro currency symbol.

Most of Windows 98 Second Edition's improvements can be downloaded for free from Microsoft's Web site, as mentioned earlier. But you'll need to shell out the upgrade dollars for the big changes, like being able to share a single modem on a network.

Watching Television on Your Monitor

Ready to relax from work and watch *Seinfeld* reruns? With Windows 98, you don't have to leave your desktop. Install a TV Tuner card, and Windows 98 not only downloads a weekly guide to upcoming TV shows, but it also enables you to search for your favorites and turn them on automatically.

Best yet, you can watch TV in a window, as shown in Figure 17-1, or let the show fill your screen.

Figure 17-1: Windows 98 lets you watch TV on your computer.

Sure, it sounds like fun — until you read the bad parts below:

✔ It ain't cheap. The procedure requires a special TV Tuner card that currently costs around $100. (That's more than a cheap TV set — and you don't get a remote control.)

✔ The TV software takes a lot of room on your hard drive. About 50MB, in fact.

✔ Television can be distracting. Can you *really* get any work done with Martha Stewart in the background talking about using sponges to paint fish on your bathroom walls?

Turning Your Desktop into a "Web Page"

Windows 98, enamored with the Internet, wants to dress itself up like a Web page, too (and if you don't believe me, check out Figure 17-2).

The trick is putting customized "shortcuts" to the Internet on your Web page. To start, right-click your desktop, choose Active Desktop from the pop-up menu, and choose Customize my Desktop. A special menu appears, as shown, in Figure 17-3. (Yours might look a little different, depending on your computer's configuration.)

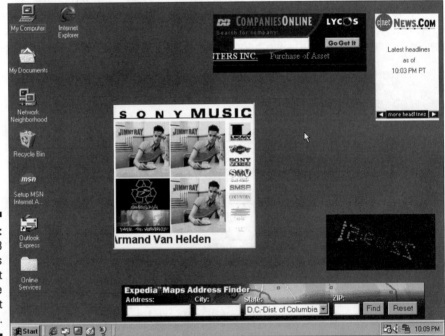

Figure 17-2: Windows 98 can make its desktop act and feel like an Internet Web page.

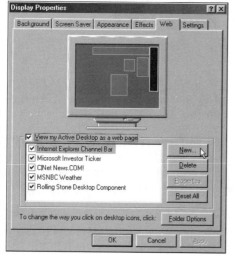

Figure 17-3:
Choose the
New button
to view your
options for
Active
Desktop
connections.

Make sure that the View my Active Desktop as a Web page button is checked, and then click the New button. If you choose, Windows uses your Internet connection to contact the Active Desktop Gallery, a site full of custom-made Internet connections for sticking to your wallpaper.

Or, after clicking the New button, click No to bypass the Active Desktop Gallery. Then, type in the name of any Web site you want to use as your own background "Web art."

✔ You'll need a pretty speedy modem connection to make the Active Desktop worthwhile.

✔ In fact, you'll probably want your computer to stay connected to the Internet 24 hours a day, so your Active Desktop will always remain up-to-date.

✔ If your computer *isn't* connected to the Internet 24 hours a day, don't be surprised to hear your computer automatically dialing up the Internet when you're nowhere near it. (It's simply keeping your Active Desktop current.)

✔ If you're into Active Desktops, you'll be into *Channels,* that menu along the side with Mickey Mouse and the Tasmanian Devil giving you the eye. Channels do basically the same thing: provide different ways to filter the Internet's informational haystacks.

Using Up to Eight Monitors at the Same Time!

Ever see the cool David Bowie movie, *The Man Who Fell to Earth,* where he sat in front of a huge stack of TV sets and channel surfed? Windows 98 supports the same degree of madness, but with a new twist.

By adding additional monitors and video cards, you can "stretch" your PC's desktop across all of them, as shown in Figure 17-4. Instead of trying to stack all your programs on a single screen, you can drag a program's windows to different monitors — or even stretch them to gargantuan proportions!

You can read e-mail on one monitor, for instance, while reading Web pages on another. Or, if you're really hip (and have a lotta extra cash lying around), you can set up a bunch of monitors for gaming: Put one monitor in front for the spaceship's windshield, and others on the left and right for side windows. Fun!

Figure 17-4:
Although Windows 98 only displays two monitors here, it supports up to eight monitors — if you have enough video cards and computer slots to support them.

- More boring uses include desktop publishing and presentations.

- Own a TV card? You can't stretch the TV's picture larger than one monitor, unfortunately. In fact, you can't even move the TV picture onto a second monitor.

- The "multimonitor" trick only works on PCI-capable cards and computers.

Keeping Windows 98 Up-To-Date through "Windows Update"

Face it: The computer industry moves so quickly that even your brand-new copy of Windows 98 Second Edition is probably out of date in some way or another. The answer? Until Windows 98, frustrated users had to search through the Internet for the "magic fix," hoping to find the up-to-date, newly improved file that would cure their systems and make Windows act normally.

Windows 98 makes searching for fixes much easier with its Windows Update program. Click Windows Update from the top of the Start menu, and Windows 98 heads for the Windows Update site on the Internet.

After you connect, little Web site gremlins diagnose your computer and present you with a list of needed repairs. You click the updates you want, and the program installs them automatically. Quick and easy.

- Best yet, the program remembers what it did so it can reverse its actions if it made things even *worse*.

- Even better, Windows Update can upgrade your Windows 98 program to include almost everything offered by Windows 98 Second Edition.

- The site contains a technical support database, where you type in questions and wait for the computer to spit back possible answers — some even understandable.

- Just got knocked on the head with a wacky word? Head for the Windows Update Technical Support Glossary. Microsoft does a pretty good job of defining the most computer terms that you come across.

The Foolproof Right Mouse Button Trick

Although mice have had at least two buttons for the past decade, Windows didn't take advantage of the right mouse button until Windows 95 came along. The index finger has done all the work, clicking and double-clicking the left button, while the middle finger rested, unused, on the right mouse button.

Windows 98, like Windows 95, puts your middle finger to work by making the right button just as powerful as the left. The buttons don't do the same thing, though, so here's the rundown:

- ✔ Click something *once* with your *right* mouse button to bring up a menu that lists the things you can do with that item — adjust its settings, for example, or copy it to another location.

- ✔ Click something *once* with your *left* mouse button to select it — to highlight an icon, for example. (If the item highlights itself before you even press the button, stop — Windows 98 has already selected it because your computer is running with a Web-style desktop.)

- ✔ *Double-click* something with your *left* mouse button to not only select it, but to also kick-start it into action — to load a program, for example, or to open a folder. (If the item is highlighted when you merely hover the mouse pointer over it, a single-click will load it; that's because your computer is running with a "Web style" desktop.)

Figure 17-5 shows the menu that pops up when you use your right mouse button to click a file in the My Computer window.

Figure 17-5:
Click a file's icon with your right mouse button and a menu appears, listing the thing you can do with the file.

When you're unsure of how to work with something on your desktop — a button, icon, or anything weird-looking — click the confusing entity with your right mouse button. Often, a menu pops up that displays a list of stuff you can do to that confusing thing. By choosing from the options, you can often bluff your way to success.

The Microsoft IntelliMouse has two buttons *and* a little wheel thingie poking out from between them. Spinning the wheel lets you do different things in different programs. In most programs, it lets you scroll up or down the page, so you don't have to click on those annoying scroll bars along the window's right side. Most programmers are now adding IntelliMouse support to their programs.

Peeking into Files without Opening Them

When faced with a plethora of files, how can you tell which one you need? For example, all the icons for files created by the Paint drawing program look the same. How can you check to see if the file named Sea Food is that lobster picture you are searching for?

You can load the Sea Food file into Paint, but Quick View provides a faster way. Click the file with your right mouse button and then click Quick View from the menu that pops up.

A new window immediately appears, like the one in Figure 17-6, showing you the file's contents.

Figure 17-6:
Right-click-
ing a file's
icon and
choosing
Quick View
causes a
window to
appear,
showing the
file's
contents.

✔ Want to open the file for editing? Click the little Paint icon in the upper-left corner of the Quick View window. Windows 98 loads Paint, along with your file. The icon for the program responsible for creating the file is always in the upper-left corner.

✔ If the file on the screen isn't the one you're searching for, feel free to drag another file's icon into Quick View's open window. Windows 98 rapidly displays the contents of that file, too.

✔ Here's the bad news: The Quick View command only works on certain varieties of files. Only the more popular formats are displayed. You can "quick view" your WordPerfect and Microsoft Word files, for example, but you can't peek inside any files created in less-popular programs, such as WordStar or XyWrite.

✔ There's another way to peek inside many graphic files. Open a folder and click <u>V</u>iew from along the top of the window. Select as <u>W</u>eb Page from the menu that falls down. Now, when you click on a file, information about the file appears in the blank space to the window's left side. Click on a graphic file to see a small picture of the file.

✔ You can find more information about Quick View in Chapter 7.

Much L-o-n-g-e-r Filenames

Somber industry analysts said it wouldn't happen in our lifetimes, but with the advent of Windows 95, people can name their files with descriptions longer than eight characters. Windows 98 also lets you use more than one word to name your files, and you can separate the words by a space!

Figure 17-7 shows a few filenames approved by Windows 98; as long as you keep the names under 255 characters, you're pretty much okay. (More detailed details on filenames are discussed in Chapter 11.)

Figure 17-7:
Windows 98 allows for longer file-names than Windows 3.1.

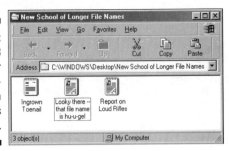

Retrieving Deleted Files from the Recycle Bin

Windows 3.1 allowed you to safely retrieve accidentally deleted files, so the concept of the Windows 98 Recycle Bin isn't new. The new part is how much easier the Recycle Bin makes it to salvage deleted files.

Whenever you delete a file, the sneaky Windows 98 doesn't *really* delete it. It just hides the file in the Recycle Bin — that green trash can sitting on the desktop. When you get that sinking feeling that you shouldn't have deleted that report on Coelacanth Tailfins, double-click the Recycle Bin, and you can find your report inside, undamaged.

The Recycle Bin doesn't hold onto deleted files forever, though. It waits until you've filled up 10 percent of your hard drive's storage capacity. For example, if you have a 10GB hard disk, the Recycle Bin always holds onto 1GB of your most recently deleted files. When you fill up that 10 percent, Recycle Bin starts shredding the oldest files, and you can't retrieve them.

That 10 percent figure is adjustable; see Chapter 10 for details.

Selecting Bunches of Icons with a Lasso

This feature doesn't really seem like much, but you'll probably find yourself using it more than you think.

Windows has always allowed several ways to select files and icons. For example, hold down the Ctrl key and click all the icons you want: Windows highlights all the icons that you click.

Or, when selecting items in a list, you can click the first item, hold down the Shift key, and click the last item in a list. Whoosh! Windows instantly highlights the first item, the last item, and every item in between.

Windows 98 can still highlight icons in those ways, but it's allows something easier. To select files or folders that are next to each other, you can drag a "lasso" around them. Point just above the first icon you want to grab and, while holding down the mouse button, point just below the last icon that you want to grab. Windows 98 draws a rectangle around the icons, shown in Figure 17-8.

Figure 17-8:
Windows 98 can drag a rectangle around files and folders to select them easily.

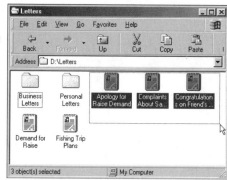

The lasso can only be rectangular, so all the files and folders have to be next to each other. But you can always lasso the big chunk and then hold down the Ctrl key to select the stragglers that are away from the main pack.

Working with Windows 98 Wizards

Windows 98 tries hard to be personal, adding human touches whenever it can. Honestly, how many times have you wished for a computer wizard to materialize and automatically make your new modem or sound card work?

Well, Windows 98 comes with several Wizards, each customized for various bits of magic. For example, the Add New Hardware Wizard, shown in Figure 17-9, searches your computer for any new gadgets you've added. When the Wizard finds these accessories, it introduces them to Windows 98 so that they can all start working together.

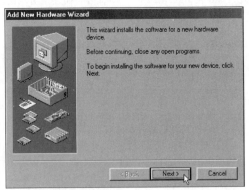

Figure 17-9:
The
Windows
Wizards can
help you
install new
parts to your
computer.

The Wizards aren't magic by any means, but they can often work wonders when you need to set up Windows 98 to work with something new.

Chapter 18

Ten Aggravating Things about Windows 98 (And How to Fix Them)

. . . .

In This Chapter

▶ Finding out your computer's version of Windows

▶ Wanting to double-click instead of click (or vice versa)!

▶ Bypassing the menus

▶ Keeping track of multiple windows

▶ Finding a missing taskbar

▶ Fixing the Print Screen key

▶ Installing a missing program

▶ Lining up two windows on the screen

▶ Updating a floppy disk's contents in the Windows Explorer or My Computer program

. . . .

*W*indows 98 would be great if only . . . (insert your pet peeve here). If you find yourself thinking (or saying) this frequently, this chapter is for you. This chapter not only lists the most aggravating things about Windows 98, but it also explains how to fix them.

What Version of Windows Do I Have?

Windows comes in more than a dozen flavors since it debuted in November 1985. Now Windows 98 comes in two versions, as well. How do you know if your new computer already comes with Windows 98 Second Edition, known as Windows 98 SE, for short?

Right-click on My Computer, and choose Properties. Click the General tab, if that page isn't already showing.

Under the word *System,* Windows 98 displays its version number. If you're using the second edition, the words *Second Edition* appear beneath the words *Microsoft Windows 98.*

I Want to Click Instead of Double-Click (Or Vice Versa!)

Slowly but surely, Windows 98 is stretching away from your desktop and onto the Internet's *World Wide Web:* A huge, worldwide network of computers stuffed with everything from movie previews to groups of people discussing eggnog recipes.

When accessing the Internet, users click *once* on icons, not twice, the way Windows users have grown accustomed. Click the Start button, choose Settings, followed by Folder Options and Web Style from the General tab.

If you prefer to "double-click" your icons to bring them to life, choose the Classic style option on the same page.

I Don't Like the Mouse!

Look closely at the words on the menu bar, along the top of each window. Somewhere in almost every word, you can spot a single underlined letter. Press and release the Alt key and then press one of the underlined letters you see in a word. Try pressing the F in File, for example. Presto! The File menu leaps into place. Look for underlined letters on the newly displayed File menu. For example, press S for Save. Presto again! Windows 98 saves the current file, without a single mouse click.

To save a file in nearly any Windows 98 program, press and release Alt, press F, and then press S. It's that simple (after you memorize the combination, that is).

You find these underlined letters everywhere in Windows 98. In fact, you can see underlined letters in this book, as well. They're the keys you can use to avoid rooting through all the menus with a mouse.

Note: A list of the most commonly used key combinations is included in the Cheat Sheet at the front of this book.

When maneuvering through the options listed in the Start menu, you only need to click once: Just click the Start button to bring the Start menu to life. All the other menus contained in the Start menu pop up automatically as the mouse pointer hovers over them. When you spot the program or choice you're after, click it, and the Start menu loads that program or choice.

✔ To move from box to box while filling out a form, press the Tab key. Each press of the key takes you to a new part of the form to fill out. Ecstasy!

✔ For some keys, you hold Alt while pressing a function key. For example, to close any Windows 98 program, hold down Alt and press F4 (Alt+F4).

✔ If you accidentally press Alt and are stuck in Menu Land, press Alt again. Alternatively, press Esc and bark loudly until it lets you out.

It's Too Hard to Keep Track of All Those Windows

You don't *have* to keep track of all those windows. Windows 98 does it for you with the taskbar. Hold Ctrl and press Esc, and the taskbar rises to the forefront. (If it doesn't, see the very next section.)

The taskbar, covered in Chapter 10, has a separate box listing the name of every window currently open. Click the name of the window you want, and that window hops to the top of the pile.

Even better, shrink all the open windows into icons except for the window you're currently working on. Then click the taskbar with your right mouse button and click one of the two tile commands to line everything up neatly on the screen.

In Chapter 7, you find more soldiers to enlist in the battle against misplaced windows, files, and programs.

The Taskbar Keeps Disappearing!

The taskbar's a handy Windows 98 program that's always running — if you can just find it. Unfortunately, it sometimes vanishes from the screen. Here are a few ways to bring it back.

First, try holding down the Ctrl key and pressing Esc. Sometimes this effort makes the taskbar appear, but sometimes it only brings up the Start menu.

Still no taskbar? Try pointing at the very edge of your screen, stopping for a second or two at each of the four sides. If you point at the correct side, some specially configured taskbars stop goofing around and come back to the screen.

If you can only see a slim edge of the taskbar — the rest of it hangs off the edge of the screen, for example — point at the edge you *can* see. After the mouse pointer turns into a two-headed arrow, hold down your mouse button and move the mouse toward the screen's center to drag the taskbar back into view.

In Windows 3.1, double-clicking the desktop brings up the Task List, which lists all the currently running programs. Double-clicking the desktop in Windows 98 just makes two clicking noises in rapid succession. (The taskbar doesn't appear.)

- If your taskbar disappears whenever you're not specifically pointing at it, turn off its Auto hide feature: Click a blank part of the taskbar with your right mouse button and choose Properties from the pop-up menu. When the taskbar Options menu appears, click in the Auto hide box until a little check mark disappears. (Or, to turn on the Auto hide feature, add the check mark.)

- While you're in the taskbar Options menu, make sure that a check mark appears in the Always on top box. That way, the taskbar always rides visibly on the desktop, making it much easier to spot.

- Running two monitors? Don't forget the taskbar can be on any monitor's edge — that includes the second monitor. Make sure that you point at every edge before giving up.

My Print Screen Key Doesn't Work

Windows 98 takes over the Print Screen key (labeled PrtSc, PrtScr, or something even more supernatural on some keyboards). Instead of sending the stuff on the screen to the printer, the Print Screen key sends it to the Windows 98 Clipboard, where it can be pasted into other windows.

- If you hold Alt while pressing Print Screen, Windows 98 sends the current *window* — not the entire screen — to the Clipboard.

- If you *really* want a printout of the screen, press Print Screen to send a picture of the screen to the Clipboard. Paste the contents of the Clipboard into Paint and print from there. (Chapter 12 explains that process.)

> ✔ Some older keyboards make you hold Shift while pressing Print Screen. You may need to hold Shift and Print Screen to send a picture of the screen to the Clipboard on these older computers.

Windows 98 Didn't Install All the Programs Listed on the Box

In an attempt to make friends with everybody, Windows 98 comes with gobs of programs — more than anybody would ever want. So, to keep from making enemies of everybody, Windows 98 doesn't fill up everybody's hard drive with every possible program.

For example, Windows 98 comes with sounds that make your computer sound like a robot or squawking bird. But it doesn't automatically install those sounds, nor does it tell you about them. If you want to add those sounds, you must go back and do it by hand.

Start by double-clicking the Add/Remove Programs icon in the Control Panel and then click the Windows Setup tab along the top. Windows 98 lists the programs it can install and offers to install them for you — a process described in Chapter 12.

(And if you want the robot sounds, double-click the Control Panel's Sounds icon and choose Robotz Sound Scheme. The birds and frogs hang out in the Jungle Sound Scheme. Beware, however: Some employers may have already deleted these fun files from your computer.)

It's Too Hard to Line Up Two Windows on the Screen

With all its cut-and-paste stuff, Windows 98 makes it easy for you to grab information from one program and slap it into another. With its drag-and-drop stuff, you can grab an address from a database and drag it into a letter in your word processor.

The hard part of Windows 98 is lining up two windows on the screen, side by side. That's where you need to call in the taskbar. First, open the two windows and place them anywhere on the screen. Then turn all the other windows into icons (minimize them) by clicking the button with the little line that lives in the top-right corners of those windows.

Now, click a blank area of the taskbar with your right mouse button and click one of the two Tile commands listed on the menu. The two windows line up on the screen perfectly.

The My Computer and Windows Explorer Programs Show the Wrong Stuff on My Floppy Disk

The My Computer and Windows Explorer programs sometimes get confused and don't always list the files currently sitting on a disk drive. To prod the programs into taking a second look, simply press the F5 key along the top of your keyboard.

Chapter 19

Ten Expensive Things You Can Do to Make Windows 98 Run Better

Give a Ford Fairlane to the right teenage boy, and he'll get right to work: boring out the cylinders, putting in a high-lift cam, and adding a double-roller timing chain. And replacing the exhaust system with headers, if his cash holds out.

Computer nerds feel the same way about getting under the hood of their computers. They add a few new parts, flip a few switches, and tweak a few things here and there to make Windows 98 scream.

Even if you're not a computer nerd, you can still soup up Windows 98 a bit. Take the computer back to the store and have the *store's* computer nerd get under the hood.

This chapter talks about what parts to ask for so that you don't end up with high-lift cams rather than more memory.

Buy More Memory

When you bought your new computer, the salesperson probably tried to talk you into buying more memory, or RAM. Windows 98 probably talks just as loudly about this issue as the salesperson.

See, Windows 98 can read and write information to RAM very quickly. The phrase *lightning quick* comes to mind. But when Windows 98 runs out of RAM, it starts using the hard drive for storage. Compared with RAM, hard drives are slow, mechanical dinosaurs. If you're short on memory, you can hear the hard drive grinding away as you switch between programs and Windows 98 frantically tries to make room for everything.

Windows 98 runs slowly on a computer with only 16MB of RAM. Twice that amount of RAM speeds things up more than twice as much. With 32MB or 64MB of RAM, Windows 98 can juggle programs even more quickly (and without dropping them as often).

If you're tired of waiting for Windows 98, toss the computer in the back seat, take it back to the computer store, and have the store people put some more RAM inside. (The price has dropped since the last time you shopped.)

- ✔ After Jeff in the back room puts the memory chips inside the computer, he'll flip some switches on the computer's *motherboard* so that it knows that the new chips are there. People who plug in the chips themselves often don't flip the right switch and then wonder why their new chips don't work. (Some newer computers don't have a switch; they know automatically when they have more memory to play with.)

- ✔ Different computers can hold different amounts of RAM. And some computers make you yank the old memory chips before you can install the newer, higher-capacity chips. Before buying more memory, check with your dealer to make sure that your computer can handle it. (You'll find more memory information in *Upgrading and Fixing PCs For Dummies*, from IDG Books Worldwide, Inc. Don't bother buying the book, just read the Chapter 11 at the bookstore.)

Shell Out the Bucks for a Bigger Hard Drive

To install every part of Windows 98, you'll need about 300MB of hard drive space. That's for Windows 98 and no other programs.

If you buy the latest version of Microsoft Word for Windows, however, that program wants almost 40MB of hard drive space, too. Add a few other hoggy Windows programs, and your hard drive can run out of room quickly.

Plus, you should leave part of the hard drive empty so that Windows 98 has room to shuffle information around.

The moral is to shop for the biggest hard drive you can afford. Then borrow some money and buy one that's slightly bigger. A hard drive that's 8GB is a good starting size these days.

Order a Faster Pentium Computer

Windows 98 works on a fast 486 computer, but just barely. The program is really designed for a fast Pentium computer.

As programs incorporate more and more sound and graphics, computers are becoming more and more burdened with computing chores. That's why you want a fast Pentium II to keep the information flowing smoothly across the screen. Balance your need for speed with your checking account balance.

You can find this computer model/Pentium stuff thrashed out in Chapter 2.

Put a 3-D Graphics Accelerator Card on the Credit Card

When tossing boxes and bars around, Windows 98 puts a big strain on the computer's *graphics card,* the gizmo that tells the monitor what information to put on-screen.

Windows 98 also puts a strain on the computer's *microprocessor,* the gizmo that tells the graphics card what to tell the monitor.

A *3-D graphics accelerator card* eases the burden on both parties. Simply put, a graphics accelerator is a hot-rod graphics card. It replaces the VGA or Super VGA card and contains a special chip that handles the dirty work of filling the monitor with pretty pictures.

The result? Dialog boxes that shoot on-screen almost instantly. You no longer have to wait for Windows 98 to repaint the screen when you move windows around. Everything just looks snappier.

- You probably don't need to upgrade the monitor when buying an accelerator card. Monitors always work fast; it's the cards that slow them down.

- Upgrading the computer from a 486 to a Pentium or buying a faster Pentium also speeds up the graphics, even if you don't buy a 3-D accelerator card.

- Computers with special *PCI* or *AGP* slots can speed up 3-D graphics the fastest. These slots can accept the speedy PCI and AGP video cards. Anything else is obsolete.

- In fact, only PCI cards and AGP slots work with the Windows 98 multi-monitor feature. If your computer doesn't have those type of slots, you can't use more than one monitor with it. Best bet: Use an AGP slot for your main monitor, and a PCI slot for your second monitor.

Beg for, or Borrow, a Bigger Monitor (Or Two)

Part of the problem with the Windows 98 stack-of-windows approach to computing is the size of the screen. The Windows 98 desktop is the size of the monitor: a little larger than one square foot. That's why everything constantly covers up everything else.

To get a bigger desktop, buy a bigger monitor. The 17-inch monitors offer almost twice the elbowroom as the standard 14-inchers. You have more room to put windows side by side on the screen, as well as more room to spread icons along the bottom. The new 20-inchers give you an executive-sized desktop, but at a mahogany price.

- If you have a stack of phone books holding up one side of your desk, buy a new desk when you buy the new monitor. Those big monitors can weigh 50 pounds or more.

- That last tip holds particularly true if you're buying into the Windows 98 multimonitor plan and you want to use two or more monitors with your computer.

- To cut down the weight — and increase the amount of space on your desktop — consider buying one of those way-cool LCD panel screens. They only weigh a few pounds, they're about 2 or 3 inches thick, and they can actually pack more information onto the screen than a "normal" monitor of the same size. Plus, there's less eyestrain and the picture's clearer. Unfortunately, they cost a lot more. . . .

Buy a CD-RW Drive

Software companies have just about given up on floppy disks. Their programs are simply too big to fit on one disk, and nobody wants to feed their computer handfuls of disks in order to install the program.

The solution? Package the program on a compact disc, which can hold the equivalent of hundreds of floppies.

And if you're getting tired of packing your own information onto those tiny floppies, check out those CD Read/Write drives. They not only read information from normal CDs, but they can write information onto special CDs costing a dollar or two.

 ✔ CD Read/Write drives can write information once onto those dollar discs. But they can erase the information and write new information onto more expensive discs costing about ten times as much. The more expensive discs that can read and write many times are dubbed CD RW; the cheaper, write-once discs are called CD-R.

 ✔ CD drives are always slower at writing information to a disc than they are at reading that information.

 ✔ Today, CD-RW drives don't cost much more than CD drives that can only read information. However, they're usually a lot slower. Expect that to change as the technology continues.

Buy a TV Tuner Card

Admittedly, a TV Tuner card could be considered an extravagance. You can buy a small TV set for the cost of a TV Tuner card.

Nevertheless, few things in life compare to watching *Three's Company* in the corner of your Windows 98 screen. And Windows 98 makes it sinfully easily. It'll even keep a running download of your area's TV programming information, so it can alert you to the next airing of *Xena: Warrior Princess*.

You'll find more information about the TV Tuner in Chapter 20, as well as in this book's more advanced sequel, *MORE Windows 98 For Dummies*, published by IDG Books Worldwide, Inc.

 ✔ Good news: Many video cards today toss on a TV tuner for just a few dollars more. Hurray! Now you just need to connect them to a cable TV outlet or rooftop TV antenna to get a decent picture.

✔ If you're using a computer for business, convince the boss you need the TV Tuner card for watching CNN business information on the stock market.

✔ If your computer's staying at home, a TV Tuner card means you'll have to upgrade your home/office chair into a lounge chair.

Snap Up a Faster Modem

Face it: The Internet isn't going to disappear, even after all the hullabaloo has died down. With the Internet's World Wide Web software, you won't have to leave the house to go to the library, read newspapers and magazines, meet people, research trips, and join I Hate Barney User Groups. You can even have food delivered while you tap the keyboard.

✔ If you find yourself using the Internet a lot, make sure that you're using a 56 Kbps or faster modem.

✔ If you find yourself using the Internet a *super* lot, call up your phone company and Internet Service Provider to see if they offer something called "ISDN service." ISDN can spew out the information a super lot faster — but at a higher price (especially because ISDN service requires special, ISDN modems — your old modem won't work).

✔ If your cable company offers it, look into the costs of a super-speedy 500 Kbps cable modem. Most offer 24-hour access through your cable line, freeing up the cost of a second phone line. Plus, you can still watch TV — even on your computer — while surfing the Net. Blatant Editorial Department: I love my Cox Cable company's @Home service. No more thumb-twiddling while waiting for weather maps!

Chapter 20

Ten Windows 98 Icons and What They Do

Windows 98 uses different icons to stand for different types of files. That arrangement means that the program is packed with enough icons to befuddle the most experienced iconographer.

Table 20-1 shows pictures of the most common icons built into Windows 98 and what the icons are supposed to represent.

Table 20-1	Windows 98 Icons
What It Looks Like	*What It Stands For*
	3½-inch floppy drive
	Hard drive
	CD-ROM drive
	Audio CD; a CD with music currently inserted in your CD-ROM drive
	Batch file; a collection of DOS commands for the computer to run automatically
	Bitmap file; graphics usually created by Paint (in Windows 98) or Paintbrush (in Windows 3.1)

(continued)

Table 20-1 *(continued)*

What It Looks Like	What It Stands For
	Cabinet file; a compressed collection of Windows 98 installation files on the installation CD. Open with Explorer
	DOS program
	Folder or directory; a computerized storage area for files
	Fonts; stored in a TrueType format that can be easily shrunk or enlarged
	Fonts; stored in an older, fixed-size format
	Help file; contains instructions stored in a special format for the Windows 98 Help system
	Hidden information; Windows keeps these important system files invisible unless the user flips a secret switch (in that case, they appear with a gray, washed-out look)
	Internet information about a Channel; a method for the Internet to make information more easily available
	Internet information; usually a map to a Web site
	Internet HTML file; opened by Internet Explorer, these look just like a Web page.
	Movie; a file usually stored in the Microsoft Audio Video Audio Video Interleave — AVI —format
	Music; a MIDI file containing specially formatted instructions that tell synthesizers or sound cards what sounds to create

What It Looks Like	What It Stands For
	Outlook Express mail; a piece of e-mail that's been cut or copied from Outlook Express and pasted to your desktop or another folder.
	Sound or video file in RealAudio format that's usually broadcast from the Internet.
	Scrap; scraps are dabs of information dragged and dropped onto the desktop: a paragraph from WordPad, for example
	Sound; a recorded sound saved as a wav file
	System file; technical files for Windows 98 to use
	Text file; settings information for a computer program or part
	Text; usually created by Notepad
	Themes; those cool backdrops and settings described in Chapter 9
	Word processor file; a file usually created by either WordPad or Microsoft Word
	A file Windows 98 doesn't think it recognizes

Chapter 21

Ten Ways to Fix Confusing Internet, Web, and Active Desktop Problems

• •

In This Chapter

▶ Understanding Internet, Web, and Active Desktop problems

▶ What happens if I don't use the Internet with Windows 98?

▶ How to remove the Internet's influence from Windows 98

▶ How to adjust the Internet's influence

▶ Do I want an "Active Desktop"?

▶ Turning off the ugly "Channels" bar

• •

*E*ager to dish out something new — and follow the latest trend — Microsoft stuffed Windows 98 Second Edition with oodles of sparkling Internet tricks. Unfortunately, plenty of people simply aren't interested in the Internet, no matter how well-washed.

In an attempt to please everybody, Windows 98 added an option that adjusts how much the Internet affects your computer.

This chapter explains how to use that option; it also explains what to do with confusing windows that say "Internet," "Web," or "Active Desktop" on them. It shows how to wring varying amounts of the Internet out of your computer until it reaches your comfort level.

Finally, it explains what would happen if you tossed all that confusing Internet stuff into the backseat, where you could simply pull out the proper chunks when you needed them.

Need a little more background material on the Internet before determining its nuisance level on your computer? Chapter 13 has open arms.

Understanding an Internet Problem

Words like "Internet," "Web," and "Active Desktop" pop up throughout Windows 98. Sometimes they ride on menus, in plain sight. Other times, they lurk in the background, waiting to leap into action.

This can be a problem to some people, especially those who've moved to Windows 98 from an earlier version — or for people who've never used the Internet at all.

Some people like the Internet, some don't, and some just like parts of it. And because Windows 98 offers so many options to appeal to all of these people, it often becomes more confusing than the Internet itself.

  ✔ Unlike Windows 95, Windows 98 rides on top of the Internet, letting you use Web pages as wallpaper and jump to the Internet from nearly every menu. (Just point and click at the little Windows icon in any folder's upper-right corner.)

  ✔ Don't know what the Internet is? Start by heading to Chapter 13 for a good-sized backgrounder. Then, after you know what it is and what it can do, this chapter shows you how to make Windows 98's Internet relationship a strong and steamy one, a gleam in an eye, or something in between.

What Happens If I Don't Use the Internet with Windows 98?

I certainly won't tell anybody. In fact, most people won't notice. That's because most people don't even use the Internet. Don't get me wrong; I use it an awful lot to look up subjects like determining the manufacture dates of potentiometers, and finding out if I should be feeding the neighborhood blue jays raw or roasted peanuts.

I also read the news, check the weather, and listen to Chinese radio stations. Yep, there's a lot of information floating around on the Internet, but it's certainly not everybody's top priority.

My point? Rest assured that Windows 98 works fine without the Internet plugged in. You can still write letters, make spreadsheets, and create databases. You can participate on networks, including ones run around the office. You can even send faxes through your modem.

However, Windows 98 is designed to run exceptionally well with the Internet. So if you like using the Internet, you'll probably enjoy the extra Internet goodies tossed into Windows 98.

✔ For example, Internet users can use Windows Update, a special place on the Internet that automatically dishes out files for helping your computer stay up-to-date with new improvements to the Windows software. While you're connected, the Update Wizard peers under your computer's hood and examines the way everything's working. Then it recommends or installs any updates your computer might need.

✔ A little leery of Mr. Update Wizard? That same Windows Update area features an Uninstall option that restores order if Mr. Wizard's tricks left things even worse.

✔ Stayed away from the Internet because it was too hard to use? The new Windows 98 Internet Connection Wizard makes matters much easier when signing up for Internet service. It automatically handles the software configuration steps necessary for gaining access to the Internet. (It'll still toss you a few jaw-dropping questions that'll send you scurrying to Chapter 13, though.)

✔ The Active Desktop, described more fully later in this chapter, customizes your desktop so you can keep parts of the Web — a stream of news or stock quotes, for example — continually running as a sort of newfangled wallpaper.

✔ The Internet Channels option puts a bar similar to the Start menu on your screen, where it sits there like a TV remote control. By clicking the channels, you can switch to your favorite Web sites.

✔ Finally — and not to be confused with the Internet Channels — comes the TV Tuner's Program Guide. Through the Internet, your computer can download the week's TV program list so you can always know when your favorite shows are on. (You can even set alarms to go off when *The Munsters* TV show begins.)

How to Remove the Internet's Influence from Windows 98

To remove most of the Internet's most unwieldy influences, follow these steps:

1. **Click the Start button and choose Folder Options from the Settings area.**

2. Click the Classic style button.

This makes Windows 98 behave more closely with its predecessors, which could be a relief to Windows 95 and Windows 3.11 users.

3. Click the OK button to save the changes.

✓ Choosing the Classic style option makes Windows 98 work less like a Web page. You double-click icons to open or load them, for instance, instead of single-click. It also removes any Web material from your wallpaper: You don't have to worry about your modem dialing the Internet if you accidentally click the wrong spot on your desktop's background.

✓ The Classic style doesn't banish the Internet completely; it's ready for use in the Windows 98 Classic style. You can still access the Web through Internet Explorer, download the program listings for your TV, and use the Windows Update to keep your computer running smoothly. Classic style simply turns off portions of the Active Desktop and the often-confusing "single-click" option.

✓ Want a ham and cheese on rye, hold the pickles? With its Internet customization feature, Windows 98 can serve up enough options to meet just about everybody's needs. To begin barking orders, click the Start button, click Settings and choose Folder Options. Finally, click the Custom, based on settings you choose option at the bottom and choose the Settings button (see Figure 21-1). Helpful instructions await in the file viewing options section of Chapter 5.

Figure 21-1:
Choose the
Custom
option to
combine the
features you
want from
both the
Web style
and Classic
style.

Do I want an Active Desktop?

The mysterious Windows 98 Active Desktop has a secret agent appeal, that's for sure. Turn the thing on to display mysterious little windows across your desktop, each displaying a different type of information.

In one corner of the background, for example, a stock chart rocks and rolls the day's movers and shakers. In another corner comes the real rock and roll: Click the little jukebox to hear current CDs broadcast over the Internet.

To start the Active Desktop, click the desktop with your right mouse button, choose <u>A</u>ctive Desktop from the pop-up menu and select <u>C</u>ustomize my Desktop from the next menu.

Click the <u>N</u>ew button, and Windows 98 hustles you off to the Active Desktop gallery to choose hip, electronic art from the Internet's walls and arrange them tastefully across your desktop. (No <u>N</u>ew button? Then click the <u>V</u>iew my Active Desktop as a web page button, right under the picture of the monitor.)

> ✔ Of course, you need to be connected to the Internet for all this fun stuff. And your phone line will be tied up for a long time with all the computer-to-computer chattering. Best bet? Check to see if your area's cable company offers cable modem turned on 24 hours a day.

> ✔ If you hear your modem dialing places when you're nowhere near your computer, chances are it's trying to keep parts of your Active Desktop up to date. To make it stop, turn off all parts of your Active Desktop, and delete any options listed on your <u>C</u>ustomize my Desktop area.

> ✔ You'll also run out of desktop space, fast. You'll work best on a 20-inch monitor running at 1024 x 768 or better.

> ✔ Better yet, get a separate video card and a second monitor. Run Windows 98 on two monitors, keeping all your Internet stuff spilled onto your second monitor.

> ✔ Words are deceiving: Your new Active Desktop can turn into a slothful desktop that spends more time talking to the Internet than listening to your own commands. To turn it off, click the desktop with your right mouse button, choose <u>A</u>ctive Desktop from the pop-up menu and select View as <u>W</u>eb Page from the next menu. That toggles the feature on or off.

Turning the Ugly Channel bar on or off

When you first start Windows 98, it thrusts an ugly, black bar along the right side of your screen that looks like a misplaced TV remote control. It's a confusing, Microsoft-devised way to reach the Internet without using a Web browser.

Unfortunately, the Channel bar takes up a lot of desktop space. To get rid of it, click the little X resting at the very top of the bar. Poof! The Channels bar disappears, leaving a question: Do you want the Channel bar to be displayed next time you restart your computer?

Click the No button, and you've banished the bar.

If you change your mind and want the Channel bar to return, follow these steps:

1. **Choose Settings from the Start button and select Control Panel.**

2. **Double-click the Internet icon.**

3. **Click the Advanced tab.**

4. **Select the checkbox marked Show channel bar at startup (if Active Desktop is off).**

5. **Click OK, close the Control Panel, and restart your computer.**

When your computer comes back to life, the Channel bar will come back to life, as well.

Appendix A

Installing Windows 98

● ●

In This Chapter

▶ Turning on the computer

▶ Deciding whether to install Windows 98 over your old version of Windows

▶ Installing Windows 98

▶ Taking the Discover Windows 98 Tutorial

▶ Leaving the Setup program

▶ Turning off the computer

● ●

*I*nstalling software means copying the program from the CD in the software box onto the hard drive inside your PC. Unfortunately, it can also mean hours of tinkering until the newly installed software works correctly with your particular computer, printer, disk drives, and internal organs. Because of the frustration potential, installation chores should usually be left to a certified computer guru. Gurus like that sort of stuff. (They even like the smell of freshly opened compact disc boxes.)

Luckily, Microsoft took mercy on Windows 98 beginners. It designed Windows 98 to practically install itself. Just slide the CD into the compact disc drive and Windows 98 should begin loading itself automatically. After that, answer a few questions and put your feet up; Windows 98 figures out the rest.

This chapter walks you through the installation process. You see how easy Microsoft made this chore, and you find out where else in the book you can turn if you need further information.

Turning On the Computer

The first step is to look for the computer's *power* switch. It's usually the largest switch on the computer. Sometimes it's red and important looking; other times, it's an itty-bitty "push on, push off" switch near the disk drives.

✔ Put your ear next to the computer's case: If the computer is not making any noise, it's either turned off or broken. Flip its power switch to the opposite direction (or push in the switch), and the computer either jumps to life or stays broken (or stays unplugged, which is why it always works in the repair shop).

✔ Turning the computer off and then immediately turning it on again can send devastating jolts of electricity through the computer's tender internal organs. Turn the computer on in the morning and off when you're finished for the day. Some sensitive people even leave their computers turned on all the time to spare them that morning power jolt.

✔ Never turn the computer off while it's running Windows 98 or any other program. Doing so can destroy data and damage your programs. If the computer is doing something weird, like freezing up solid, try the less disastrous disciplinary measures described in Chapter 14.

✔ Turn on your computer's monitor in much the same way: Push in its On switch, and it should jump to life.

✔ Finally, when installing Windows 98, tell it to keep your old version of Windows hanging around, as described in Step 6 of "Installing Windows 98," later in this chapter. Windows 98 then compresses your old Windows version and hides it in a secret directory on your hard drive. Later, after you've had time to play with Windows 98, you can tell Windows 98 to purge your old version for good. (Or, if Windows 98 doesn't meet your needs, you can tell it to resurrect your old version, removing itself in the process. Whichever your choice, it takes place in the Control Panel's Add/Remove Programs area.)

Removing the Wrapper from the Box

Pick up the box that contains the Windows 98 software and look for where the plastic bunches up in the corners. With your incisors, bite into that little chunk of bunched-up plastic and give it a good tug. Repeat this procedure a few times until you've created a finger-sized hole. Then peel back the plastic until the box is free. Be careful of your gums.

Upgrading to Windows 98

Forget those awkward experiences setting up metal Christmas trees or listening to your car make funny noises. Windows 98 caters to beginners with an installation program that checks under your PC's hood and sets up itself automatically, adjusting the fluid levels as needed.

Here's how to pull into the full-service lane:

First, make sure that your computer is turned on; then make sure that anything plugged into your computer is turned on, as well. That includes modems, printers, compact disc drives, yogurt makers, and other goodies. Plug in your joysticks, too; Windows 98 actually recognizes them. Hurrah!

Finally, a word of caution. Windows 98 often uses different tactics when installing itself onto different computers. Don't be surprised if your computer skips some of these steps, changes their order, or even slips in a new step.

1. **Start your current version of Windows, put your Windows 98 Installation disc into your computer's CD-ROM drive, and then open the Start menu's Run box.**

   You might get lucky right away. If your computer usually starts playing songs automatically when you insert an audio CD, then the Windows 98 installation program should begin automatically, as well. Rejoice, and climb the ladder to Step 3. Otherwise, move to Step 2.

2. **Type the letters** D:\SETUP **in the Run box that appears, and click the OK button.**

   Be sure to change the drive letter — D, in this case — to match your own compact disc's drive letter. For example, if your CD-ROM drive is drive E, type this in the Run dialog box shown in Figure A-1:

   ```
   E:\SETUP
   ```

Figure A-1:
If your
CD-ROM
drive is E,
type
E:\SETUP
into the Run
dialog box
and click
the OK
button.

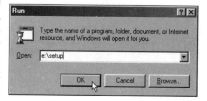

All this :\ stuff too much for you? There's hope. Windows 95 users can merely open My Computer and double-click their CD-ROM drive icon (unmistakable, the shiny icon looks like a CD). Double-click the word Setup from the file listings and the wheels start churning. Earlier-era Windows users can launch File Manager and double-click the CD-ROM drive icon — an odd-looking icon with a CD protruding from a drive like a tongue. Double-click the word Setup from the file listings, and you're out of the gate.

When Setup begins, the first taste (and sound, in some cases) of Windows 98 leaps to the screen. The window merely announces that Windows 98 will check your system for any problems before continuing. It also breaks the news that you may be sitting in front of your computer for anywhere from 30 minutes to an hour, depending on how smoothly the installation process goes. Call ahead to pick up a sandwich.

3. **Click Continue, and Windows 98 examines your computer.**

   If Windows 98 finds anything wrong with your hard disk, it says so and promptly fixes the problem.

   If Windows 98 said it found something weird, you may want to click the Details button to see what's up. You can usually get away with clicking the Continue button and pressing forward, however.

   Windows 98 then loads its own Windows 98 Setup Wizard program to ensure everything proceeds without problem.

   If Windows 98 asks you to close down any currently running programs, do so. The Windows 98 Setup Wizard doesn't want mere *programs* mingling at such an important event; the Wizard wants the computer all to itself while patching the operating system. If you're running any other programs in the background, shut them down. (**Hint:** Holding down the Alt key and pressing Tab cycles between programs; close each program as it appears.)

   Finally, rustle around for the CD case or little envelope that held your Windows 98 disc. You'll probably need to type in the envelope's secret "Product ID" code. (Microsoft's afraid that people will make illegal copies of its disc, so it came up with the secret code idea to stop the "bootleggers.")

   If Windows 98 ever asks you to choose the "FAT32 system" as it installs itself, choose "No." That FAT32 stuff's not for beginners, as it can cause awful problems.

4. **If asked, click I accept the Agreement in the License Agreement dialog box, and click the Next button.**

   Here's where Microsoft tosses you a stumper, shown in Figure A-2. Unless you agree to abide by Microsoft's special Windows 98 terms, the install process simply stops and leaves the room like a surly bellhop who only got a dollar tip. Promise to play by Microsoft's rules by clicking in the circle where it says I accept the Agreement.

   Windows boldly knocks about inside the computer's hard drive, taking measurements and preparing for its big move in.

Don't have an earlier version of Windows on your hard drive? Windows 98 asks you to insert the first disk from your *old* version of Windows into a disk drive so that it can verify that you're merely upgrading an older version of Windows. Without that older version of Windows, you won't be able to install the Windows 98 upgrade, unfortunately. Better head back to the store for the more expensive version of Windows 98 — not that less-expensive upgrade for an already purchased product.

5. **Enter your Windows Product Key and click Next.**

   Even if you agreed to abide by the License Agreement, Microsoft doesn't trust you. No, you still have to enter a customized Windows Product Key. The secret code containing letters and numbers is usually stamped on the back of your CD's container. Other times it's stamped on the cover of the software manual.

   Without the key, you're stuck: Windows 98 refuses to install. With the key, Windows 98 continues its preparations to install itself onto your hard drive.

6. **Choose your geographical location from the box, and click the Next button.**

   Windows needs to know your geographical information so it can set up the correct time zones, currency, Internet information, and other stuff pertaining to your area.

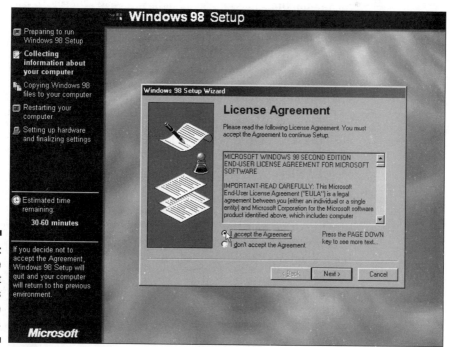

Figure A-2:
Click in the circle next to the words I accept the Agreement.

Legal gibberish and licensing terms that leap out during the installation

By choosing the I accept the Agreement option, you're essentially telling Microsoft that you agree to the following things:

✔ You won't make copies of your software and then rent, sell, or give them away to friends.

✔ In fact, you don't even own your copy of Windows. You just own the rights to use one copy of it. Microsoft holds the copyright to any images, photographs, animations, video, audio, music, text, programming, and anything else that could possibly have commercial value.

✔ You won't take Windows 98 apart to see how it works, and even if you did, you couldn't make any money off of it.

✔ It's got a 30-day warranty; if you bought a mouse along with it, you're lucky. Microsoft's warranty for hardware is a year.

✔ Finally, understand that you're the one punching the keyboard, so Microsoft isn't responsible if the software completely destroys your computer, your business, your data, and your love life.

Welcome to Windows 98!

---

7. **Decide whether or not to save your old DOS and Windows system files so you can uninstall Windows 98, and click Next.**

   If you're skeptical about Windows 98, choose the Yes option. Choose a drive, and Windows 98 copies your old system files to a secret folder where it can reinstall them if need be.

   See the buttons marked Back and Next along the bottom of the window? Throughout the next few steps, you can click the Back button to go back to your last step. So don't feel that you've blown it if you accidentally click the Next button before you're ready or if you want to go back and change something. Just click the Back button, and Windows 98 goes back a step.

8. **Make a Startup Disk.**

   As shown in Figure A-3, this "fix-it" disk contains programs for repairing problems that might occur later on. Even if you can't figure out how the disk works, a fix-it friend may need it to fix potential problems. Label a disk "Windows 98 Startup Disk," put it in drive A, and click OK to create the disk.

   Actually, you can write anything you want on the Startup disk's label. However, you *must* insert it into Drive A. No other drive works.

Figure A-3:
Create a
Windows 98
Startup Disk
for possible
trouble-
shooting.

Any existing files on your floppy disk are deleted when Windows 98 makes the startup disk. Don't use a disk with important files on it.

9. Click the Next button to begin copying files.

Just clicking the Next button, shown in Figure A-6, tells Windows 98 to install itself onto your computer. Windows 98 flashes some pictures of happy people on the screen as it begins the laborious chore of extracting, decompressing, and copying every chunk of Windows 98 to the hard drive. Now's the time to pick up that sandwich you called ahead for when beginning the Setup process. Windows 98 installs itself automatically, leaving you nothing else to do for at least the next half hour.

While installing itself, the Windows Wizard kicks the computer's tires a few times, even restarting the computer once or twice as it looks in the windows to see what's installed. After the program discovers the brand names and models of the computer parts, it tries to connect them automatically so they'll talk. (This is an enormous growth in computer savvy over the past two or three years.)

10. Sign on to Windows 98.

Congratulations! You've installed Windows 98. Type in your user name, and strangely enough, Windows 98 Second Edition will look almost identical to Windows 98. Actually, it still looks almost like Windows 95. Kind of makes you wonder what you paid for, eh?

Should you install Windows 98 over your old version of Windows?

Should you copy this new version of Windows 98 over your older, faithful version of Windows 3.1 or Windows 95 — a version that serves you so well except when it crashes?

Yeah, go ahead. The new version won't wipe out the important parts of the old version. The desktop will have the same programs as before. In fact, if you don't install Windows 98 over your old version of Windows, you must reinstall all your old programs by hand.

To be on the safe side, copy your important data files to floppy disks before you begin. You've

probably been backing up your work anyway, so copying the files shouldn't take long.

✔ If you haven't been copying your important files to floppy disks for safekeeping, head to the store and ask for a backup system that's compatible with Windows 98.

✔ When you're ready to delete the old version of Windows and free up some hard drive space, head for the Control Panel's Add/Remove Programs icon.

Click the words *Discover Windows 98* in the Welcome to Windows 98 box (see Figure A-4) for a quick look at the new goodies in Windows 98. If you have a modem, clicking the Online Registration button lets you give Microsoft your name and address so that it can send you junk mail about new software — Microsoft will also ask permission to grab your computer's parts list for use with the Windows Update program. (Click Update from the top of the Start menu to start the program.)

Finally, Windows 98 sometimes wants to restart the computer one last time to set things straight. Just click the Yes button and wait patiently.

Leaving Windows 98

After you're finished with Windows 98 and are ready to turn off your computer, click the Start button, located near the lower-left corner of the screen. When the menu sprouts upward, click the Shut Down option.

A window pops up, leaving you three options:

✔ **Shut down?:** Choose this option if you want to turn off your computer for the day and do something more constructive.

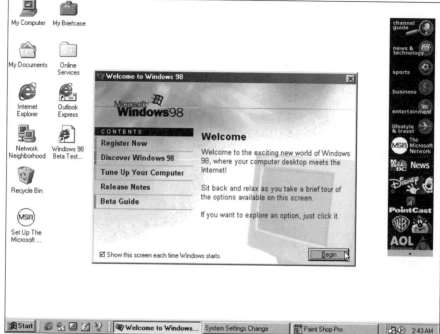

Figure A-4:
Click the
words
Discover
Windows 98
for a tour of
what
Windows 98
can offer.

✔ **Restart?:** This option works well if Windows 98 is acting funny; it tells Windows 98 to shut down and then come back to life, hopefully in a better mood.

✔ **Restart in MS-DOS mode?:** You may never have to use this option — unless you're trying to run an antique DOS program that just won't run when all the Windows 98 graphics are waiting in the background. (Type **exit** at the DOS prompt to make the prompt disappear and the windows reappear.)

Turning Off the Computer

If you're finished computing for the day — and you've told Windows 98 to shut down — turn off the computer. Find that switch you used to turn it on and flick it the other way. (Or, if it's a push button, give it another push.)

Never turn off the computer while Windows 98 is running. Use the Windows 98 Shut Down command and wait until Windows 98 flashes a message on-screen saying that it's safe to turn off your computer.

Appendix B

Glossary

*W*indows 98 buried its Glossary program in two ways. First, if you spot an unfamiliar word in the Help program — and it's underlined — click the word, and Windows 98 defines it for you.

The second method is more complicated. Choose Help from the Start button, click the Index tab, type Glossary into the box and press Enter. Windows will bring up the term Glossary of Terms. Click the words Click here on the right side of the Help page.

That brings up yet *another* Help page, and this one lists the word Glossary at the bottom. Click on Glossary to find the deeply buried definitions of many words in Windows 98.

Or you can find many of those words listed right here.

Active Desktop: A feature to transform Internet Web pages into wallpaper, where they can be updated automatically in the background.

active window: The last window you clicked — the one that's currently highlighted — is considered active. Any keys that you press affect this window.

Apply: Click this button, and Windows 98 immediately applies and saves any changes you've made from the current list of options.

AUTOEXEC.BAT: A file that old, pre-Windows computers read when first turned on. The file contains instructions that affect any subsequently running MS-DOS programs — and older Windows programs, as well. Windows 98 no longer needs an AUTOEXEC.BAT file, but it keeps one around in case older programs may need to use it.

bitmap: A graphic consisting of bunches of little dots on-screen. They're saved as bitmap files, which end with the letters BMP. The Windows 98 program called *Paint* can create and edit BMP files.

border: The edge of a window; you can move the border in or out to change the window's size.

cache: A storage area where Windows temporarily memorizes recently used files so they can be retrieved quickly if needed.

case-sensitive: A program that knows the difference between uppercase and lowercase letters. For example, a case-sensitive program considers *Pickle* and *pickle* to be two different things.

Classic style: Like Classic Coke, the Windows Classic style forgoes any fancy Windows 98 frivolities and makes Windows 98 operate like good ol' Windows 95.

click: To push and release a button on the mouse.

Clipboard: A part of Windows 98 that keeps track of information you've cut or copied from a program or file. It stores that information so that you can paste it into other programs.

command prompt: The little symbol that looks like C:\ > or A:\ > or something similar. It's the place where you can type instructions — *commands* — for DOS to carry out.

CONFIG.SYS: A file that your computer reads every time it boots up. The file contains information about how the computer is set up and what it's attached to. Both DOS and Windows programs rely on information contained in the CONFIG.SYS file. Windows 98 no longer needs a CONFIG.SYS file, but it keeps one around in case other programs need one.

cursor: The little blinking line that shows where the next letter will appear when you start typing.

default: Choosing the default option enables you to avoid making a more-complicated decision. The *default option* is the one the computer chooses for you when you give up and just press Enter.

desktop: The area on your screen where you move windows and icons around. Most people cover the desktop with *wallpaper* — a pretty picture.

Dial-Up Networking: A way to connect to the Internet through a modem and a telephone line.

directory: A separate *folder* on a hard disk for storing files. Storing related files in a directory makes them easier to find. Windows 98 no longer uses the word *directory* and prefers the word *folder,* instead.

document: A file containing information like text, sound, or graphics. Documents are created or changed from within programs. *See* program.

DOS: Short for Disk Operating System, it's a very old operating system for running programs. Windows 98 can run programs designed for DOS, as well as programs designed for Windows.

double-click: Pushing and releasing the left mouse button twice in rapid succession. (Double-clicking the *right* mouse button doesn't do anything special.)

download: To copy files onto your computer through phones lines or cables.

drag: A four-step mouse process that moves an object across your desktop. First, point at the object — an icon, a highlighted paragraph, or something similar. Second, press and hold your left mouse button. Third, point at the location to which you want to move that object. Fourth, release the mouse button. The object is dragged to its new location.

drop: Step four of the *drag* technique, described in the preceding entry. *Dropping* is merely letting go of the mouse button and letting your object fall onto something else, be it a new window, directory, or area on your desktop.

DRV: A file ending in DRV usually lets Windows talk to computer gizmos, such as video cards, sound cards, CD-ROM drives, and other stuff. (DRV is short for *driver.*)

FAQ: Short for Frequently Asked Questions, these text files are usually found on online services. Designed to save everyone some time, the files answer questions most frequently asked by new users. The Scanners FAQ explains all about scanners, for example; the Xena FAQ would trace Xena's history, starting with Hercules.

file: A collection of information in a format designed for computer use.

firewall: A combination of hardware and software on a corporate network that keeps both employees and outsiders from having unauthorized access to all parts of the Internet.

folder: An area for storing files to keep them organized (formerly called a directory). Folders can contain other folders for further organization. *See* subdirectory.

format: The process of preparing a disk to have files written on it. The disk needs to have "electronic shelves" tacked onto it so that Windows 98 can store information on it. Formatting a disk wipes it clean of all previous recorded information.

highlighted: A selected item. Different colors usually appear over a highlighted object to show that it's been singled out for further action.

icon: The little picture that represents an object — a program, file, or command — making it easier to figure out that object's function.

infrared: A special way for computers to communicate through invisible light beams, infrared ports (IR ports) are found frequently on laptops and printers.

INI: Short for *initialization,* INI usually hangs on the end of files that contain special system settings. The files are for the computer to mess with, not users.

Internet: A huge collection of computers linked around the world. The *World Wide Web* rides atop the Internet along with other computer transactions. You can connect to the Internet's World Wide Web by paying a fee to an Internet Service Provider — much like paying a monthly phone bill.

lasso: Grabbing a bunch of items simultaneously with the mouse. Point at the bottom right corner of the items and, while holding down the left mouse button, point at their top left corner. Lassoing the items highlights them for further action.

maximize: The act of making a window fill the entire screen. You can maximize a window by double-clicking its title bar — that long strip across its very top. Or you can click its maximize button — that button with the big square inside, located near the window's upper-right corner.

memory: The stuff computers use to store on-the-fly calculations while running.

minimize: The act of shrinking a window down to a tiny icon to temporarily get it out of the way. To minimize a window, click the minimize button — that button with the horizontal bar on it, located near the window's upper-right corner.

multitasking: Running several different programs simultaneously.

network: Connecting computers with cables so that people can share information without getting up from their desks.

operating system: Software that controls how a computer does its most basic stuff: stores files, talks to printers, and performs other gut-level operations. Windows 98 is an operating system.

path: A sentence of computerese that tells a computer the precise name and location of a file.

PC card: Used mainly by laptops, PC cards can house modems, memory, network parts, or other handy items.

Plug and Play (PnP): A sprightly phrase used to describe computer parts that Windows 98 is supposed to be able to recognize and install automatically.

program: Something that enables you to work on the computer. Spreadsheets, word processors, and games are *programs*. *See* document.

RAM: Random-Access Memory. *See* memory.

scrap: When you highlight some text or graphics from a program, drag the chunk to the desktop, and drop it, you've created an official Windows 98 *scrap* — a file containing a copy of that information. The scrap can be saved or dragged into other programs.

search engine: A program for searching the Web for information that meets your special needs. It can search for all Web pages mentioning both Sea Monkeys and bananas.

Shortcut: A Windows 98 icon that serves as a push button for doing something — loading a file, starting a program, or playing a sound, for example. Shortcuts have little arrows in their bottom corners so that you can tell them apart from the icons that *really* stand for files and programs.

shortcut button: A button in a Help menu that takes you directly to the area you need to fiddle with.

shortcut key: As opposed to a Shortcut, a shortcut key is an underlined letter in a program's menu that lets you work with the keyboard instead of the mouse. For example, if you see the word Help in a menu, the underlined H means that you can get help by pressing Alt+H.

Shut Down: The process of telling Windows 98 to save all its settings and files so that you can turn off your computer. You must click the Shut Down option, found on the Start menu, before turning off your computer.

Start button: A button in the corner of your screen where you can begin working. Clicking the Start button brings up the Start menu.

Start menu: A menu of options that appears when the Start button is clicked. From the Start menu, you can load programs, load files, change settings, find programs, find help, or shut down your computer so that you can turn it off.

subdirectory: A directory within a directory, used to further organize files. For example, a JUNKFOOD directory may contain subdirectories for CHIPS, PEANUTS, and PRETZELS. (A CELERY subdirectory would be empty.) In Windows 98, a subdirectory is a folder that's inside another folder.

taskbar: The bar in Windows 98 that lists all currently running programs and open folders. The Start button lives on one end of the taskbar.

VGA: A popular standard for displaying information on monitors in certain colors and resolutions. It's now being replaced by SVGA — Super VGA — which can display even more colors and even finer resolution.

virtual: A trendy word to describe computer simulations. It's commonly used to describe things that *look* real, but aren't really there. For example, when Windows 98 uses *virtual memory,* it's using part of the hard disk for memory, not the actual memory chips.

wallpaper: Graphics spread across the background of your computer screen. The Windows 98 Control Panel lets you choose among different wallpaper files.

Web browser: Software for maneuvering through the World Wide Web, visiting Web pages, and examining the wares. The Microsoft Web browser, Internet Explorer, comes free with the latest version of Windows 98 or can be downloaded for free from the Microsoft Web page at `www.microsoft.com`. (Other people may have bought Internet Explorer in the Microsoft Plus add-on package for Windows 98.) Netscape, a competing browser, is losing popularity.

Web page: Just as televisions can show bunches of different channels, the World Wide Web can show gazillions of different *Web pages.* These screenfuls of information can be set up by anyone: The government can display county meeting schedules; corporations can project flashy marketing propaganda; publications can display online versions of their works. (Or, the Cushmans can put up a Family Page with pictures of the baby at Disneyland.)

window: An on-screen box that contains information for you to look at or work with. Programs run in *windows* on your screen.

Wizard: Helpful Windows program that takes over the chores of program installation and setup.

World Wide Web: Riding atop the Internet's motley collection of cables, the flashy World Wide Web works as a sort of computerized television, letting you jump from channel to channel by pointing and clicking at the pages. Also known simply as "The Web."

Index

• J •

• K •

• L •

• M •

IDG BOOKS WORLDWIDE
BOOK REGISTRATION

Register This Book and Win!

We want to hear from you!

Visit **http://my2cents.dummies.com** to register this book and tell us how you liked it!

- ✔ Get entered in our monthly prize giveaway.
- ✔ Give us feedback about this book — tell us what you like best, what you like least, or maybe what you'd like to ask the author and us to change!
- ✔ Let us know any other *...For Dummies*® topics that interest you.

Your feedback helps us determine what books to publish, tells us what coverage to add as we revise our books, and lets us know whether we're meeting your needs as a *...For Dummies* reader. You're our most valuable resource, and what you have to say is important to us!

Not on the Web yet? It's easy to get started with *Dummies 101*®: *The Internet For Windows*® *98* or *The Internet For Dummies*®, 6th Edition, at local retailers everywhere.

Or let us know what you think by sending us a letter at the following address:

...For Dummies Book Registration
Dummies Press
7260 Shadeland Station, Suite 100
Indianapolis, IN 46256-3945
Fax 317-596-5498

™

**BESTSELLING
BOOK SERIES
FROM IDG**